Indian Documentary Film and Filmmakers

Indian Documentary Film and Filmmakers

Independence in Practice

Shweta Kishore

EDINBURGH
University Press

Edinburgh University Press is one of the leading university presses in the UK. We publish academic books and journals in our selected subject areas across the humanities and social sciences, combining cutting-edge scholarship with high editorial and production values to produce academic works of lasting importance. For more information visit our website: edinburghuniversitypress.com

Edinburgh University Press Ltd
The Tun – Holyrood Road
12 (2f) Jackson's Entry
Edinburgh EH8 8PJ

First published in hardback by Edinburgh University Press 2018

Typeset in Monotype Ehrhardt by
Servis Filmsetting Ltd, Stockport, Cheshire

A CIP record for this book is available from the British Library

ISBN 978 1 4744 3306 8 (hardback)
ISBN 978 1 4744 3307 5 (paperback)
ISBN 978 1 4744 3308 2 (webready PDF)
ISBN 978 1 4744 3309 9 (epub)

Contents

Figures

Acknowledgements

This book is a bid to try and understand the complexity of defining independence, a question I struggled with during my experience of making three documentary films in India between 1999 and 2007 and in interactions with many of the individuals, groups and institutions that have been and continue to be intrinsic to the field and culture of independent documentary in India.[1]

My independent documentary film practice, which was self-managed and self-financed and operated in collaboration with individuals and grassroots community groups, would often run up against questions and contradictions. Independence seemed an ambiguous notion in the shifting contours of media production where filmmakers regularly approached state and civil society institutions for financial support and for exhibition platforms. In the Indian context, where independent documentary filmmaking was historically and colloquially perceived in terms of social activism, advocacy and public communication rather than as a cultural or artistic form, partnerships with social sector NGOs seemed to fix further the documentary form within alternately pedagogical and utilitarian frames. In this equation, the voice and expression of the filmmaker were submerged within the production of effective social messages. These messages, while frequently progressive and socially developmental, were invisible as a critical discourse in their own right. Insofar as it enabled the production of politically radical messages, independence was valued and acknowledged for its representational possibilities.

At the same time, the strengthening neoliberal economic order manifested in the growing numbers of private television channels, production companies and media training colleges, who measured rewards and success through the greater accumulation of economic and social capital but against which independent filmmakers were constructing their own individual systems of personal rewards. The combination of the relative invisibility of the authorial status of the documentary filmmaker in the public domain and the limited economic and professional rewards associated with independent practice raised a series of questions regarding the motivation to pursue this mode of filmmaking. Which forms of rewards propelled independent filmmakers? Through what forms of experiences and reflections did filmmakers constitute alternate cultural and economic paradigms in a social order increasingly defined through neoliberal values? What strategies did filmmakers develop in order to resist the overarching systems, structures and practices that authorised normative cultural and aesthetic expression? What were the political meanings of independent filmmaking in systems governed by political, economic and scientific rationality? It is these questions and reflections that formed the beginning of this research and also provided the grounds for the methodology centred upon practice, its heterogeneous arrangements and modes. At the same time, this book extends and substantiates studies of independent filmmaking as a site of resistance located within the overarching systems of political, economic and social rationality. It offers ways of thinking about practice as a system that produces not only aesthetic objects but that also engages with larger questions of subject positions, cultural and personal freedoms and democracy.

I am sincerely indebted to each filmmaker at the heart of this book. K. P. Jayasankar, Anjali Monteiro, Amudhan R. P., Rahul Roy and Paromita Vohra not only contributed their time for several interview sessions over the course of two years, but trusted me with their personal stories. I thank them for their willingness to share their experiences and their archive of still images included in this book. I thank Pankaj Butalia, Surya Shankar Dash, Saba Dewan, Deepa Dhanraj, Akhila Ghosh, Avik Ghosh, Shohini Ghosh, Sabina Kidwai, Anand Patwardhan and Surabhi Sharma for sharing their films, opinions and experiences, allowing me to understand the wider history and struggles of this community.

I am grateful for the tremendous support of Associate Professor Deane Williams and Associate Professor Belinda Smaill for guiding this project, first as a PhD thesis and later as a book. Their comments on the drafts were invaluable at every stage and have enhanced the quality of the book. I am indebted to Professor Ravi Vasudevan for his insightful advice in the early stages of my field work, and later for his insightful feedback about my findings. I would also like to thank Dr Rashmi Desai for his ongoing advice and Dr David Hanan for his perceptive comments on the early drafts.

I appreciate the support of family and friends – my sister Pallavi Kishore, Yask Desai, Simon Wilmot, Asif Ahammed, Paola Sophia Bilbrough, Masha Davidenko, Victor Albert, Greg Armstrong, Tyson Wils, Angus Nichols and Soe Tjen Marching, for enabling this research intellectually and emotionally.

This book is based on data collected during two extended fieldwork visits to India in 2013 and 2014 where SARAI at the Centre for the Study of Developing Societies, Tata Institute of Social Sciences, and Magic Lantern Movies generously extended invaluable support. I am grateful to Professor Rosie Thomas, who supported my visiting scholar position at the India Media Centre at the University of Westminster, London.

Finally, this book is dedicated to my parents, who have offered unwavering and limitless support and encouraged me to pursue reason and knowledge.

Note

1. Many of the questions that I address in this book emerged from my personal experience of filmmaking in India. Beginning in 1999, I codirected three films with Yask Desai: *The Great Indian Yatra* (1999), *Of Bards and Beggars* (2004) and *The Rising Wave* (2008). Each of these films was self-funded and distributed. During their making we encountered many independent filmmakers who were confronting the issues and dilemmas that are discussed in this book, to which each had an individual and reasoned response, allowing all of us to inhabit this space in our own way.

Introduction

We Are Independent Filmmakers

In May 2015, an email arrived on the Vikalp Films for Freedom listserv, a community of over 300 documentary filmmakers dispersed across India. The communication, written by a well-known filmmaker, described a humiliating confrontation with the police and mainstream press as the filmmaker was attempting to film a public protest. Labelled 'faker' by the policemen and journalists, a reference to his non-affiliated, independent status, the filmmaker was accused of filming the public events for personal profit. He was asked to prove his professional identity and eventually forced to delete the footage he had recorded. The filmmaker ends his email with a noteworthy question indicative of a discourse of legitimacy employed to distinguish independent from authorised or official media producers:

> We filmmakers don't make films for our personal interest, we make films to seek the truth and present it to our audience to see and act upon it. But the real question is, why one has to be a journalist or a reporter to make films. But we as independent filmmakers want our own rights to shoot wherever we want when making films for public interest. [*sic*][1]

Amongst the Vikalp community, the email reignited demands for the public recognition of independent documentary filmmakers as legitimate media producers, bringing to the fore key dimensions of the practice of independent documentary in contemporary India. The discussion underlines the interventionist public objective of many independent documentary filmmakers and the struggle against forces that seek to curtail this socially committed media practice. On a more fundamental level, the filmmaker's questions touch deeper issues about the ambivalence surrounding the identity of independent cultural producers in a public domain where professional identities are defined and approved through institutionalised processes which mediate the scope and nature of functions performed by individuals. As the email indicates, even as the independent filmmaker and journalists witness and record the same phenomenon, it is the professional journalists who are granted police sanction to report the events and thus construct its public narrative. Independence, as the abovementioned filmmaker articulates, is a position located external to the organised and officially sanctioned systems of media and information production. Therefore, the extent to which independent filmmakers interrogate social injustice through their choice of content, their unconventional methods and non-industry location poses larger political questions about the exclusionary and distortionary effects of power within the field of cultural production and what it means to be a cultural producer, working through unconventional, non-standard practices and means.

In India, 'independent documentary film' is a term that signifies a body of films that first appeared in 1975 during the Constitutional Emergency, a period when the repressive exercise of state authority threatened the democratic political foundations of the nation (Monteiro and Jayasankar 2015).[2] With *Waves of Revolution* (1975), Anand Patwardhan demonstrated a way of making political documentary through political means of guerrilla filming on a borrowed Super 8 camera, improvised editing and underground exhibition (Monteiro and Jayasankar 2015; Kishore 2016).[3] Choosing to locate their practice outside the Films Division of India (FD), the nationally dominant state-run documentary production and distribution agency, Patwardhan and later in the 1980s, Deepa Dhanraj, Suhasini Mulay, Tapan Bose, Manjira Datta, Mediastorm Collective, Saba Dewan, Rahul Roy, Vasudha Joshi, Ranjan Palit, K. P. Sasi and others, claimed independence in industry terms and from the itineraries of state propaganda and paternalism that plagued state documentary. Established in 1948 during the post-independence nation-building phase, Films Division is identified as a key institution through which the Indian state constructed and communicated its identity as an 'authoritative representative' of the nation (Roy 2007). Through its vast multi-language documentary output distributed nationally in complex institutional and infrastructural configurations with state governments, government departments and commercial cinema theatres, the institution played a significant role in establishing the vocal and visual identity of the Indian state (58). The term 'independent' came to be authorised in subsequent years as a category of privately produced, politically conscious documentary films, financed and distributed through means alternate to the organised structures of state production and exhibition or commercial financing and theatrical distribution.

This book is about independent Indian documentary and its meaning as a practice that not only produces political representation but opens up new material relations between culture, society and the individual. It is inspired by independent cinema imaginaries and practices that have accompanied one of the most decisive periods of modern Indian history, known as the post-reform period, beginning in 1991. Spurred by the New Economic Policy, this phase is identified by a fundamental move towards a neoliberal socio-economic system whose institutional forms and mechanisms of governance form the context against which the meaning and function of independence becomes worthy of consideration.[4]

The need for this book arises from two interrelated grounds. In terms of organisation, the initial usage of the term 'independent' to denote a production category located strictly outside of state structures is now arguably a misnomer. In the post-reform landscape, independent filmmakers operate with greater flexibility and multiple forms of interdependent and mutually cooperative forms of organisation between filmmakers, the state, international and domestic NGOs, private institutions and individuals are commonplace. Furthermore, the relations between independent filmmakers and the state demonstrate a degree of interplay that complicates the notion of independence couched in purely oppositional or politically adversarial terms. The conferment of the prestigious 2014 Lifetime Achievement Award of the Films Division upon internationally renowned political documentarist Anand Patwardhan is indicative of this ambivalence. In the last four decades, Patwardhan stands out as the most prominent filmmaker in the battle against state censorship, confronting the Central Board of Film Certification (CBFC) through judicial means on no less than eight occasions. In this sense, an adversarial framework no longer captures the meaning of 'independence' when the state is able to acknowledge, if not the political voice, then the cultural value of independent documentary cinema.

Second, in terms of industry organisation, the arrangement of Indian independent documentary differs notably from the organised production systems in the United States of America (USA) and Europe, which predominantly avail of a blend of private and public arts and television funding. In India, public funding of documentary film is limited to the Films Division within a primary mandate to commission films that contribute to creating a 'positive image of the nation', a criterion that effectively translates into a thematic focus on subjects of national artistic and cultural heritage, including India's cinematic heritage (Films Division 2017, 'Citizen's Charter'). Established in 2000, the Public Service Broadcast Trust occupies a prominent place in promoting independent documentary;

however, a broadcast partnership with Doordarshan, and funding arrangements that include state departments and international NGOs, have led to concerns about editorial polices. Many independent filmmakers voiced doubts about the organisation's viability to support the production of independent films with wide-ranging political viewpoints and aesthetics. The dearth of formalised public support has produced a system of private non-government organisation (NGO) sponsorship that contributes to the production and exhibition of Indian independent documentary.[5] The beginning of the partnership between independent filmmakers and NGOs coincides with the rising popularity of video technology during the 1980s and its adoption for the needs of 'development communication', or the use of communication technology to facilitate social development (Monteiro and Jayasankar 2015; Wolf 2013). Given that a significant number of documentary films are financed through a combination of formalised and informal arrangements by NGOs involved in the delivery of a range of social development programmes, this relation is of vital significance to the organisational forms and the artistic and political possibilities of independent filmmaking in India. Foremost, it introduces an institutional pressure in a field considered autonomous of systemised organisation, formalised structures and obligations by placing documentary film under one of several institutionally defined functions like public communication, advocacy, documentation, instruction, strengthening of public sphere and cultural preservation.[6] In this historical–industrial context, independence, I would suggest, is a complex phenomenon arranged through alternative systems, perhaps not of commercial evaluation but equally subject to practices, discourses and structures of institutional authority. The blurring of the distinctive categories of independent and mainstream production, of adversarial and cooperative rhetorical positions and of public and private objectives prompts the current need for an alternative definition of independent documentary that takes into account what appear to be contradictory positions between independence and institutional alliances. As with private modes of production, in this book I am equally concerned with the institutional modes of production and circulation within which independence articulates as a practice centred around a social agenda but against which it reflexively attends to historical discourses of power, systemisation and hierarchy produced by institutions.

My aim in this book is to conduct a cultural analysis of independent documentary from the standpoint of media arts practice to propose that in addition to films themselves as objects of meaning, the organisation of concrete practice produces alternative social meanings and subject positions. From this premise, I argue that the relationships, techniques and structures that form around the independent mode of practice not only implicate textual expression but transform the very meaning and purpose of cultural production and the relation between culture, cultural producer, society and social actors. Hence, the meaning of independence is identified through critical political positions and textual properties, equally as the tangible and effective relationships, structures and actions through which documentary production and circulation is organised. This is especially significant when examined against functions of encouraging consumerism and the production of aspirational consumption ascribed to culture under neoliberalism, the socio-economic dominant in India (Harvey 2005). Despite the proliferation of media technologies, the neoliberal mode of cultural production has moved towards greater concentration of ownership and growth of transnational media corporations creating new anxieties around shifting subjectivities, the blurring of public and private and national and global socio-economic agendas (Kapur and Wagner 2011). Therefore, central to my study is the contention that Indian independent documentary practice as part of the communication and media sphere of a liberal democracy is shaped as much by its structures and institutions as the critical analysis and resistance to its social and political forms of governance, organisation and discourse.

In the wider context of South Asia and the Global South, which share histories of colonisation, postcolonial nation-building and ongoing debates regarding identity, resource allocation and sustainability, I am concerned with revisiting established concepts and signifiers that develop situated meanings refracted equally through the historical struggles within national contexts, as engagement with and critique of disciplinary theories and concepts. While producing knowledge about Indian independent documentary, I attempt to continue the work of 'provincialising' European and North American documentary studies to demonstrate the importance of studying documentary from a range of location-specific perspectives (Chakrabarty 2000). Discussions of concepts and functions such as 'documentary ethics', 'documentary subject', 'documentary audience' and 'documentary filmmaker' demonstrate the diversity of meanings attached to these terms, which are interpreted through different histories and cultural perspectives as compared to the original context of their production. This work has already begun in South Asian documentary scholarship. In her recent study of Pakistani independent documentary, Imran (2016) outlines a specific form of feminist documentary in Pakistan that represents feminist issues as human rights issues in a Muslim society rooted in histories of Muslim women's struggles against religious fundamentalism. Hence, this book should be seen as not only an account of a national discourse of documentary cinema but one that critiques and extends the existing meanings and usage of concepts and terminologies in the broader field of Documentary Studies from a historical and geopolitical perspective.

Defining 'Independence': Culture, Industry and Practice

A field of production

The notion of independence is pervasively associated with a sphere of artistic production focused upon the expression of critical aesthetics and artistic points of view. Pierre Bourdieu's (1993: 112–14) propositions around the 'autonomisation of cultural production' define the industrial location of 'independence' as a field that lies outside dominant modes of production, 'the economic world reversed', but is nevertheless part of the social order and subordinate to the systemic norms of the social and economic fields within which all cultural production takes place. Drawing a homology between the field of cultural production and of class relations, Bourdieu observes that in the way that economic capital shares a linear relation with dominant classes in society, in the field of cultural production too, economic capital increases as one moves to the field of heteronomous or mass art production. Symbolic rather than economic capital is the determinant of what may be legitimised as avant-garde or art for art's sake (39). Bourdieu argues that works of art are 'symbolic objects' that exist as art only if they are recognised and socially instituted as such and this status is accorded not only by the producer but the producers of meaning and value of the work (critics, reviewers, curators) (37). The theorisation permits a critical understanding of independence not as a utopian ideal, but as a dynamic field of shifting and contested power relations. It provides a way of thinking about an artistic field in relational terms as a structured terrain of interrelated positions produced by a distribution of capital within a larger field of economic and political relations. Importantly, it allows for the conceptualisation of independence not as an absolute overthrow of authority but as a series of shifting relationships which form through economic and political interests and an ongoing struggle to define the position of the field and its functionaries in relation to dominant notions of culture.

The system of rewards is one such principle through which Bourdieu makes a distinction between mass producers and autonomous artists who focalise artistic freedom and therefore reject systems of valuation 'external' to their artistic field (112). Rather than seek the adulation of non-producing mass public the artists privilege critical recognition and cultural legitimacy. In India, the absence of studios, broadcast networks, ratings systems, audience research, market surveys and commercial sponsorship in the field of independent documentary depicts this crucial element of an autonomous field in which the authority of external commercial 'rules' is significantly diminished. The relationship between independent documentary and the mass cultural industries is understood as one of critique; while the cultural industry of Bombay cinema aims for box-office success, independent documentary has skirted market-based measures of success. While success itself is an unstable notion constituted through the values and beliefs of individual filmmakers and the cultural milieu, in this alternative system of validation and legitimation, critical acclaim is only one amongst several determinants of success. Nevertheless, the cultural field theory indeed provides a partial framework to rethink the relation of hierarchy that has characterised much of the cultural discourse about the relation between independent documentary and the dominant cultural industries. But what Bourdieu's key determinant of autonomy, or an internally generated notion of cultural value, does not fully account for is the complicating presence of social sector NGOs in Indian documentary. Particularly as independent cultural producers are frequently located at the intersection of artistic production and social participation, the measurements of success frequently include contribution to public debate and social movements. In these intersectional areas, cultural production exceeds discourses of artistic or critical appreciation to provoke new questions about forms of valuation, audience, aesthetic and the role of cultural producer as independent documentarists seek both cultural and historical outcomes.

Independence as text and industry category

In the case of narrative cinema, the debate on independence centres on its symbolic relation or distance from dominant national cinema industries. Studies of American independent cinema identify independent film and filmmakers by its spatial location outside of the industrial economies of studio production systems and critically in expressions of stylistic innovation, and critique of mainstream narrative forms (Insdorf 1981; Holmlund and Wyatt 2005; Berra 2010; King 2012; Ortner 2012). Not surprisingly, the debates are complicated by the expansion of major Hollywood studios into the ownership of independent production labels rendering independence as a co-opted brand or category (King et al. 2013). And while interpretations of independence from the standpoint of aesthetic critique offers valuable insights into artistic thought, contextual information about the structure of the field allows us to identify the materiality of independence as a practice and the text as a series of struggles.

In this regard, recent studies of independent cinemas of East and Southeast Asia and China offer a productive expansion by framing independence as a sphere that cuts across texts, practices, authors, economic and social spheres (Jaffee 2006; Berry et al. 2010: Baumgärtel 2011; Ingawanij and McKay 2012; Robinson 2013). Acknowledging that the relations between independence and the dominant social, cultural and industrial systems are diverse and complex rather than binary, these studies pay considerable attention to localised factors that shape the development and culture of independent film cultures and films. The growth of digital video technology, access to internet and informal working methods, for instance, are considered crucial factors enabling the expansion of an independent film culture, aesthetics and publics. Notwithstanding the significance of transnational alliances and networks, the development of specific forms of regional and national independent cinema cultures makes evident the fundamental role of historically specific social and political contexts, histories and visual cultures in shaping this process.

Cultural and industrial context provide a significant axis to identify and map the meaning of independence in national and regionally specific contexts. Chris Berry (2003) takes a comparative approach to argue for a 'relational' conceptualisation of independent documentary interconnected with the examination of historical, social and ideological contexts of production and circulation. In a discussion of East Asian independent documentary practices, he identifies the practice as one relatively independent of capitalist structures and motivations, in which filmmakers view themselves as 'part of the community' and the production process as one of self-mobilisation rather than profit-making (Berry 2003: 141). Notably, Berry's account foregrounds a critical site where the theory and practice of independence is formulated; the relationship between the filmmaker's subject position, artistic practice and the institutionalised systems governing documentary production and exhibition. For Kleinhans (1984) the filmmakers' critical self-identification in relation to dominant political, social, historical and institutional conditions constitutes the primary index of an independent position, a discussion that I will continue in Chapters 2 and 3. By drawing together the standpoints of historical contexts and subjectivities into the study of independent film, we are asked to dwell upon the multiple levels and dimensions of relationality or structural relations – visible and invisible – that produce the historically and culturally specific nature of what may be considered independent. In national contexts, where films are cultural objects reflective of political, cultural, industrial and social histories and struggles for meaning, it becomes difficult to sustain definitions over time, particularly when nations and societies undergo vast cultural and institutional change. What is considered independent in one culture or historical period defies an easy transference across nations, contexts and histories. The identification of independence therefore becomes a historically situated consideration of specific national, cultural, political and industrial contexts and individual filmmaker practices.

Independence as mode of practice

In Waugh's (2011: 242) foundational study, Indian independent documentary is framed as a revolutionary project, 'a countercinema' that connects with the liberatory politics of a 'domestic third world cinema' in contrast to the aesthetic project of state-subsidised art cinema. Considered an expression of political dissent, scholars perceive Independent Indian documentary film as cultural text that offers diverse views, discourses and representations of history to constitute an alternative record of the nation's struggles from non-official viewpoints (Lal 2005; Kapur 2006; Ghosh 2009; Deprez 2015; Monteiro and Jayasankar 2015). The method of representational 'reading' continues an established mode of film scholarship where independence is interpreted through political position-taking within the conceptual framework of the the nation-state. As political–aesthetic critique, the studies reinforce a discursive identification of independent documentary as an ideological form of filmmaking concerned with the representation of history but whose materiality – how it looks and operates on the ground, and the diverse meanings of resistance it offers beyond spectatorship – remains obscured.

In recent developments, a measure of attention has come to be focused upon issues of practice signifying the importance of this area to documentary studies (Dutta 2007; Kapur 2008; Swami 2008; Vohra 2011; Gadihoke 2012; Sen and Sen 2012; Monteiro and Jayasankar 2015). In addition to filmmaker Anand Patwardhan, whose practice continues to attract significant critical attention, practice forms an important component of feminist writing on independent documentary.[7] Beginning in the mid-1990s, feminist contributions to Indian documentary cinema and later to scholarship have consolidated discussions of practice as legitimate sites to examine the meaning and politics of independent documentary as a series of texts and practices (Rajagopal and Vohra 2012; Sarkar and Wolf 2012b). The accounts offer intimate personal insights into the role played by video technology, institutions, policy, censorship and gender in the formulation of concerns and aesthetics as well as modes of production and circulation. Particularly revealing are the accounts of collective filmmaking provided by Deepa Dhanraj of Yugantar Collective (Dhanraj 1986) and members of the Mediastorm Collective (Ghosh et al. 2012). The accounts outline multiple scales of collaboration amongst women filmmakers and between women filmmakers and women's groups. Indicative of moves towards 'deinstitutionalisation' marked by consensus-based decision-making, the practices militate against hierarchical and bureaucratic structures of state and corporate media organisations (Atton 2002: 5).

Neoliberalism and Cultural Contexts of Media Production and Circulation

The objectives of social critique and more radical social transformation foregrounded by independent Indian documentary are historically positioned against a framework of neoliberalism that shapes media and public cultures. The growth of neoliberalism arguably would be impossible without the assistance of commercial media industries that promote ideologies of consumption and self-building through consumption practices. The introduction of neoliberal market reforms in 1991 brought in a range of economic adjustments including the reduction of subsidies, creation of a flexible labour market and privatisation of public sector industries. The role of the state was reinvented in contrast to the statist vision of nation-building of the post-independence Nehruvian mixed economy, where the state occupied the 'commanding heights' from where it planned and governed economic growth while allowing private enterprise to participate in economic activity. The Nehruvian state assumed a direct and major role in national economic production by taking ownership of heavy industries, power generation and all manner of economic production determined to be essential for the growth of consumer-focused industries. According to Kaviraj (2010: 67), Nehru used an ingenious mix of Left ideas from Marxist analysis of economic systems and Fabian concern with economic redistribution but above all, sought to dispel the economic and political dominance of the West through achievement of true economic independence brought about by industrial modernisation. In 1991, forced to avert a foreign exchange crisis, India adopted a New Economic Policy in agreement with the standard structural adjustment measures advised by the International Monetary Fund and the World Bank based upon neoliberal economic policy (Ahmed et al. 2010).

The benefits of liberalisation are debatable and critics have focused on the rising social inequality accompanied by the growth of an aspirational and consumption-motivated middle class as a result of market-focused policies (Ganguly-Scrase and Scrase 2008; Kaviraj 2010; Ludden 2015). Contrary to celebratory narratives that highlight the dynamism of the private sector, large-scale retrenchment and unemployment confronts the organised labour sector, a group that was securely employed in state sectors on the basis of Nehruvian socialist-influenced labour policy (Kaviraj 2010). An unfolding crisis in the rural farming sector has triggered rising rates of rural poverty, growing farm debt and falling assets culminating in the suicides of hundreds of thousands of farmers in different Indian states (Patnaik 2007). In *Nero's Guests*, veteran Indian rural affairs journalist P. Sainath offers a trenchant critique of the globalised agriculture economy through the scathing analogy of a debt-ridden, hungry Indian farmer who wishes to be reborn as a protected, well-fed European cow.

The construction of an Indian enterprise culture is an extremely revealing phenomenon to analyse the mechanics of the cause and effects of widespread public consent for neoliberalism (Gooptu 2013). Consent is given primarily by the growing Indian middle class experiencing new forms of leisure and consumption resulting from growing levels of wealth and individualist beliefs in living the good life (Brosius 2012). Brosius' consideration of neoliberal Indian urbanism, symbolised by privatised urban territory comprising shopping malls, parking lots, gated residences and luxurious green parks patrolled by security guards, testifies to the spatialisation of individualism inscribed in urban areas. The production of neoliberal subjectivities emphasises the individual as key social protagonist who takes accountability for his or her own choices, decisions, success or failures. Foregoing systemic analysis, the active enterprising citizen makes few claims on the state, and is a self-regulated and self-governed individual (Gooptu 2013). The rationale of neoliberal governmentality requires autonomous individuals to govern themselves in the context of a reconceptualised state project and in this process, the regulatory functions of the state are transferred onto 'responsible' and 'rational' individuals (8). According to Gooptu, in India subjectivities are produced in negotiation with multiple state and non-state agents and institutions which create aspirational horizons that promote the engineering of the self through a number of instruments (9). This includes the salutation of successful entrepreneurs, start-up cultures, skill-building and self-improvement industries, beauty and fitness industry, educational system and government policy through which identities are untethered from the collective context of social organisation.

Media, and in particular television, forms a key instrument to communicate neoliberal constructions of subjectivity through the relations fostered between audiences and screen representations. The privatised model of media ownership that took hold in the 1990s entailed a different imagination of the state–citizen relationship once the media abdicated its nation-building function to promotion of market-based ideologies (Rajagopal 2001; Mehta 2008; Athique 2012). Beginning with the cautious opening up of national television broadcaster Doordarshan to limited private programming in the 1980s, the arrival of Hong Kong-based Star TV in 1991 on the heels of the New Economic Policy triggered the rapid proliferation of local network cable and satellite television. In 2015 India had 869 registered TV channels, with nearly 300 around-the-clock news channels (TRAI, report). Grounded in the democratic discourse of press freedom, traditional and online media have continued to expand together in India. Nevertheless, media criticism highlights the underlying bias within Indian media industries and systems of governance that parallel and reflect social hegemonies of caste, class and gender (Rao and Wasserman 2015). Lack of representative media content, reproduction of social disparity and inequality in media industry governance and representation, and a marked disinterest in issues of poverty and marginalisation are viewed as the effects of an increasingly privatised media economy focused on growing market share (ibid.). For Indian independent documentary makers, the tightening 'interlinking' of media industries including film, television, multiplex and advertising has provided little comfort as closed regimes of franchised content flow across screens and spaces. The possibilities for alternate forms of viewing, reflection, and dissent necessary for the construction of public opinion decline with the increasing emphasis on monetisation of time, space and people. The expansion of the internet and new media technologies in the new millennium holds the promise of a dynamic democratic public sphere outside of the authorised media spaces. However, together with issues of access, this optimism is now paired with deepening concerns regarding internet censorship, the rampant use of public security and defamation laws to manage counter opinion, and the growing sophistication of online government surveillance (Pandit 2011; Iosifidis and Wheeler 2016; Litton 2015).[8]

Expectedly, documentary continues to be an 'outsider' in this cultural economy. But equally, the concept of flows in the new global economy understood as a complex, 'overlapping, disjunctive' order, creates openings for subversions through fluidity and movement of ideas, images, objects and people. The expanded space of 'imagined worlds' extends far beyond the conceptual, geographical and political boundary of nation and in these worlds, individuals are able to contest the imaginations of the official mind and of the entrepreneurial mentality that surround them (Appadurai 1990). Improved access to affordable digital video technology, national and transnational finance through NGO, web-based crowdfunding, international television and arts funding, the availability of new digital and physical exhibition platforms, and expanded access to media training and education in India and overseas present new opportunities and possibilities for independent Indian documentary filmmakers. Arranged through overlapping motivations and discourses of art, information, politics and activism, beyond its initial representational focus upon historical crisis and avowedly political address, independent Indian documentary encompasses contemporary explorations of private and artistic subject matter, and intimate vocabularies of poetic, personal and critical filmic grammar.

The Study of Practice

From the practices of everyday life to the complex structures and patterns of activity in institutional settings, practice is a distinct area of theorisation that attempts to understand social organisation through a study of concrete practices (Bourdieu 1977; Polanyi 1998; Schatzki 2001). Practice theorists explicate the wide range of meanings denoted by the term itself, such as 'tradition, tacit knowledge, *Weltenschauung*, paradigm, ideology, framework, and presupposition' (Turner qtd in Rouse 2000: 500). The practice approach is underpinned by a belief that phenomena such as knowledge, meaning, human activity, language, social institutions and historical transformation occur within and are aspects of the constitution of the field of practices.

Addressing the limitation of studying human activities through the means of texts and knowledge forms encoded in language, the practice idiom calls attention to important aspects of human life that include tacit and linguistically inexpressible gestures, bodily skills, practical knowledge and spontaneous responses (Rouse 2000: 500). The study of practice begins with a sociological understanding of society and culture as a realm constituted according to rules and consequential performances instead of objective or biological facts; of actions according to norms and rules rather than instrumentally related events. In pursuing knowledge through the study of practice, I focus on two dimensions of specific relevance to the study of independent artistic practices. The first relates to the social and public aspect of practice, a performance that is publicly accessible, unlike a private mental state or internal thought process. Without discounting the agency of intent, this refers to the ways in which rules, norms and concepts are embodied in publicly comprehensible activity. In other words, the social dimension is articulated and given aesthetic form or vocabulary through practice, inextricably linking practice to a performed and public dimension (Taylor 1985). The second consideration relates to the historical specificity of practice-theoretical approaches to the study of society and social organisation. It is understood that practices occur against the background of social structures and cultures; however, these formations are understood to be dynamic rather than stable and fixed (Turner 1994). Instead of positing a monolithic or uncontested conception of culture, practice theorists recognise the co-existence of 'alternative practices' within a cultural setting (Rouse 506). The study of a discipline through practice is thus the creation of knowledge focused on actions; of externalised performances that are arranged in relation to historically specific governing structures and rules.

It is important to point out that unlike auteurist studies of individual authors, the study of practice draws attention to the relation between filmmakers as individual subjects but also as members of a collective public located at particular historical moments. Michel de Certeau (1988) views practice as the terrain where those collectively subordinated under the term 'consumers' in modern societies 'disguise and transform' themselves in order to survive (xi). In India, 'the practice of everyday life' extends from social practices to complex political practices where individuals and groups develop operational logics to reorganise, for instance, oppressive bureaucratic and governmental regulations and norms. In his study of urban media practices, Ravi Sundaram (2009) offers us an example of practices of the everyday or innumerable minor practices of informal urban growth in New Delhi following a period of rigid control during the period of Constitutional Emergency. Minor practices are evident in the way that those excluded from authorised systems of land allocation in the urban planning blueprint, the Council Masterplan, innovatively recombine and redefine space to create what Sundaram terms a 'pirate city' that is officially declared as unauthorised (81).

For documentary practitioners, the strength of everyday practices lies in their productiveness; their unsystematic and adaptive character that bypasses disciplinary and normative socio-economic rationalities. These actions, detours and appropriations of regulations and parameters offer productive sites for an examination of the nature of 'independence' as it applies to documentary practice and further afield to media production and social relations.

Filmmakers and Films

The mixed methods approach to research combines critical textual analysis from the standpoint of documentary theory and on-site empirical research, posited as an important form of cultural inquiry. Both methods inquire into the work practices and social interactions of cultural producers to render transformative potential into observable information. I chose an empirical method for the study of localised fields and processes as it makes fewer assumptions about individuals, practices and relationships to draw its findings and produce 'grounded theory' (Davis 2008: 60). In a departure from 'theoretical bricolage', the empirically grounded methods of this study are consistent with David Bordwell's (1996) definition of 'middle level research' as a counter-approach to the study of non-Western cinemas ignored by 'orthodox film history' (28). Therefore, emphasising site and historical specificity, empirical evidence together with critical analysis forms the bulwark of the concepts proposed in this book (29).

The findings in this book are drawn from the analysis of several extended unstructured interviews with documentary filmmakers and my personal observations conducted during two field visits to India between February 2013 – January 2014 and October 2014 – January 2015.

The task of translating and deriving concepts from dispersed and unsystematic practices presented me with several challenges. The first involved determining an appropriately sufficient corpus of texts and of individual filmmakers to draw meaningful conclusions. The second challenge concerned the selection of filmmakers which, whilst not claiming to be representative, would reflect the diversity of individuals, positions and practices of independent documentary filmmaking at this present time in India. To address these questions, I selected filmmakers who offer a range of positions in relation to modalities of practice from privately financed to NGO-sponsored filmmaking, express wide-ranging thematic concerns distributed across historical politics to image semiotics, and finally, reflect the gender diversity of those engaged in the practice. The selected filmmakers, New Delhi based Rahul Roy, Chennai resident Amudhan R. P., Mumbai resident Paromita Vohra and, also residing in Mumbai, the filmmaking partners Anjali Monteiro and K. P. Jayasankar, are recognised for a substantial body of films in the post-reform phase and share a deeply reflective relation with their practice.

Chapter Organisation

This book is organised into five chapters. Apart from Chapter 1, which identifies key historical and theoretical foundations, each chapter is conceptually sectioned into three parts. The first section is a contextualising discussion about the historical and disciplinary debates that frame the focus area of the chapter. In the second section I construct an analytical description of the work practices of individual filmmakers based upon primary research in the form of interviews with filmmakers, film participants and relevant individuals involved with the production and circulation of independent documentary. My attempt here is to construct an ongoing critical dialogue between broader concepts of documentary studies and the situated perspectives that emerge from individual accounts and the analysis of films. These accounts highlight the historical significance of documentary as a space of oppositional representation, but also how the practice of independence is structured in relation to institutions, industry practices, individual subjectivities and technology in post-reform India. In the final section I analyse and theorise each focus area which illuminates the culturally specific dimensions of Indian independent documentary.

In order to outline the specific cultural terrain and meaning of Indian independent documentary, my first chapter addresses the period from the 1980s onwards to the present day, beginning with an outline of the self-conceptualisation of 'independence' by Indian documentary filmmakers. Disclosing foundational democratic values of free speech, equal representation and civic associations, the formulation is propelled through representational practice and equally, the substantive means of organising and social participation undertaken by documentary filmmakers. Examining diverse events including the formation of collectives, alternative film festivals, citizen partnerships and other forms of democratic petitioning including public protest, I consider the importance of 'relationality' or 'bundles of relations' as the underpinning fundamentals of the practice (Bourdieu and Wacquant 1992: 16). I then move on to identify the context-specific functioning of the three central concepts of documentary studies as identified by Bill Nichols (1991): the position of the filmmaker, the politics of textual representation and the position of the documentary spectator. Taking advantage of a conceptual approach, I examine a wide range of historical and textual documents using the lever of reflexivity as a method to delineate key theoretical and pragmatic debates that structure standpoints in independent Indian documentary. Hence, I trace the conceptualisation of 'documentary filmmaker' formed in dialogue with the values of Third Cinema, the feminist 'documentary text' that critiques media representation and ideologies, and finally, the problematising of 'documentary spectator' evident in the methods of participatory video producers. Together these debates portray the historical, cultural and social concerns that are important to understand independent Indian documentary, and particularly its non-procedural and self-aware character.

In Chapter 2, my focus is on the concrete ways in which independent filmmakers have crafted non-standard methods and artistic vocabularies to realise a form of 'independence' that frequently runs counter to commodity relations which position cultural production in terms of consumption and cultural producers as industry professionals. Speaking to the questions I raised in Chapter 1 regarding professionalised identities like media producer, scriptwriter, artist, journalist or activist, stabilised through industrial functions and accountabilities, I identify the ways in which independent practice is constituted with consideration to individual capacities, goals and ethos. Critical discourses in documentary have historically defined the limits of theory and practice, an issue I address in this chapter by employing a methodological framework which incorporates film content as one element in an inquiry that is equally interested in the work practices and social biographies of filmmakers as major functionaries of an independent documentary culture. I argue that as a practice, independent Indian documentary has developed an artisanal mode of production that is deprofessionalised in contrast to the focus on professional specialisation and standardisation of creative processes in industrial modes of media production. This is a critical feature as it permits a radical reimagination of documentary as signifying practice existing in the everyday that produces a system of references to interpret social process and actors, dismissed by mainstream media representation.

In Chapter 3, I focus on documentary financing and two forms of organisation, an institutionally managed and a private self-managed mode of production initiated in response to the chronic and historical lack of production support for documentary from the industry and public sectors. My focus is upon the concrete actions which filmmakers create to resist an instrumental framing of documentary film under a range of social functions and communication discourses in an ongoing struggle for artistic expression. I examine the organisational arrangements that form around independent documentary to argue that 'independence' materialises through a series of de Certeau's (1988) 'ruses'. Involving principles of de-economisation and decapitalisation, filmmakers primarily work in non-industrial non-profit settings but through distinct forms of patronage. Independence becomes visible in a series of tactical adaptations where standardised media practice is displaced by the formation of cooperative social alliances, the reduced significance of capital in the production process and non-monetary rewards. These reworked practices implicate the mode of documentary inquiry, textual aesthetics and political position-taking to render possible the expression of representational and semiotic concerns within institutional production environments.

In Chapter 4, I examine the structures and practices of independent documentary circulation and exhibition in a bid to discuss the ways in which independence is asserted within and against the institutional systems of film and video circulation and the rules of censorship. Taking into account the tactical and innovative ways in which filmmakers resist assigned peripheral modes and spaces of cultural circulation, I demonstrate the operation of an idea critical to independence, that of resistance to the commercially reified roles of consumer–producer assigned to the artist–audience relationship. Circulation, I contend, is reframed as a forum for dialogue that creates 'involved' publics rather than limited to frameworks of cultural dissemination marked by logics of quantity, profit and markets (Atton 2002: 25). I argue that the construction of participant-publics and the re-evaluation of cultural ownership or 'copyright' repurpose both technological and historical norms, giving shape to Garcia and Lovink's (Garcia and Lovink 1997) proposition of tactical media through which filmmakers create alternative systems of exhibition containing the vital potential to disrupt a highly regulated public domain.

My final chapter examines the nature of social associations between documentary filmmakers and documentary participants, and the types of knowledge these associations reveal about the social relations imagined and constructed by the practice of independent Indian documentary. Particularly in the industrial and social context of the NGO-dominated production and distribution environments where governmentality produces specific subject relations and discourses of subject positions (donor, recipient, client, expert), these relationships function as a lens to bring into focus the reorganisational scope of independent documentary practice and its potential to challenge socially assigned identities, relations, functions and thus social relations. From this position, I argue that at least in the practice and works of the filmmakers examined, alternate grounds of 'interdependent filmmaking' are noticeable, often formed between socially disparate groups by means of reorganised processes such as 'negotiated consent'. When projected alongside broader historical practices of documentary, the relationships point towards 'interdependent filmmaking' predicated upon horizontal linkages between filmmakers, individuals and communities, organised around diverse commitments to documentary production that critique reified roles and knowledge hierarchies of media producer, media participant and audience ascribed through discourse and institutions.

The study of practice offers one amongst many methodologies for constructing knowledge about independent cultural production. It is predicated upon the idea that the organisation of independent modes of cultural production offers a particularly useful insight to enable us to think about the fundamentally organising and liberatory potential of independent practice in relation to the governmental neoliberal systems of social, economic and political organisation. It is a partial account from a particular standpoint that is interested in revealing and making visible the structures, language and performances which allow institutional systems to organise, manage and arrange individuals, culture and ideas, and the ways that exercise of power also produces resistance at the very site that it is exercised. The struggle against forms of 'subjection', against subjectivity and submission, which Foucault (1982) identifies as one of the three types of struggles against domination, forms the core of the artistic and social concerns across which I will identify 'independence'.

Notes

1. The original email and subsequent circulation include the filmmaker's name; however, I exclude this information here for ethical and privacy reasons, as I was unable to contact the filmmaker directly to obtain permission for its use.
2. On 25 June 1975, Prime Minister Indira Gandhi suspended the civil rights and constitutional liberties guaranteed by the constitution of India to all citizens. During this period, which is referred to as the Constitutional Emergency, democracy was brought to a halt, conferring upon Gandhi the power to rule by decree.
3. The film documents the popular student movement in Bihar led by its Gandhian leader J. P. Narayan, whose popular call against the 'corrupt' regime of Indira Gandhi led to the proclamation of the Emergency.
4. The New Economic Policy, adopted by India in 1991 as a way to avert a foreign exchange crisis, was in agreement with the standard structural adjustment measures advised by the International Monetary Fund and the World Bank based upon neoliberal economic principles. See Ahmed, Kundu and Peet (2010) and Kaviraj (2010) for detailed analysis of the wide-ranging political and social effects of liberalisation.
5. NGOs are variously defined as 'private, voluntary, nonprofit groups' or as 'humanitarian organisations' that are granted 'NGO status' by intergovernmental organisations such as the United Nations (UN) or European Community (EC), by NGOs in developed countries, or by national governments (Khagram, Riker and Sikkink 2002; Sen 1993). I agree with Sen's identification of NGOs in India as large and medium-sized developmental and empowerment-oriented non-profit organisations which receive foreign funds. NGOs operate in a wide range of sectors, including health and education.

I am interested primarily in social sector national and international non-governmental organisations that aim to publicly influence some form of social change. These are identified as key organisational forms that can implement the global commitment to 'bottom up' development, in contrast to the efforts of experts from large bureaucratic institutions (including the state) (Kamat 2004).

6. The protean view of documentary can be seen in the Kabir Project, an ongoing media production initiative headed by singer–filmmaker Shabnam Hashmi and financed by four organisations, including the Ford Foundation. With multiple purposes that include documentation, cultural preservation and public communication, in the Kabir Project documentary film is located at the intersection of several functions.
7. For references to interviews with Anand Patwardhan, see interviews with him by Ruth Vanita (1986), Robert Crusz and Priyath Liyanage (1983), John Akomfrah (1997), Kathleen Maclay (2004) and Georgia Korossi (2015). For references to scholarly writing about Patwardhan's cinema, see Bhrigupati Singh and Ashok Bhargava (2002), Vijay Prashad (2007), Geeta Kapur (2008) and Catherine Bernier (2013).
8. A. Litton (2015) and S. Ghosh (2013) provide a comprehensive analysis of the Centralised Monitoring System, a system that would be capable of conducting multiple privacy-intrusive activities involving sifting through large amounts of data, ranging from call data record analysis to social media mining, access to private email and location-based monitoring.

CHAPTER 1

Histories and Cultures: Space, Filmmaker, Text and Spectator

The heterogeneous practice of independent Indian documentary is scarcely amenable to the construction of a systematised historical narrative and therefore in this chapter I take a conceptual approach to identify positions and debates integral to the formulation of its central concerns, beliefs and idioms. I specifically focus upon its dialectical relation with discourses of art and media, and social and political institutions during the formative decades of the 1980s and 1990s. Heterogeneity or diversity is perhaps the operative concept here, for in this historical analysis, documentary film is both a semiotic project, a site of cultural critique as well as a form of representative social communication. Patently the practice critiques mainstream media representation and the narrowness of public debate but there also exists a relation of reflexivity within its practices and discourse that encourages a recurring mode of self-awareness and critique. The presence of reflexivity prevents independent Indian documentary from acquiring a generic character concerned merely with reproduction, multiplication and output, to instead remain attentive to considerations and debates around its identity, symbols, meanings and relations in society.

As an artistic undertaking, even as documentary may perform diverse functions and attract various forms of valuation, it contains the grounds for a distinctly 'reflexive practice', understood as one in which the artist and subject not only comprehend a depicted world but reflect upon their historical and social position in the world (Feige 2010: 134). Focusing on the concept of reflexivity allows for a conceptualisation of independent documentary as a set of practices whose form and politics are in a state of critical dialogue with society and its own histories and canons, rather than a free-standing mode contained within a rigid oppositional horizon. In a foundational essay, Dana Polan (1974) explicates the aesthetics of the dynamics of reflexivity in three steps. First, a distance from worldly reality is inherent in art and its language of codes and constructions – a distance which allows the work to articulate as a form of knowledge and establish an entity as a mediated representation of reality, rather than reality itself. Second, is an attitude of self-reflexivity, a distance in which the work glances at itself and enunciates its arrangement of artistic codes and beliefs. This is the text estranging the viewer from its own formal devices. Finally, and perhaps most significant to the discussion of documentary film, reflexivity is a gesture out of the self-enclosed world of the artwork toward a real world which the mediations of art usually leave behind. In other words, the dynamics of reflexivity can foreground the relation of the documentary towards the world it is drawn from, towards concrete forms of action, building of solidarities and material possibilities of transformation. By pointing inwards to the power relations within the film and outwards to the world within whose formal power structures the film is situated, reflexivity offers both symbolic and material ways of engaging the spectator. Insofar as critical modes of viewing provoke the interrogation of representation, by positioning the film within a historical movement, event or phenomenon, documentary materially connects the spectator's world with the actuality of the depicted world. Reflexivity, when foregrounded as dynamic relation of the film with the world, is substantively relevant to define the scope of independent documentary which is perennially defined in relation to an Other (mainstream, dominant). Rather, Chris Berry resolves the fundamental problem through a 'relational' episteme of independence which recognises the shifting and fluid nature of what constitutes the 'dominant' in different nations (2006: 112). Reflexivity demonstrates the inherent relationality or dependence of independence configured by its relation with the historical and contemporary, society and art, structures and interpretation, and technologies and agents, revealing itself as 'existing only in and through its relation with other properties' (Bourdieu 1998: 6).

Eschewing the limits of historical chronology, in this chapter I employ the productive quality of reflexivity as proposed by Polan as a mechanism to examine how it has activated artistic reflection and new formulations as filmmakers respond to historical conditions as well as visual cultures and representational systems. Independent filmmaking in India encompasses more than a semiotic undertaking and documentary filmmakers frequently share a personal stake in the issues and people they choose to portray. Indicating a significant extra-textual social realm or network of relations, my account extends to these processes and relations that form outside of the text to reveal the ways in which independent filmmaking is inextricably tied with social process. In the first section of the chapter, I sketch a brief account of events and discourses about how filmmakers have self-conceptualised the meaning of 'independence' and its close relation to a primary belief in the institutions and processes of democracy. In Section 2, I bring together Polan's mediations on reflexivity to identify the context-specific functioning of the three fundamental concepts of documentary studies as identified by Nichols (1991): the position of the filmmaker, the politics of textual representation and the documentary spectator. I trace the specific conceptualisation of 'documentary filmmaker' formed through engagement with Third Cinema, the critique of media representation expressed by feminist filmmakers and finally, the problematising of documentary spectator evident in the methods of participatory video producers. Together these debates portray the historical, cultural and social dialogues that have contributed to the development of the forms and cultures of independent Indian documentary.

Public Space and Democratic Instruments

In a mediatised and regulated public domain, two instances of associational or cooperative activity persuasively illustrate the social agenda of independent Indian filmmakers who employ representational practice in contiguity with more material methods of organising. Drawing additional strength from unity, collective forms of action are noteworthy for their profound democratic significance as a working model and to promote socially important issues. Two important actions by filmmakers stand out in this regard and depict a firm belief in the democratic instrument of collective action. In 1996 independent filmmakers formed the Forum for Independent Film and Video, issuing a vision statement that outlined a national agenda for independent documentary filmmaking. The second and more visible action in the form of a campaign against state censorship mounted in 2004 made use of collective resistance and protest to trigger both short- and long-term shifts within the field of independent documentary and its wider exhibition and viewing cultures. Both actions allow us to witness the 'relational' nature of independent documentary culture at once organised and distributed across values of social activism, constitutional rights and artistic freedoms.

The Forum for Independent Film and Video (FIFV) built upon a history of film collectives like Yugantar (f. 1980, Karnataka), Mediastorm (f. 1986, New Delhi), the Prakrit Media Collective (f. 1987, Ahemdabad/Bangalore), the Alternative Communications Forum (f. 1980s in Kerala as Media Collective) and the Drishti Media Collective (f. 1991, Ahemadabad), which deinstitutionalised the processes of film production. Collective modes of filmmaking paralleled the rise of film activism elsewhere in Asia, which was identified as a revolt against an 'original sin' or the birth of cinema in the context of 'atomised individuals' in a Western capitalist society (Park 2011: 196). In Korea, these advocates of collective filmmaking drew upon folk cultures that ascribed to group rather than individual authorship. In India, collectives organised themselves around alternate relations of collective labour, shared capital resources and joint decision-making, in contrast to the labour hierarchies of commercial studio and public sector film production. Founded by independent documentary filmmakers in 1996, the New Delhi-based FIFV published a proposal for an alternate media formation entitled 'A Vision for Television', which principally demarcated independent documentary from profit-oriented industrial media and from state propaganda. Central to this distinction was a historical–critical evaluation of post-reform shifts in media broadcasting from a state-managed activity to a market-driven economic activity focused upon 'delivering audiences to advertisers' (2). Following the implementation of the New Economic Policy, the arrival of satellite channels in the early 1990s began to blur the categories of voter and consumer through ratings-driven news, current affairs and entertainment programming (Rajagopal 2001; Jeffrey 2008). For FIFV, the closer ties between commercial media, realpolitik and a mediatised social sphere came at the detriment of public debate and free spaces for the formation of public opinion.

Critiquing emerging media platforms and practices, FIFV questioned the curtailment of a representative public sphere in the face of proliferating commercial media ownership. Hence, from its politically and commercially independent location outside the 'giant broadcasting and production companies', the group insisted on independence as a precondition to democratic free speech and the freedom to express social and personal concerns (13). FIFV's anxieties were not unfounded. In his extensive analysis of this period of Indian television broadcasting, Rajagopal argues that liberalisation was accompanied by complex alliances between right-wing religious Hindutva groups and the market that played out through the content of television. Inherently 'contradictory', these affiliations simultaneously promoted individualism and consumption-based modernity while being 'aggressive, exclusionary, and hostile to individual expression' (26). Media technologies like television became a primary instrument to create consent for new market-driven practices of consumption and for the construction of self and subjectivities. Viewed in terms of a partnership relation, both television and the market economy disseminated information to help circulate goods as well as to socialise members of society, explains Rajagopal (4). Advertising formed the motor of an economic process which produced audiences to serve sponsors. In the 1990s, large-scale expansion in television advertising was driven by the change in government policy on foreign ownership of advertising agencies (Ciochetto 2009). During this period, advertising contributed to the process of social and cultural changes that complemented globalisation in India by foregrounding and endorsing values of competition, individualism, consumerism and the promotion of new icons of corporate success and consumer lifestyles (ibid.).

In contrast to what it considered a homogenising and hegemonic mediated public domain, FIFV expressed its commitment to a public form of representative documentary cinema related to the everyday realities of marginalised communities and individuals (13). The model laid its foundation in an imaginary of genuinely multiple 'democratic media', where all participants would have access to common channels with equal capacities to communicate and receive responses. Hence its proposal for an autonomous public service broadcasting unit dedicated to the provision of programming in the public interest was similar to the USA-based Public Broadcasting Service.[1] FIFV argued that the parallel broadcasting system would guarantee a high degree of autonomy to filmmakers from systems of market and state control, whilst also supporting non-standard modes of documentary from the avant garde to the activist. Regrettably, the group tailed off over the next two years; nevertheless, continuing its public itinerary, many of its members were to reconvene eighteen years later, along with a broader coalition of intellectuals to stage a more visible and direct confrontation with the state in another public intervention.

In 2004, a determinedly visible public action by independent documentary filmmakers yields further evidence of principled investment in the institutions of representative democracy beyond the limits of electoral instruments. The formation of Mumbai-based Vikalp Films for Freedom in 2004 is viewed belatedly by Geeta Kapur as the 'occasion for the documentary movement to erupt'; however, the importance of this moment cannot be underestimated in defining the political relationship between independent documentary, public domain and the nation-state (Kapur 2008: 39). Filmmakers directly confronted the state when the government-run 2004 Mumbai International Film Festival of Documentary and Short Films (MIFF) rejected several politically volatile films on ambiguous grounds. Following a series of failed negotiations, the unofficial exercise of censorship became the flashpoint for a larger debate on constitutionally guaranteed free expression and democratic rights, particularly under governments inclined towards authoritarianism (Monteiro and Jayasankar 2015). Direct action by filmmakers in the form of rallies and public debates culminated in the constructive formation of Vikalp (Alternative), an alternative film festival whose first programme included all the censored films accompanied by discussions and public debates about the public effects of

Figure 1.1 Filmmakers (Anjali Monteiro and Anand Patwardhan) hold signs promoting Vikalp – the Alternative Film Festival in Mumbai in 2004. Photo courtesy of Ashish Avikunkthak.

censorship and the need to protect freedom of expression. Proposed by thirty-five filmmakers from across India, the festival management drew upon voluntary effort from filmmakers and supporters, demonstrating a form of direct action, at once a model of collective organisation and an example of cultural practice that blurs distinctions between art and society. The successful staging of Vikalp in February 2004 has since encouraged coalitions of filmmakers like the Vikalp city chapters and Docuwallahs, an online community where members share information and mobilise action against instances of censorship and broader issues of cultural freedom in the larger South Asian region.

The struggles against censorship that led to the formation of Vikalp are instructive to our understanding of independent documentary film as a terrain for the staging of alternate social subjectivity beyond that of individual self-interest. On an organisational level, it is indicative of a form of filmmaking that foregrounds historical coalition-building as legitimate instrument of civil society. An institutional component of the political structure of liberal democracy, civil society plays a vital role in maintaining a dynamic public sphere and the formation of public

Figure 1.2 The B. P. Gupta Bhavan in downtown Prabhadevi, which also houses the Lokvangmay Griha (or House of People's Literature), functioned as the alternative venue for Vikalp in 2004. Photo courtesy of Ashish Avikunkthak.

Figure 1.3 Spectators watch *A Pinch of Skin* at the monthly Vikalp documentary screening series at Prithvi Theatre in Bandra, Mumbai in 2013.

opinion through the culture of debate. The rise of 'associational life' based on a 'secular-associational model' instead of caste- or religion-based identity is a fundamental foundation of civil society in India (Jayal 2007: 143). Non-party political formations, grassroots movements and new social movements that target historical forms of injustice have historically inhabited this civic associational space. Connected through shared participatory principles, Vikalp and subsequent groups model civic associations that promote the functioning of democracy through cultural means. Initiatives in this direction have substantively attempted to expand audiences for documentaries, built alternative cultures of viewing and mounted resistance towards official and unofficial forms of censorship.

Fostered through access to social media and digital technology, a contemporary form of participatory association involves coalitions between independent documentary filmmakers and ordinary citizens. Especially significant is the way that these coalitions are organised by radically involved methods of organisation that mobilise citizens not only as viewing publics but as agents in the construction of an alternative viewing culture. The circulation of *Muzaffarnagar Baaqi Hai/Muzaffarnagar Eventually* (2015), a film that interrogates the role of Bharatiya Janta Party (BJP) cadres in stirring sectarian violence against Muslims in the northern state of Uttar Pradesh, illustrates the operation of new modes of participation that respond to restrictive power formations and policy action. In early August 2015, acting without official sanction, Akhil Bharatiya Vidyarthi Parishad (ABVP), the youth cadre of the ruling right-wing BJP government, disrupted public screenings of the film at campuses of Delhi University. Responding to the unofficial nature of the action, an appropriate extrajudicial response was formulated and spearheaded by the Cinema of Resistance, a volunteer group of cinema activists in coalition with filmmaker Nakul Sawhney, film societies, student groups and people's organisations. Organised by means of social media applications like Facebook, WhatsApp and online blogs and email, an alternate programme of screenings was proposed and communicated to citizens nationwide. On the nominated date of 25 August 2015, fifty screenings across forty-four towns were organised to an audience of nearly 7,000 viewers mobilised through web-based communication and the participation of ordinary citizens taking decisive roles.[2] To the degree that the film itself constructs arguments against a divided polity, the relations mobilised in the joint filmmaker–citizen partnerships propose to reclaim divided publics implicating social relations as much as documentary cultures.

An 'Involved' Filmmaker

Insofar as independent Indian documentary cinema responds to socio-historical conditions and the culturally dominant visual politics of institutional documentary, there are also substantial sites of exchange with international documentary cultures. I am particularly concerned with the values and concepts through which the subject position of the documentary filmmaker in relation to self, art and society has been debated. The practices and theories of Third Cinema are a critical site in this regard as evident in the localised translation and adaptation of the discourse in the practice of Anand Patwardhan, considered the stalwart of Indian political documentary. According to Getino and Solanas (1976), the work of a revolutionary cinema is to bring the intellectual or artist stationed behind 'universal art and models' with the reality of people's struggle to produce cultural counter-practices from a position of common interests (5). In Patwardhan's practice, localised translations of Third Cinema enact critical departures from the Griersonian documentary producer who functioned with the 'general sanction' of the state apparatus to firstly fulfil its needs, rather than to promote the cause of the documentary participants (Aitken 2013: 190).

Anand Patwardhan's *Waves of Revolution* (1975) is considered an international exemplar of the localised translation of New Latin American Cinema and its political aesthetics (Hanlon 2014; Kishore 2016). Patwardhan's own writing about his filmmaking philosophy refers specifically to two radical manifestos of New Latin American cinema. The first, 'Towards a Third Cinema', is an essay written by Octavio Getino and Fernando E. Solanas following the making of *The Hour of the Furnaces* (1968), and the second is Julio García Espinosa's 'For an Imperfect Cinema'. For Patwardhan, both documents offer theoretical positions that 'justify and demarcate the emergence' of a guerrilla cinema in the Third World (1984: 446). In terms of film models, Patwardhan has consistently cited Patricio Guzman's *The Battle of Chile* (1975) as a film that presented to him the possibility of adopting cinema as a cultural instrument of protest (Korossi 2015).

Casting a terrain for the independent filmmaker, Patwardhan's turn towards Third Cinema is a critical push against the Griersonian mode of authoritative 'oratory' adopted by public service documentary aimed at building national consensus between the state and citizens. In the period of postcolonial nation-building, documentary production and exhibition acted as a vital tool of domestic policy objectives to unite the nation behind a national identity coincident with the Indian state (Roy 2007). Consequently, the responsibility for the production of public service documentary was given to the Films Division of India, an institution governed by the Ministry of Information and Broadcasting, directly under the command of a high-ranking civil servant, the Chief Producer. Annual film production output and content were jointly determined by the central government and state governments who took into account the priorities of the centralised Five Year Plans, events of national importance and political exigencies to distribute and allocate personnel, resources and stock.[3] In contrast, Third Cinema offered a method for conceptualising a direct relation between the intellectual or the documentary filmmaker, art and social participation. Confronting the cultural horizons of paternalistic public utility filmmaking and the detachment of Direct Cinema, New Latin American cinema questioned the separation between intellectual cultural activity and social participation. Paul Willemen (1989) interprets this practice of politically committed art as an 'end to the division between art and life and therefore between professional, full time intellectuals such as film-makers or critics and the people' (5). In Patwardhan's film practice, these conjectures were resolved through a method that collapsed the distance between image-making, political commitment and direct modes of resistance.

Patwardhan's *Bombay Our City* (1984), winner of the 1986 Best Non-Feature Film award given by the Directorate of Film Festivals, bears witness to a complex interplay between political commitment and cinematic form. The film emerged from the filmmaker's membership in the Mumbai-based Nivara Hak Suraksha Samiti (Committee for the Protection of the Right to Shelter), an umbrella group of twenty organisations opposed to the slum demolition activities of the Bombay Municipal Council. United by the demand for alternative housing to replace demolished slum dwellings, the committee also responded to crisis situations as demolition teams arrived to destruct dwellings. Together with political commitment to the fair distribution of urban space, the film is constructed from Patwardhan's personal knowledge of and experience within this resistance movement.

To the degree that commitment to direct action alongside film subjects is a complex issue implicating documentary ethics, truth and neutrality, it also evokes significant textual issues, and what becomes apparent in Patwardhan's films is the relative reorganisation of social function and visual style. In an interview with Sean Cubitt about *Bombay, Our City*, Patwardhan reflexively identifies the materialisation of an aesthetic of active participation, not of perfection or visual order but of the partial, the opportune and the chanced-upon. He describes,

> At the same time, the roles between film-making and activism are constantly changing. Has the organisation suffered? I definitely would have got better footage – zooms,

> hidden mics, dramatic shots of bulldozers clearing people out of their shanties at dawn – but instead we warned the people that the demolitions might happen and tried to organise resistance . . . The most dramatic footage would have been the panic as the demolitions started, but it is too hard to sit by and watch, because there were people there we had come to know. We are organising demos and also filming them (1986: 63).

Testifying to this ethical dilemma between intervention and reporting, in *Bombay, Our City*, the camera rarely captures the beginning of the moment of crisis; the arrival of bulldozers, frenzy of violence and actual demolition are nearly absent from the visual narrative. Unlike the planned pre-scripted official documentary, visual forms in these independent films embody traces of the conditions and constraints of the filming location, events and recording technologies.

Patwardhan's disavowal of critical or aesthetic valuation in favour of political efficacy resonates with Third Cinema's key arguments against 'critics (mediators)' as arbiters of artistic value (Espinosa, 3). In one of the most cited sequences from the film, the filmmaker avowedly expresses a position of representative significance rather than semiotic or critical importance, which nevertheless the sequence has acquired over time. The sequence begins with a shot of hundreds of slum evictees camped on the pavements of South Mumbai under the pouring monsoon rain. As the camera tracks across, a distraught homeless woman holding an infant confronts the filmmaker:

> 'Where can we go? Do you have a solution? You just want to earn a name taking photographs, what else can you do? Don't just take photographs of the poor.' (*Bombay, Our City*).

The filmmaker includes the provocative visuals that compel a consideration of the possible exhaustion of representation against the lived material dimensions of human crisis. On a critical scale, the sequence invokes formal self-reflexivity, a key area of interest in documentary studies and art criticism. Reflexively, the sequence visualises the political issues of class privilege between the filmmaker, spectator and the marginalised film subject to raise questions of voice and power in documentary representation and subjectification. It raises fundamental doubts about the effectiveness of filmmaking and film viewing as political practices. Crucially, Patwardhan reads the sequence differently and moderates metacritical concerns with political impact, 'I toyed with ending with that scene . . . But finally the main contradiction is not between the filmmaker and the filmed, but between them and the landowners' (1986: 64). Thus what might have foregrounded meaning of a critical–theoretical nature is rendered peripheral as a symptomatic response of ineffective liberalism from the standpoint of Patwardhan and Third Cinema.

A further materialist resonance between New Latin American filmmakers and Patwardhan's practice can be found in a coincident perspective regarding a functionalist view of cinema as an object of social intervention. Solanas and Getino explicitly exhort cooperation between filmmakers, organisations and the public to address the insufficiency of 'individual rebellion' (52). Organisations involved in direct political struggles fail to attend to the cultural needs of the people and the revolution, creating an imperative for filmmakers to join as co-revolutionaries, they argue. In Patwardhan's case, coalition-building encompasses public persuasion through representation, as well as direct participation alongside social actors. For instance, the rushes from *Bombay, Our City* were successfully used as evidence by the People's Union for Civil Liberties to obtain a temporary reprieve against slum demolitions. However, two years later, after the completion of the film in a merging of art and political action, the filmmaker continued to participate in the movement. In February 1986, Patwardhan courted arrest with 150 slum residents against the demolition of dwellings in the Sanjay Gandhi Nagar slum, and in May he joined a hunger strike with three slum residents to demand alternate land allocation. This form of visible action, while gathering direct support for the cause, also attracts the attention of a broader group of socially connected agents. The support of the educated middle class, civil liberties activists, lawyers and journalists forms an important weapon in the larger struggle. Filmmaking and participation in these conditions, observes Patwardhan (1986), play equal roles in targeting public opinion:

> Well, if this kind of work was not carried on, public opinion, which is already violently against slum dwellers, would be even worse than it is today. The fact that demolitions are protested, keeps public opinion from being totally reactionary and also keeps authorities on their toes. (Vanita 1986)

The conscious ethos of personal involvement was central to a growing culture of non-institutional social documentary in India during the 1980s. The merging of the political and the artistic, of ideas and action, responded to an institutionally constrained mode of documentary through a 'committed' form of filmmaking, whose instruments were both cultural and historical. As Waugh (2011: 6) suggests, committed filmmaking is an 'ideological undertaking' that attempts to not only document but transform the socio-political site where it intervenes. For filmmakers like Patwardhan who arrived from solid experience within political movements, documentary filmmaking was an extension of social participation and thus work practices, methods and objectives were formulated in activist rather than dispassionate terms. This is marked clearly in the films from this phase which can be identified with specific social campaigns and diverse work practices, for instance, solidarity with people's movements and struggles in the films of K. P. Sasi, Vasudha Joshi, Ranjan Palit and Manjira Datta, the campaign for women's constitutional rights in the films of the Mediastorm Collective, and feminist critique of women's labour and domestic relations in films made by Yugantar Collective. For Deepa Dhanraj, feminist filmmaker and co-founder of Yugantar Collective, who was addressing entrenched gender oppression in the domestic and labour spheres, a participatory mode of working with women's groups was the natural outcome of shared objectives. Dhanraj explains:

> We did not come to a ready-made understanding of documentary practice; we were creating a process as we worked. When we started this collective, our intention was to be collaborative and to stand with the women, not only to transmit their story (Kishore 2014).

The politically committed mode was noteworthy for providing a direction forward from neutral observationalism, informational reportage and elitist oratory of public utility documentary. In these films the social world was not only abstracted as object of analysis but critically recognised as the concrete relations and organising system within which documentary functioned.

Text, Representation and Reflexivity

> The reference by one character in a novel to another character in a novel marks the access of the novel to a reflexivity that, as we know, is one of the foremost manifestations of the autonomy of a field: the allusion to the internal history of the genre, a sort of wink at a reader able to appropriate the history of these works (not only the story/history recounted in this work). (Bourdieu 1996: 101)

The arrival of filmmakers from feminist, literary, political and artistic movements during the late 1980s and the 1990s corresponded with the growth of women's studies as a discipline and introduced new concerns about the politics of representation and truth-making in independent Indian documentary. Independent cinema assumed a mode of self-reflexivity where the object of documentary examination expanded from historical phenomenon to include the scrutiny of its own material and symbolic practices and textual forms. Excellent examples of self-reflexive films from this period include *Eleven Miles* (Ruchir Joshi, 1991), *Tales From Planet Kolkata* (Ruchir Joshi, 1993), *Saa* (R.V. Ramani, 1991), *Kamlabai* (Reena Mohan, 1992), *The Hidden Story* (Shikha Jhingan and Ranjini Mazumdar, 1995), *Three Women and a Camera* (Sabeena Gadihoke, 1998) and *Kumar Talkies* (Pankaj Rishi Kumar, 1999). Each is constituted through diverse modes of reflexivity: autobiographical, performative, theatrical and self-reflective. Reflexivity, contends Bill Nichols (2010), asks us 'to see documentary for what it is: a construct or representation' where the authority of the film itself is called into question (194). Speaking to issues I raised in the introduction, a series of questions become evident at this juncture: is the documentary a creative or representative form? Is its purpose to persuade or to provide pleasure? Is it possible to incorporate self-awareness in the diegesis? These questions are directly related to the politics of representation and the self-identification of independent documentary, and continue to be debated in the field.

Before proceeding further, I will establish a distinction between deliberate attention to the cultural potential of reflexivity and the routine deployment of reflective elements as organising narrative devices. While reflexive techniques are present in the earliest independent films including *Waves of Revolution* (1975), where Patwardhan's reflexive narration draws attention to the fraught production schedule of the film, the considered discourse of self-reflexivity draws attention to an examined relation between documentary inquiry, truth and history (Ruby 1980: 157). Hence, I suggest that what distinguishes independent Indian documentary from other forms of non-fiction media representation such as current affairs, reportage, journalism and factual entertainment is the critical engagement with the aesthetic politics of its own historical truth claims and of the invisible yet authoritative position of its agent-filmmaker. Against a history of authoritative claim-making by public service and institutional documentary, reflexivity permits the opening of new epistemological sites beyond narrative facts. The imaginative use of reflexivity creates opportunities for representational and historical critique that are illustrated in *Seven Islands and a Metro* (2006), a film that explores the symbolic gaps between the official and lived histories of Mumbai. Director Madhusree Dutta fictionalises the personae of twentieth-century Urdu authors Ismat Chughtai and Sa'adat Hasan Manto as protagonists to dramatise the experience of migration to a city.[4] The choice to cast the legendary authors known for progressive social critique permits Dutta to script penetrating first-person accounts evocatively arranged through poetic and idiosyncratic expression. Rather than the logos of fact-based techniques, the theatrical interludes activate affective modes of perception towards the fragmented experiences of displacement and optimism that accompany migrant journeys. Not surprisingly, the codification of the real world and persons through the rigid complex of values, technologies and visual language of documentary troubles Dutta:

> My discomfort is about this proclaimed 'unobtrusiveness'. Why do we have to be unobtrusive? Why does the protagonist need to become unmindful of the camera or at least become comfortable with the camera? Could we say that the protagonists must remain 'small' in their screen appearances in order to be part of a larger world order/discourse/visual practice? (qtd in Sarkar and Wolf 2012a: 24)

Reflexivity mounts a determined challenge to the historical realist lineages of social documentary as well as the process of historical narrative construction by foregrounding the movements around enunciation as a central epistemological concern.

Drawing intellectual solidarity, the reflexive methods of feminist filmmakers especially from the Global South, such as Trinh T. Minh Ha's self-aware methodologies of text-making, become equally as significant as their representative concerns with women's struggles and gender inequality. In a reflective essay about the experience of staging a cultural intervention at the 2004 World Social Forum, feminist filmmaker and curator Madhusree Dutta (2004) expresses deep misgivings about the standardisation of resistance. Citing this quote by Trinh T. Minh-Ha from *Framer: Framed*, Dutta raises a number of questions about the need to examine the ethics and aesthetics of representation:

> The work of critical inquiry cannot be content with fixed anti-positions, which were, in their own time, necessary (in regard to the war in Vietnam), but need to be problematised in the context of contemporary histories of political migration. (Minh-Ha quoted in Dutta 2004)

Dutta subsequently proceeds to question the 'fixed anti position' of political arts where the intellectual and social processes of making are hidden in the smooth surfaces of finished cultural forms. Artistic display, she argues, is little more than a cathartic device that must be interrogated to reveal deeper politics of representation, hegemony and objectification. Dutta's pertinently feminist concerns indicate a critical filmmaking practice organised through an interrogated relationship with research, production and representation.

The growth of Western 'film feminism' during the 1960s and 1970s occurred alongside the consciousness-raising action by women's groups in workshops, conferences and political campaigns. Raising diverse issues related to women's oppression such as domestic abuse, rape and the right to abortion, this politicisation of domestic and personal spheres hailed the much-recognised axiom of 'the personal is political'. In a truly feminist cinema, Johnston argued, 'any revolutionary strategy must challenge the depiction of reality . . . so that a break between ideology and text is effected' (1985: 215). In India, the growth of feminist documentary coincided with the emerging field of women's studies in the 1980s and many of the historical and representational issues were identified and debated in a dialogue between feminist theory and practice.[5] The dialogue encompassed critical examination not only of gender stereotypes, but of textual and iconographic conventions that placed females in subordinate positions. Many of the critical approaches to documenting reality in independent Indian documentary began to draw upon feminist theory and visual practice: the interrogation of modes of power in speaking and listening, the favouring of personal histories and the use of fictional elements to blur the boundary between fiction and non-fiction.

The interaction between feminist film theory and cinema occurred in spaces of practice and criticism; amongst cinephile circuits in journals like *Deep Focus* (Geetha 1992; Mohan and Choudhuri 1996), in academia, at a series of Indian Association of Women's Studies (IAWS) conferences, and through educational exchanges.[6] Founded in 1982, the IAWS was a scholarly association that followed the first National Conference on Women's Studies at Bombay in April 1981. The annual IAWS conferences consolidated the discipline of women's studies, which permitted 'the pursuit of a more comprehensive, critical and balanced understanding of social reality', wrote feminist historian Vina Mazumdar (1985). To accomplish this objective, Mazumdar assembled an interdisciplinary realm of practitioners, scholars and activists from women's political groups encompassing feminist knowledge and action.

The Fifth National Conference of IAWS at Jadavpur University, Kolkata in 1991 occupied a pivotal position in bringing together feminist theory and cultural critique, elements that encouraged political analysis of the history and aesthetic of independent documentary cinema. The nearly 600 participants included feminist and gender activists Flavia Agnes, Vina Mazumdar, Urvashi Butalia, Ritu Menon and Kamla Bhasin, women's studies scholars Professor Bharati Ray, Professor Jasodhara Bagchi, Uma Chakravarti and Vina Mazumdar, social workers, researchers and social documentary practitioners. Members of the feminist Mediastorm Collective, Shohini Ghosh, Ranjani Mazumdar and Shikha Jhingan participated as speakers, while Mazumdar and Jhingan also screened their documentary *The Girl Child: Prisoner of Gender* (1991). The conference was sectioned into nine sub-themes. Sub-theme III was devoted to the analysis of mass media representation. The analysis of women's representation in film and television concluded that the operation of a 'grand signifier' mediated the representation of Indian women into normative patterns of subjectivity. Constructed during colonial rule, this was believed to be the main conceptual organiser of gender representation in modern mass media forms (IAWS Newsletter).

The epistemological encounter between feminist theory and media representation became evident in an emerging form of feminist film criticism and feminist praxis. In a paper titled 'Dialectic of Public and Private', Ranjani Mazumdar (1991) draws upon Cora Kaplan's *Essays on Culture and Feminism* to analyse the representation of women in two art-house feature films, *Bhoomika/The Role* (Shyam Benegal, 1977) and *Mirch Masala/Spices* (Ketan Mehta, 1987). In her critique of *Bhoomika*, Mazumdar finds that representations of gender fall short of the complex plurality of identity:

> Concepts of natural, essential and unified identities, a static femininity and masculinity prevent us from getting to the core of the issue. Masculinity and femininity are not pure binary forms but [are] arranged, organised and situated through various social, cultural and political categories. (Mazumdar 1991: 83)

Further on in the paper, Mazumdar comments specifically upon the realist modes of representation in *Bhoomika*. Beyond the possibility of passive modes of identification, she states, realism offers 'no scope for interaction, participation or alternative action' for spectators (84). Together with fellow IAWS 1991 participant Shikha Jhinhan, Ranjani Mazumdar went on to make *The Hidden Story*, a documentary that examines historical gender relations with a critical examination of the realist regimes of documentary representation. The narrative unfolds not in the moment of a social crisis but makes visible the many instances of subordination and resistance in the everyday lives of four rurally located Indian women. As a system of visual representation, the realist text hierarchically defines itself by an 'empirical notion of truth' (MacCabe 1974: 8). Insofar as spectators are concerned, realism fixes subjects in a point of view that fails to reveal the constitutive ideologies of representational forms that require 'certain strategies of subversion' (19). The subversion of documentary realism in *The Hidden Story* takes the form of a reflective first-person voice-over that opens out into an interpretative space between the historical real and its narrative reconstruction by the filmmakers. Decentring their authority, the filmmakers reveal the limitations of their speaking positions as urban dwellers instead of professing complete knowledge of the experiences and struggles of the village-dwelling film subjects. Reflexivity in this film takes the form of a meta-narrative where the filmmakers reflect upon their own learning, questions and doubts as the narrative progresses, and thus make possible reflective ways of viewing and interpretation.

The simultaneous recuperation of political and sexual subjects in feminist films worked dialectically. First, it emerged as a thematic concern in films about issues of identity, gender equality and sexuality, and second, it provoked a poetics of reflexivity that questioned conventions of social documentary with reflexive, reflective and personal forms of artistic expression. Thus films including *Memories of Fear* (Madhusree Dutta, 1995), *Adha Aasman/Half the Sky* (Samina Mishra, 1996), *Tales of the Night Fairies* (Shohini Ghosh, 2002), *Sita's Family* (Saba Dewan, 2002), *Majma* (Rahul Roy, 2001) and *Many People, Many Desires* (T. Jayashree, 2004) decentre discourses of heteronormativity, gender roles, sexuality and the body. The filmmakers are concomitantly self-conscious of their own status as authors and speakers as well as acknowledging their entry into the world of the subject.

Culture is a site of struggle between the ideologies, ideas, functions and imaginations of society. In the field of communication, the struggle, suggests Williams, is between the idea of a generalised public, the object of mass communication, and the construction of 'an actual community' based on a genuine 'theory of communication' (1983: 313). In the field of cultural production, specifically independent Indian documentary faced similar struggles with regard to purpose, relations and politics that echoed the wider debates in the field of documentary studies where documentary straddled both historical and cultural terrains. What the feminist-theorised forms of documentary disputed was a view of documentary as neutral communication whose speaking positions and politics of enunciation were obscured in its seemingly noble purpose of education and advocacy. And while both committed and feminist filmmaking understood documentary as a set of aesthetic and formal relations, participatory video embodied a radical reconceptualisation of documentary, spectator and audience spurred by the mobility of portable video.

Spectator and Horizontal Communication

The availability of portable video recording and playback systems during the 1980s was a significant enabler in the consolidation and expansion of Indian independent documentary production and circulation (Monteiro and Jayasankar 1998; Gadihoke 2003; Rajagopal and Vohra 2012; Dutta 2013; Battaglia 2014). Video technology is central to the practice of independent filmmakers, and each of the filmmakers I interviewed either initiated their film practice with analogue video or later migrated with the availability of digital video. Notably, video was placed in a discourse of development communication in 1973 as a form of inexpensive 'little media' which shaped its use as a form of two-way communication technology between media producers and publics (Schramm 1973). Development communication mediated the arrival of video in India and authorised a discourse of participatory communication that formed around the technical and social functions of video. What was noteworthy in these emerging media practices was the shifting position of the documentary spectator, whose capacities, needs and experiences became central to the form and practice of media communication. NGOs and community-level organisations viewed media in predominantly utilitarian terms and played an organising role in this emerging culture, where independent Indian documentary became entangled with values of media communication.

According to Larkin (2013), all infrastructures, including technological infrastructures, generate forms of address and subject positions in a relay with social and political conditions. Unsurprisingly, upon its arrival portable video was quickly subsumed within a variety of utilitarian discourses similar to the imagination of 'useful cinema' constructed by educational institutions and social development organisations (Acland and Wasson 2011: 3). By focusing on the historical site and social context, it is possible to identify the institutional and technological factors that secured the usage of video primarily as a horizontal communication channel between participants and spectators. The Centre for the Development of Instructional Technology (CENDIT), India's first video training and tape dissemination agency, was a staging ground by virtue of its numerous training programmes and field projects led by filmmakers and community workers dispersed across Northern Indian states. The independent filmmaker from this period assumed the role of 'a mediator', located outside the flows of power that he or she was representing, and seemingly relinquished his or her agency to technological apparatus and social communication needs (Monteiro and Jayasankar 2015: 61).

The understanding of the filmmaker–subject–audience relationship at CENDIT was filtered through the theories, objectives and practices of participatory video. Unlike the top-down communication flows of mass media or educational video, participatory video was founded upon models of 'horizontal communication' (White 2003: 70). In these projects, the immediate playback function of video confirmed it as a medium for the exchange of information between socially related groups with the utopian goal 'to promote self/other respect, a sense of belonging' (White

65). Participatory video was part of the toolkit of development communication, an alternative formulation concerned with the reorganisation of uneven social structures that emerged in 1976 with the publication of Everett Rogers' *Communication and Development: Critical Perspectives*. The reorganisation involved greater use of communication technology to bring about large shifts in emphasis from measurable indicators of growth towards qualitative criteria such as the 'exchange of ideas', 'social conscience' and 'social change', with a new focus on the achievement of a 'higher quality of life and social justice' (Moemeka 1994: 13).

In development communication theory, electronic media technologies of video were positioned in a discourse of communication flows and its direction, purposes and agents. The diffusion (monologic communication) and participation (dialogic communication) approaches generated specific arrangements of video methods, language and mobilisations in contrast to uses such as public relations, journalism or adult education (Mefalopulos 2008: 58). Each of the two approaches authorised particular technical and social uses of video, governed by their underlying social objectives. In contrast to the planned, one-way communication flow of the monologic mode, the dialogic mode brought the participatory discourse of video to the forefront. In this two-way communication model, the scope of communication was open-ended and people's participation was promoted and captured for purposes of project feedback and improvements (Mefalopulos 2008: 23). The key components of participation and micro-level communication suggested a fertile ground for thinking of video as a medium for social communication. Rather than the creation of theoretical or academic knowledge, visual methods and technologies were deployed for community-level problem-solving through the use of shared and participatory methods of knowledge production. Participatory production functioned as a mode of social intervention where video not only produced affective and aesthetic media objects but through its democratic process, addressed social inequalities.

CENDIT's critique of state-managed mass communication methods motivated it to place faith in the use of communication technology as an instrument of participatory democracy. The critical perspective was empirically supported by concrete data from observations and surveys, including a crucial study conducted in Sultanpur, Western Uttar Pradesh, in 1973. Commissioned by the Family Planning Foundation, the survey focused on the reception of sixty-four documentary films on the subject of reproductive planning, meant for audiences in the Hindi-speaking rural and urban areas. With the majority of rural audiences alienated by the urban social values, living conditions and domestic relations portrayed in the films, the findings reported a 'lack of rural identification' (Ghosh 1974: 18). The study provided the concrete field data required to justify alternative approaches while affirming the importance of social context to the success of the communication process. Therefore, in its own projects, CENDIT built alliances with grassroots and community advocacy groups and adopted socially cooperative means of media production for community determined uses. Numerous videos like *Hum Bhi Insaan Hain/We are also Human* (1980, CENDIT and Delhi Dehat Mazdoor Union/Delhi Rural Worker's Union), *Dohra Bojh/A Double Burden* (1982, CENDIT and Delhi Dehat Mazdoor Union/Delhi Rural Worker's Union) and *Mahila Mela Tilonia/Women's Fair Tilonia* (1985, CENDIT and Social Work and Research Centre) were cooperatively produced with people's groups and trade unions, and aimed to promote grassroots democracy.

The translation of participatory impulse relied primarily on the pivotal role of portable video technology, which reframed media audience from a passive receiver to an active participant. In July 1975, in the CENDIT newsletter *Nigah*, the organisation's co-founder Rajive Jain recorded his experience of screening celluloid films amongst rural communities in the Saharanpur district of Uttar Pradesh:

> The nature of the film medium is such that it breeds passivity in the viewer . . . The heavy weight technology required for even sixteen millimetre projection with 2 ton generators, cumbersome cables, critically sensitive lamps and the requirement of darkness turn any film screening into a 'tamasha' [spectacle]. (Jain 1975: 49)

On the other hand, with the reduced demands of infrastructure and expertise, video encouraged the group to trial new practices that would lead towards lateral shifts in the subject position of the viewer. The simplified and basic operations of recording and immediate playback were central to this encounter, where audiences turned hands-on producers. Jain describes this pioneering moment:

> We allowed the community to dictate the content of the programmes. A few of the villagers began to make their own tapes. Many discovered that they had hidden talents. Some sang and acted out film scenes, and others preferred a more documentary approach taping harvest scenes, wrestling matches and other village activities. (Jain 1975: 49)

Whilst making no general claims, notably, Jain's accounts substantiate the narrative of community video practices occurring elsewhere. In *A Brief History of American Documentary Video*, Deirdre Boyle notes the emergence of similar community video initiatives in the USA during the 1970s, staffed by unskilled community producers where the purpose was not so much 'to experiment with a new medium' as to use video to effect social change (1990: 59). For independent documentary, a most complex challenge was the emerging symbolic contrast between the practice of documentary filmmaking and participatory video. At stake was authorship, since community video viewed itself as an instrument to mediate the transfer of agency to its subjects such that they 'control how they will be represented' while documentary emphasised ideas, critique and analysis associated with definite subject positions (Lunch and Lunch 2006: 10). Moving towards collective forms of making, a singular point of view became incompatible with the social objectives of participatory projects. This is marked in many of CENDIT's videos that dismiss individual production credits for technical and editorial functions.

From the perspective of circulation, CENDIT's screening practices speak of the social mobilisation of video in a bid to construct modes of cognition and subjectification that situated audiences as members of a specific group in precise, named geographies. Addressing the critique of mass media that conceptualised audiences as a homogeneous and generic group, CENDIT mobilised publics around common interests and shared contexts. Interlinked through existential conditions but produced by means of technology and media circulation, the small, dispersed and active publics were framed as the first and most important audience of media communication. *Hum Bhi Insaan Hain* (1980), a documentation of the struggles of landless peasants in the Mandi village outside Delhi, depicts the goal of horizontal group formation across geographies, an ambition extended through video screening apparatus. The video features conversations with several landless peasants and was circulated in a neighbouring village in the same district, at a fair organised by the labouring poor of the area. Another particularly telling example comes from Ferozabad in Uttar Pradesh. Akhila Ghosh (1984) notes that a video programme was made about a group of Dalit women who organised themselves into a sewing cooperative in a village-level social action programme. The video was transported 450 kilometers to Pather village and a screening was organised for a group of Muslim women who were struggling to initiate a cooperative group. Here, video was not only a form of technological hardware; its practices and functions enabled the flow of information between geographically separated but similar groups, making a bid to render change imaginable and to impart instruction.

The imagination of social documentation at this juncture did not identify itself through the discursive documentary form and while not related to the latter directly, it consolidated the framing of an objective of social emancipation and socially constituted vision of media producer and audience. In addition to communication discourses, it created positions regarding viewing practices which decried specialised spaces of cultural consumption. Instead, the geographically dispersed non-metropolitan circulation combined with limitations of infrastructure brought into being a space of exhibition governed by the principles of access instead of quality, profit or customisation. Thus an improvised circuit of community halls, school halls, training centres and village squares functioned as screening venues. Evidently, over the longer term this led to the systemisation of media viewing and audiences to the extent that the video catalogue *The Other Picture* (CENDIT, 1993) includes 'Instructions for Viewing', anticipating lack of technical knowledge and media equipment. The section entitled 'Notes on organizing a video screening session' begins with a basic introduction to the PAL video system and VHS systems. A note on 'Place of Screening' recommends, 'Ensure adequate ventilation', 'the audience should not be made to sit facing the Sun' and 'in case of outdoor night screening keep it away from ditches, holes etc. because people might fall in them in the dark' (p. 216). The focused attention to the conditions of viewing depict the multidimensional and yet site-specific ambit of participatory media and its intention to mediate localised transfers based on first-hand knowledge and direct contact.

How appropriate were these models for independent Indian documentary, and what is their contemporary relevance in an increasingly mediatised society where the distinction between producer and viewer is in the paradoxical state of continuous flux? I would argue that rather than the discursive focus on an institutionalised form of participation, an 'alternative media' approach productively explains the sharper focus on process and relation (Atton 2002). Industrial media creates notions of target audiences, distributed in spatial (national, regional) or social (gender, age, income) categories, reified through the norms of advertising (Busch 2016: 213). Primarily constructed as consumers or as paternalistic subjects of development by public service media, the emerging participatory discourse instead idealised audiences as active participants in social change and media construction. The value of alternative media is their capacity to give voice to the 'Other', the 'native informant' for the construction of 'heteroglossic' (multiple-voiced) text realised through transformation in the organisation and production of media (Atton 2002: 9). The complete transfer of apparatus and authority to people was an idealistic goal that faced many obstacles, not least in terms of resources, but for independent documentary it opened out a democratic mode of filmmaking and film exhibition in close alliance with its participant-subject and whose social needs determined the objective of the film. Examples of these films include *Voices from Baliapal* (1988), the documentation of people's struggle against a missile testing range in Orissa, and more recently *Development at Gunpoint* (2007), the documentation of people's uprising in West Bengal against a proposed SEZ, and *Radiation Stories* (2010–12), the documentation of a popular movement against nuclear power plants in Tamil Nadu.

Conclusion

In this chapter I have mapped the theory and practice that contoured an emerging discourse of independent documentary in a period where practitioners were formulating a symbolic terrain, voice and aesthetic form. While Anand Patwardhan, Deepa Dhanraj, Suhasini Mulay, Tapan Bose, Manjira Datta and others showed the possibilities of a film practice avowedly resistant towards hegemonic structures of social and institutional authority, this idealised practice of independence was rearranged by the development communication discourses during the late 1970s and '80s that dominated within media training institutions. Moreover, the arrival of video and its dispersal into private hands that could conceivably pursue alternate aesthetics continued to struggle against the overbearing postcolonial anxieties of what Srirupa Roy describes as 'national backwardness and lack' that had beleaguered FD films (110). Hence, while tying the format to prevailing instrumentalist perspectives of progress, the categories of educational video and participatory video constructed a utilitarian horizon around the techniques, operations and outlook of independent documentary.

One of the critical effects of the developmentalist imaginary during the 1970s and 1980s relates to the allocation of roles to social actors, infrastructure and culture in independent documentary during this period. The persistence of fixed social identities and relations between the poor and marginal who were perceived as the subjects of development and the filmmaker as the bearer of knowledge were expressed in objectivist representational regimes. Notwithstanding the urgent forms of video-based social activism that emerged in this phase, debates about the ideological construction of visual representation, the instability of language and the subjective position of the speaker were subsumed into narratives of social change. This discourse also consolidated the public instead of the private as the idealised space for documentary intervention.

These stabilised forms of documentary inquiry, expression, rhetoric and purpose were opened out for critique through feminist interventions during the late 1980s and early 1990s and continue to the present day.

The notion of objectivity so central to the construction of public address was opened up as a site for semiotic interrogation. In films such as *The Hidden Story*, the notion of truth itself was examined through attention to performativity, speaking position and construction of documentary representation. The effects and relations of power were understood not only in historical terms but also in terms of the cultural relations between the addressor and addressee, between text and reading, and between fact and rhetoric that set it apart from other non-fiction media representation.

In the next chapter I introduce the filmmakers at the core of this book through a discussion of their social biographies, which will not only provide insight into their artistic concerns but also allow us to view closely the dialectical relation between social and aesthetic orders, subjectivities and documentary cinema. To the extent that the histories of independent documentary are shaped through multiple practices, beliefs, assumptions and purposes, as outlined in this chapter, the next chapter will allow us to situate the filmmakers and define their practice against these many contending and overlapping factors.

Notes

1. PBS is a private, non-profit corporation, founded in 1969, whose members are America's public TV stations – non-commercial, educational licensees that operate 350 PBS member stations and serve all fifty states. Comprising documentaries, non-commercial news programmes and features, PBS aims to use media to educate, entertain and express the diversity of perspectives that would contribute to the democratic and cultural strength of the USA.
2. 'Documentary on Muzaffarnagar Riots Screened at 60 Venues across 50 Towns in Protest' (2015).
3. Five Year Plans are policy documents that outline the planned and coordinated programme of priorities and resource allocation of the Indian government for a five-year period. They are formulated by the central Planning Commission, which was set up in 1950 by Jawaharlal Nehru. Sudipta Kaviraj (2010) argues that from the second Five Year Plan in 1956 onwards, the state rapidly constructed a public sector of state-run industries in a commitment to distributive justice.
4. Ismat Chughtai (1915–91) and Sa'adat Hasan Manto (1912–55) are recognised as two of the four pillars of Urdu Literature whose progressive works questioned the operation of social taboos and the hegemony of religion and patriarchy. For biographical information about Chughtai see Pandey (2017) and for critique of Chughtai's writing see Kiran (2016) and Patel (2001). Koves (1997) provides an informative discussion of Manto's thematic concerns of partition and war.
5. The discipline of women's studies was based in the women's movement of the

1980s. The main concerns of the Indian women's movement were to challenge culturally prescribed gender roles which faced the exaggerated influence of religion, culture and social attitudes. The continued invisibility of women in roles/sectors was also questioned with a focus upon bringing the real-life experiences and issues of the majority of women into the public domain. See Vina Mazumdar and Indu Agnihotri's chapter on the Indian Women's Movement 1970s–1990s, 'Changing Terms of Political Discourse: Women's Movement in India 1970s–1990s', for an informative account of the debates and ideas that informed the movement.

6. Filmmakers from this period pursued advanced education in film studies, initiating transnational flows of theory and practice. Members of the Mediastorm Collective include Shohini Ghosh, who graduated with a Masters in Communication from Cornell University in 1989; Ranjani Mazumdar, who completed a Ph.D. in cinema studies in 2001 from New York University; and Shikha Jhingan, who in 1988 achieved a Master of Fine Arts majoring in film from the University of Wisconsin at Milwaukee. Upon return to India, each undertook to pursue documentary in various combinations of film practice, scholarship and criticism.

CHAPTER 2

Method and Meaning

> It transforms another person's property into a space borrowed for a moment by a transient. Renters make comparable changes in an apartment they furnish with their acts and memories; as do speakers, in the language into which they insert both the messages of their native tongue and, through their accent, through their own 'turns of phrase', etc., their own history; as do pedestrians, in the streets they fill with the forests of their desires and goals. (de Certeau 1988: xxii)

Why do people make documentary films? Rather open-ended, this question is one that directly relates to the issues this chapter addresses. Discourses of activism and art are often attributed to independent Indian documentary defined in relation to thematic concerns, aesthetic treatment and spaces of circulation. Effectively, as a set of ideas and terminologies both discourses close off deeper analysis of the relation between documentary and the world by attributing notional functions and qualities to films, filmmakers and spectators. Instead, I propose a methodological framework that incorporates film content as one element in an inquiry that is equally interested in the work practices and social biographies of filmmakers as major functionaries of an independent documentary culture. By incorporating these additional sites in contiguity with representational inquiry, I hope not only to re-assess these discursive categories but to show that independent films constitute a form of response to the world that has the capacity to generate political meaning equally through methods of creation and circulation as with content.

The need for biographical methods arises from documentary studies' narrow focus on critical textual analysis as the primary tool to access the complex nature of documentary's relation with the world.[1] While axiographics, or the visible ethics of representation, positions the documentary filmmaker as the bearer of an involved gaze whose artistic decisions reflect a relation with the world, framed in textual terms any interpretation assumes the text as a stable set of aesthetic relations (Nichols 1991: 79). For instance, it is entirely possible that Nichols's concept of 'accidental gaze' predicated upon textual evidence of 'accidentalness' like 'chaotic framing, blurred focus' and the 'sudden use of zoom lens, jerky camera movements' may symbolise inexperience or formal experimentation in diverse viewing contexts (83). Critical discourses in documentary have historically outlined the limits of theory and text, an issue that feminist scholars and filmmakers (Armatage 1979; Lesage 1984; Juhasz 1999) have tried to address in their scholarship by drawing method into the ambit of analysis. In '*Feminist Film-making: Theory and Practice*', Armatage outlines four central questions – about representation, identification, apparatus and method – that allow her to 'make political films politically' (49). From this premise, my focus in this chapter is on the concrete ways in which independent filmmakers have crafted non-standard methods and artistic vocabularies as a function of 'independence' which often runs counter to commodity relations that position cultural productions as commodities and cultural producers as industry professionals. Speaking to the questions I raised in Chapter 1 regarding professionalised identities like media producer, scriptwriter, artist, journalist or activist, stabilised through industrial functions and accountabilities, the issues I address are directly related to these concerns. I wish to address the ways in which practice is not simply contained within the rules of an industrial process but constituted through considerations particular to individual capacities, goals and ethos.

At the same time, it is important to remember that individuals who choose to work independently as documentary filmmakers are largely members of what Chuck Kleinhans (1984) identifies as the 'petty bourgeoisie', which grants them access to the means of 'production and dissemination of ideas' that may include skills, resources and networks (330). Whilst not specific to India, this observation is eminently true of Indian filmmakers as the majority belong to a privileged intellectual class identifiable by their Western-style education, urban upbringing, progressive values and significant social capital connected with networks amongst the state bureaucracy, education and civil society. In the 1980s, as functionaries of a 'domestic third world cinema', Indian filmmakers were perceived as agents struggling for emancipatory objectives of giving voice to the silenced colonial subject (Waugh 2011: 251). Nearly two decades later, Geeta Kapur complicated this relation by taking into account the issues of class, privilege and social hierarchy to assert that Indian artists, including filmmakers, occupied the position of a 'sovereign subject' in the social order (2008: 37). This is a position of power, whereby filmmakers have the privilege to be 'inside' the nation space but 'outside' the governing rationale of the state in their interpretative rendering of politics (37). It is clear that filmmakers operate dialectically as subjects and agents of power. Undeniably, access to social capital plays an important function insofar as it determines access to resources, recognition and spaces for circulation. While an in-depth examination of the politics of this relation remains outside the scope of this present analysis, I would suggest two criteria to assess the ethos and politics of this relation: the degree of reflexive awareness of class privilege on the part of filmmakers, and in social terms, the long-term cultural and social consequences of this mode of practice upon meanings attached to cultural production and cultural producers. In other words, do independent cultural producers perform an organising purpose to the extent that they transform or realign the relation between cultural production, culture and society? These private and public questions are essential to a rethinking of the social significance and value of cultural production and the forms of reorganisation it entails.

The examination of material and symbolic domains of ideas and actions is epistemologically useful for it extends beyond the rewards of cultural critique which may further solidify the discursive categories of art, politics and activism to instead disclose the concrete means through which filmmakers are able to reconceptualise these in relational and interrelated frames. This is widely significant for documentary studies in general but South Asian documentary in particular, whose discourse so far largely positions independent documentary within the horizon of functional value as activism (Imran 2016) and resistance (Monteiro and Jayasankar 2015). These discussions unfold over the rest of the chapter, divided into two broad sections. The first is dedicated to individual filmmakers where the intersection between the biographies, practice and films of Amudhan R. P., Rahul Roy, the filmmaking partnership of Anjali Monteiro and K. P. Jayasankar, and Paromita Vohra reveals a central focus on 'cultural autonomy' as asserted by each filmmaker in specific ways. In the second part, I contextualise individual practices alongside the wider field of media production in India to argue that as a practice, independent documentary has developed an artisanal mode of production in contrast to the industrial emphasis upon specialisation, professionalisation and codification of cultural production. Further, this mode of production permits a radical reimagination of documentary as signifying practice existing in the everyday with citizens and social process as its functionaries and materials. Instead of suggesting an essential causality between films, individual experience and social conditions, I hope that the relationships attempt to open out into further discussions of the relation between artistic expression and the *dispositif* of culture, historical conditions and institutions particular to historical periods and individual filmmakers.

Filmmakers, Histories, Concerns, Aesthetics

Amudhan R. P.

My introduction to Amudhan was through his film *Notes from the Crematorium* (2005), a sombre portrait of Dalit (ex-untouchable) men involved in one of the most invisible and socially despised forms of labour in society: the cremation of unclaimed corpses, many of which are victims of disease and decay. Thematically, issues of caste-related social discrimination, industrial negligence and exploitative labour relations are at the forefront of Amudhan's filmic concerns. Born in 1971 in the southern Indian state of Tamil Nadu, Amudhan began making films in 1996 and currently has nineteen documentaries to his credit. He is variously described by critics as 'a rebel', 'an activist' and 'a filmmaker'. Amudhan's filmography is a catalogue of dissent against acts of private, state and social injustice, a political ethnography of the marginalised (Velayanikal 2012). His commitment to documentary cinema extends to building a broader documentary culture; in 1998 Amudhan founded the Madurai International Documentary and Short Film Festival, and in 2013, the Chennai International Documentary and Short Film Festival.

In his biography, what surfaces are political beliefs equally grounded in theory as first-hand participation in social and intellectual movements. Documentary filmmaking for Amudhan is an exercise of political conscience reflected in visible position-taking, deliberate method and an 'urgent' aesthetics. Amudhan's working practices consist of extended periods of filming, lengthy and repeated interactions with film participants and observational camera work. In relation to style, Amudhan's films are an excellent example of the inseparability of method, form and content, chiefly as 'style' is not predetermined but a response to the conditions, dialogues and truths contingent upon the nature of the profilmic encounter with the world.

Caste as opening act: ethics, histories, objectives

The Dalit upsurge of the 1990s in Tamil Nadu is central to Amudhan's political subjectification as reflected in his trilogy of films on caste discrimination (*Notes from the Crematorium*, 2005; *Shit*, 2003; *Serruppu*, 2006). Informed by the political legacy of an earlier Self-Respect Movement, a historic social struggle to overthrow the cultural and social dominance of Brahamanism in Tamil society, each film mounts a comprehensive argument against institutionalised caste discrimination and its effects on individuals, communities and society.[2] In a society where religion and caste identities determine essential vectors of kinship and social networks, Amudhan grew up in a communist household which identified itself as atheist. Later, a master's degree in development communication from Madurai Kamaraj University drew Amudhan's interest towards intersecting issues of 'social development, gender, identity and environment'.[3] The ideas of social thinkers like Gabriele Dietrich, the scholar of Dalit feminism, and B. R. Ambedkar, author of the influential polemic against the Hindu caste system *Annihilation of Caste*, are reflected in Amudhan's intersectional politics in which social citizenship forms the basis and precursor to democratic participation.

In Amudhan's political view, social discrimination is a function of economic relations (*Mercury in the Mist*, 2011; *Dollar City*, 2015) and histories of social conflicts that form around caste discrimination, gender discrimination (*Leelavathi*, 1996) and an authoritarian Indian state (*Radiation Stories I, II and III*, 2010–12). As a result, Amudhan's film subjects are expectedly drawn from oppressed and socially weaker groups, but he is alert to group identities and the significance of cultural histories and practices to an assertion of citizenship in a globalising nation. In *Serruppu/Footwear* (2006), a film about the caste exploitation of the Arundhatiyar (former Dalit) community of Tamil Nadu, Amudhan engages with the history of religious conversion in a bid to understand the practice from a sociological standpoint as a critique of historically institutionalised social inequality. Confronted by the social violence of the caste system, many of the Arundhatiyar communities have converted to Christianity but continue to face discrimination within their new adopted religion. Engaging with the hegemonic practices of organised religion, the film documents threats to cultural identity that erupt from majoritarian sanctions against food practices like the consumption of beef in a Hindu-dominated region as well as the second-grade treatment by local parish authorities. At the same time, intersectional concerns motivate Amudhan to open out the discussion to an examination of the forces of globalisation, shown to reorganise both socio-economic structures and cultural identity. In a social order where identity is tied with community livelihood practices, the Arundhatiyars are struggling economically and culturally against their rapidly disappearing small-scale leather industry. At microcosmic levels, caste discrimination takes economic form when individuals are unable to access bank loans and forced to turn to loan sharks for small sums of money. The complex network of oppressive factors implicates the state, social institutions and the market, raising pertinent questions that go to the core of contemporary struggles over the meaning of nation, citizenship identity and democratic rights.

Importantly, whilst Amudhan's body of work is geographically situated within Tamil Nadu, it is far from regionalist or purely vernacular in its political scope. Countering limitations of regionalist readings, represented issues are framed against the constitutional guarantee of equality and therefore connect symbolically to people's struggles in other parts of the nation. It is important for the films to avoid regionalist labels in order to access nationwide publics and build a broader political community. Insofar as Amudhan's nation framework continues established documentary tradition of historical critique, it creates significant opportunities to summon national audiences connected through social and political histories of oppression. Not surprisingly, Amudhan is acknowledged for bringing localised issues into public discourse. Following the National Jury Award at the 9th Mumbai International Film Festival awarded to his documentary *Pee* (*Shit*, 2003) on the topic of manual sanitation work, a reviewer noted 'For documentary filmmaker R. P. Amudhan, things which fail to draw the attention of commoners always catch his eye' (Saravanan 2006).

Insofar as Amudhan's film subjects are drawn from socially marginalised groups, representation becomes an ethically fraught terrain, given the filmmaker's privileged social status as public intellectual and his non-Dalit caste identity. The politics of who speaks on whose behalf and who is represented is an issue of moral concern in documentary studies, and Amudhan is clearly conscious of these issues. Gayatri Spivak's (1988) deconstruction of the epistemology of the subaltern elucidates this dichotomy where the substantive concern for the politics of the oppressed potentially conceals the ways in which the intellectual speaker gains privilege from speaking on behalf of the oppressed. In the case of Dalit representation, evidently the disjuncture between the filmmaker and the participant on the scales of social capital, networks, agency and media access raises similar questions, and thus Amudhan's position as speaker is admittedly tenuous. But speaking to the position of an involved filmmaker I discuss in Chapter 1, for Amudhan, filmmaking is more than a semiotic exercise, and the struggle as he understands it is not only representational but historical. In response to this criticism, Amudhan reframes his films as a form of personal citizen protest rather than staking the bigger claim as 'representative' or 'spokesperson' of the Dalit movement. According to Amudhan:

> If a Dalit man or woman makes the film on caste issue, definitely it will be different, I don't dispute that but I will make a film. While it is their point of view and I don't disapprove, I say we need more films on this issue, so we should make them. It is my contribution to the fight against the caste system and I won't claim anything beyond this.[4]

Admittedly the filmmaker disavows the authority conferred by the role of spokesperson; nevertheless, harking back to its historical origins as official state speech, the issue highlights the cultural tension surrounding the public identity of a documentary filmmaker even as Amudhan attempts to express a personal interpretation of the world.

Filming solo: influences, choices and form

Amudhan's film practice performs an emblematic departure from public service documentary, addressed towards an undifferentiated audience and assembled through systemised production processes that together congeal in texts intended for didactic pedagogy. Amudhan frames his films as forums for critical dialogue, stating that 'in documentary there is a space and an opportunity for intellectual discourse. It gives the freedom to expand the possibility of intellectual capability.'[5] By idealising critical dialogue, Amudhan discloses an attentiveness towards the consciousness of the spectator as a key participant in the construction of meaning and as such a perceptive and cognitive entity. As I will lay out, a dialogic formulation of documentary as a space of positions, rather than a determinedly functionalist object, anchors the relation between Amudhan's artistic intention, work practices and aesthetic vision.

Amudhan's method of filmmaking is avowedly inspired by the methods of filmmakers like Anand Patwardhan and Dennis O'Rourke, who frequently govern major aspects of their film practice to create strongly authored works. The appeal of this method lies in its spontaneity as a form of personal response to the world and the accompanying freedom to exercise editorial independence. From research and shooting to editing, exhibition and publicity, Amudhan controls each function and determines the scope of the collaborative partnerships that he invites from individuals and community groups. The most significant overlap between Amudhan and the independent practice of Anand Patwardhan is the prioritisation of editorial freedom above economic rewards, to the extent that Amudhan does not participate in industry pitching and co-production events, and to date none of his films have been financed by corporate, governmental or civil society agencies. While initially documentary funding was not forthcoming, subsequently Amudhan chose not to pursue fundraising for extended periods at the cost of sacrificing pressing film-worthy issues. At present, with a large body of work behind him, Amudhan continues to locate his filmmaking practice outside an economic discourse, a discussion that I will take up further in Chapter 3.

In Amudhan's films, the politically urgent visual theory of Third Cinema stalwarts Patwardhan and Patricio Guzman often sits uneasily with the ethnographic visual expression of Dennis O'Rourke. Nevertheless, beyond the judgement of aesthetic criticism, the visual dialogues are notably indicative of a reflexive engagement with the theory, politics and history of documentary. The mediation of the real in Amudhan's films draws upon diverse cinematic legacies in an ongoing reflective conversation between rhetorics and aesthetics. Foremost, Amudhan's style suggests an obvious relation to cinéma-vérité, which he describes as 'no music, no commentary, no tripod, no light', reminiscent of Patwardhan's utilitarian 'whatever is necessary' counter-aesthetics (1984: 446). Most evident in films like *Nuclear Stories Part 3: Koondankulam*, part of a trilogy about the hidden human and social costs of India's nuclear power plants, Amudhan employs a hand-held camera to record lengthy unstructured testimonies with the victims of nuclear contamination and to patiently observe everyday individual struggles. Refusing to edit out incidental sounds and images reminiscent of Patwardhan's *Bombay, Our City*, the camerawork aims to dissolve itself in its refusal to stage and arrange aesthetic compositions. Frequently participants continue their work routine as they speak to the camera or express their surprise at being chosen as a speaker. From Guzman's *Battle of Chile*, Amudhan utilises the epistemological possibilities of the serialised chapter structure evident in the caste trilogy (*Notes from the Crematorium*, *Seruppu* and *Shit*) and in the nuclear energy trilogy (*Radiation Stories 1*, *2* and *3)*. The structure allows temporal exploration and the development of an argument through a wide range of symbolic inquiry points between individual voice and social observation. The absence of voice-over is a common feature that binds Amudhan's films; nevertheless, the filmmaker's corporeal presence in films such as *Mercury in the Mist*, *Seruppu* and *Notes from the Crematorium* produces textual asides or a glimpse into the process of filmmaking and the intersubjective relations between the filmmaker and the film participant. More importantly, self-inscription also contests the truth claims of verismilitude associated with instrumental imaginaries of documentary film.

Amudhan's biography offers us a number of ways to contemplate the development of social and subjective dimensions behind the construction of an individual documentary practice. The expression of independence in Amudhan's films takes form in artistic fluidity to resist categorisation under the genre classification of expository, journalistic, personal or agit-prop documentary. Stylistic hybridity, experimental visual aesthetics and movements between public discourse and private subjectivities express Amudhan's unconventional artistic independence where each film is constituted as a factor of method, the pro-filmic world and intent.

Rahul Roy

New Delhi-based Rahul Roy is widely acknowledged as a key contributor to a consolidating discourse of masculinities in the Indian context. Roy's ethnographic filmic studies of the lives of four young men, filmed twelve years apart in *When Four Friends Meet* (2000) and *Till We Meet Again* (2013), portray a complex social-subjective terrain where masculine subjectivities are negotiated and assigned. At the same time, together with *Majma* (2001) and *The City Beautiful* (2003), Roy's body of work is determinedly place-specific. Set against the changing urban spatial and social formation of New Delhi, a city where Roy has himself lived since 1978, the films consistently investigate and probe the city as a mediator of subjectivity and social identity. Roy's thematic concerns regarding cultural and social forms of subjectification are located within a larger semiotic concern with documentary representation as a means of assigning particular identities. Roy states,

> Now, everything is political. The real battle has been to try and resolve the question; if a documentary film is self-avowedly political, what happens to the film subjects?[6]

Roy's questions about the semiotic dimensions of representation of specific individuals, ethnicities and identities marks an ethical terrain of representational inquiry that effectively resonates with 'discursive and semiotic struggles' that trouble engagé cinema (Naficy 2001: 48). In Roy's biography, of greatest interest is the determined movement from an initial 'instructional' media practice towards an independent practice recognised for complex explorations of identity, subjectivities and intimately observed domestic relations. As I probe the rationale behind the shift in Roy's practice, it becomes apparent that Roy is extending cultural debates concerning the organisation of power, authorship and representation in documentary theory.

Enter cinema and politics

Delhi University's film society Celluloid, which commenced in the late 1960s, is described as a 'home' and 'an intellectual world' by film scholar Ravi Vasudevan (2011: xiii). Managed by cinephiles with films sourced from diplomatic and cultural missions located in the national capital, the screenings attracted a diverse membership that included Roy. Here, spectators encountered the world of the French Nouvelle Vague, German expressionism and cinema from the Eastern bloc countries. At the same time, the 1980s were bursting with expressive possibilities unveiled by the portable video camera and the charge of political and cultural movements.

As a history undergraduate at Delhi University between 1981 and 1984, Roy was politically active, participating in student protests in solidarity with the Delhi University Teachers' Union action against violence on campus. In 1984, anti-Sikh riots erupted in the wake of the assassination of Prime Minister Indira Gandhi and Roy volunteered for the relief and rebuilding initiatives in North East Delhi's Farsh Bazaar rehabilitation camp for several months.

The 1980s were a period of cultural activism in Delhi, which included radical forms of political theatre and feminist activism. Theatre activist Safdar Hashmi and his group Jan Natya Manch rejected proscenium confines to perform theatre on the streets, outside factory gates and in working-class colonies, to express solidarity with labour and trade unions. The feminist journal *Manushi* brought women's writing, personal experiences and narratives into the public sphere, and when the team decided to perform *Ahsaas* in 1984, Roy was part of the cast. Based on an earlier play, *Om Swaaha* (1980), that had been performed by the feminist group Stree Sangharsh, *Ahsaas* deals with the social ills of gender inequality and dowry. Social participation and cultural activism propelled Roy towards the Mass Communication Research Centre (MCRC), a media training institution where media technologies were positioned in the service of public communication and social development.

MCRC provided Roy with a socially progressive setting in which Canadian documentarist and co-founder James Beveridge introduced the students to social documentary. Politically, the institution situated itself in a space of of Nehruvian nation-building and aspired to build an educated, democratic and rights-based society through effective communication. This objective prevailed against what Arvind Rajagopal views as the rising 'third phase of Hindu nationalist development' from 1980 onwards that sought to expand the ideology of Hindu nationalism amidst the denunciation of Nehruvian Socialist beliefs (57). In contrast, MCRC alumnus and Roy's peer Saba Dewan recalls that MCRC maintained 'continuity with the Left, liberal very Nehruvian ideals; Nehruvian socialism and Nehruvian secularism'.[7] The cinematic translation of democratic social engagement was evident in the diverse spectrum of visiting documentary filmmakers. Between James and Margaret Beveridge and Anwar Jamal Kidwai, the centre invited distinct filmmakers like Mira Nair, who screened *India Cabaret* (1985), Deepa Dhanraj and Navroz Contractor, who screened *Kya Hua Is Shhahar Ko* (1986), and Anand Patwardhan, who screened his newly completed *Bombay, Our City* (1984). Just as memorable was a screening programme of Dennis O'Rourke's films. 'We were enchanted with *Half Life* (Dennis O' Rourke, 1986)' recalls Dewan.

For Roy, the first opportunity to make a professional video programme came with the University Grants Commission's Country-Wide Classroom educational television broadcasts and was followed by commissions from civil society and non-governmental agencies. Many of these early productions with Saba Dewan proved formative for Roy's practice. *Invisible Hands, Unheard Voices* (Dewan and Roy, 1988), a film commissioned by the Indian Council of Agricultural Research on the subject of the role of technology in women's participation in agriculture, set many foundations of independent documentary practice for Roy. It was filmed over a period of four months across the length and breadth of the nation, and halfway through the filming Roy decided to operate the video camera himself, a practice that continues to this day. Research inaugurated important social alliances with individuals and organisations that propelled the city-based filmmakers into the radical and interconnected world of feminist activism, rural women's groups and civil society agencies. These groups proved to be useful allies in introducing the filmmakers to communities, individuals and neighbourhoods for subsequent film projects. For instance, *Barf/Snow* (1997) and *When Four Friends Meet* emerge from Dewan and Roy's alliance with Action India Foundation, which proved an important stage for collaborations with the workers and member constituencies of the agency to explore issues of gender construction and urban politics.

The 'ethnographic turn'

Surprisingly, commissioned work was a source of discontent and questions for Roy. Roy and Dewan's first independent documentary, the anti-sectarian *Dharmyuddha/Holy War* (1989), was produced in association with the Mediastorm Collective and Sampradayikta Virodhi Andolan (Movement against Communalism), and followed by *Nasoor/Festering Wound* (1991). Both independent films were what Roy considered 'satisfying, politically hot'.[8] Therefore, it was not the secure commissioned films but the fledgling independent practice that brought critical appreciation, and this is where Roy was to find artistic motivation. The turn towards a determined independent practice was further secured by Roy's ambivalence about the didactic instrumentalities imposed by commissioning organisations.

> In an unconscious way, commissioned films somewhere showed us that no one was really interested in people's lives – what and how they lead their lives and the complication of their struggles. They wanted to set up projects, show how successful they are and how wonderful their impact is. People and their lives had to somehow support this process. If you start looking at documentary film, then it's almost a parallel. Then one starts thinking, are films really interested in people's lives or in filming the filmmaker's agenda?[9]

Questions that surfaced at this juncture, about the role of ventriloquism promoted by organisational agendas, the dissonance between the complexities of lived experience and its flattened audiovisual representation, remain key aesthetic and political struggles in Roy's documentary films.

A crucial interior process of self-reflection helped to mediate a turn in the entire direction and scope of Roy's practice. Encounters with diverse and provocative documentary imaginaries like Nilita Vachani's *Eyes of Stone* (1990), an observational film about the possession ritual of rural women in Rajasthan and the 1992 winner of the Basil Wright Prize at the Royal Anthropological Institute Film Festival, Manchester, 'completely shook us out of our comfort zone and made us question our own work', says Roy.[10] Dewan recalls the impact of the film upon the young filmmakers: 'Why was I choosing to move away from this neat happy world that I had of funded films? I was considered a very good filmmaker within that circuit' (2010).

The movement across early protest cinema towards engagé cinema was mediated through ethnographic filmmaking, methodological dimensions of which underpin Roy's visual representation of the everyday lives and struggles of people. Insofar as ethnographic filmmaking has provided Roy with an alternative conceptual framework to documentary's representational crisis, it is the cinema philosophy of David MacDougall that resonates with Roy's audiovisual exploration of individual subjectivity. After meeting MacDougall in New Delhi in 2002, Roy closely studied the filmmaker's films and writings. In 2008, Roy collaborated with the Department of Sociology at the University of Delhi to coorganise the Delhi International Ethnographic Film Festival. The co-authored curatorial note states:

> The ethnographic film emerges from a sustained social relationship between the researcher and her objects and subjects of investigation. This document, however, is not so much a supplement to the ethnographic record as a function that is located at the limits and possibilities of the spoken and written word. (Roy et al. 2008: 5)

Framed within the epistemological and methodological category of ethnographic filmmaking, the ethical–power equation of the filmmaker–film subject relationship has become of primary significance to Roy, a position that also resonates with the feminist documentary ethic (Lesage 1984). One of the struggles for ethnographic films, suggests MacDougall (Grimshaw and Papstergiadis 1995), is that of breaking the rules of didactic film, particularly through 'the portrayal of people as individuals rather than as social actors or as types' (qtd in Grimshaw, 29). Reflection upon the power dimension of representation is evident in Roy's ambivalent and complex characters, who are presented as more than social representatives or social types. Roy's engagement with the urban geography and social space of New Delhi provides the social–historical context to explore the private and psychological worlds of his working-class film subjects: Sanju, Bunty Sanjay and Kamal in the series *When Four Friends Meet* and *Till We Meet Again*, and Hira Lal, Shakuntala, Radha and Bal Krishan in *The City Beautiful*. However, paradoxically, ethnographic methodology does not extend to textual self-reflexivity, and Roy's personal experiences and relationships with the film subjects are not probed consciously, but accidentally revealed in the narratives.

In Roy's engagé cinema, concern with emerging modes of neoliberal subjectivities unfolds through considered observations of individual embodied experience and emotion that open out into unexpected narratives. In addition to representational significance, Roy's turn towards ethnographic methods provides us ways to consider the function of reflexivity in the conscious definition of one's artistic self and artistic practice. The conditions that made this turn possible indicate Roy's personal authority over his filmmaking practice, which does not guarantee autonomy in complete artistic or ideological terms but centralises Roy's desire to self-define his practice. These tensions between autonomy and subordination are explored more fully in Chapters 3 and 4, where we closely examine the tensions underlying Roy's institutional alliances and relationship with film subjects.

Anjali Monteiro and K. P. Jayasankar

The professional partnership of Anjali Monteiro and K. P. Jayasankar commenced in 1987 with the documentary *The Young Workers*, and has yielded thirty-eight films so far.[11] As well as being life partners, both are senior media studies faculty at the School of Media and Cultural Studies (SMCS) at the Tata Institute of Social Sciences (TISS) in Mumbai, and have together pursued contemporary issues of cultural politics, identity, urban relations and gender politics in their video and social activist work. The most persuasive element of their joint practice is an ongoing engagement with issues of cultural politics, from agitating against the curbs on freedom of expression (as co-founders of Vikalp) to the audiovisual narratives that militate against the submergence of working-class urban cultures in *Saacha/The Loom* (2001) and *Naata/The Bond* (2003), represent marginal cultural voices in *SheWrite* (2005), *Our Family* (2007) and *YCP 1997* (1997) and vocalise marginalised cultural histories in *Kahankaar, Ahaankar* (1995). Industrially, their films are produced within the symbolic

Figure 2.1 K. P. Jayasankar, Anjali Monteiro and M. Harikumar make their way to Bhadreswar in Kachchh in 2009 for an ongoing video documentation project of Sufi music traditions in the region.

confines of TISS, their institutional employer and yet both have continued to engage with documentary filmmaking, informed by politically left-wing and poststructuralist cultural theorisation. What is of interest in their biographies is the relationship between cultural theory and practice, a unique combination where the conceptualisation of each film is distributed between historical, theoretical, methodological and, in particular, deeply personal concerns. The intersection between cultural theory and media practice constitutes a praxis that attempts to address critical documentary cultures both through textual means and through the evocation of critical viewing practices. For instance, the use of traditional narrative storytelling structures in *Kahankar Ahankar* works as a cinematic critique of the nation's official histories that identify with industrial, economic and social modernity. 'Modernity has always positioned tradition as a chief enemy in Nehruvian ideas,' says Jayasankar, 'Where modernity is seen as a liberating force, it is important to discover and see what these traditions can offer.'[12] Stylistic elements drawn from traditional narrative forms, believes Jayasankar, offer the 'reflexive spaces' to critique the discourses of certainty and evidence valued by modernity.

Made in Mumbai

Documentary filmmaking is the audiovisual extension of the filmmakers' broader cultural activism organised through diverse textual forms (cinema and writing), teaching practice and material participation. Mumbai, where Monteiro and Jayasankar live and work, is an ongoing site of inquiry for the filmmakers, a space they traverse in several films including *Naata*, *Saacha* and *Irani Restaurant Instructions* (2008) to interrogate its transforming social and cultural identities and ephemeral spaces. In relation to representational politics, the socially framed questions demonstrate a kind of politics that John Corner describes as a 'dimension' or 'level' that offers the possibility of politicising the world by using its representations to show the hidden politics beyond the normative (2009: 115). Tracing the changes wrought by neoliberal economics, urbanisation and sectarian politics upon quotidian spaces and relations is a means of politicising the world and revealing the structural arrangements of power that arrange social relations and subject positions in this shifting formation.

Monteiro and Jayasankar share a personal involvement with Mumbai's working-class communities, cultures and neighbourhoods. Anjali Monteiro has worked in adult education and community awareness programmes in the working-class areas and slum communities of Mumbai since 1977. Employed initially with the Marxist Science Education Group and later as media producer with the Xavier Institute of Communication between 1979 and 1983, Monteiro's focus on issues related to gender and reproductive health provided first-hand evidence of the social and domestic struggles faced by working women. Direct contact with her brother Vivek Monteiro's labour rights activism in his role as Secretary of the Maharashtra State Centre for Indian Trade Unions created a set of conditions where lived experience and political movements coalesced. For Jayasankar, the cultural efflorescence of the Second New Wave of Malayalam Cinema that began in 1969 drew him towards cultural inquiry, meanings and representations. Later, after moving to Mumbai and finding employment at an oil refinery, Jayasankar gravitated towards left working-class politics. During this period, personal participation in the organised protest movements against the violence of slum eviction laid a robust foundation for Monteiro and Jayasankar's enduring cinematic and personal relation with Mumbai.

Their attention to the paradoxical effects of economic modernity and discourses of consumption extends to the filmmaker's critical concern for shifting urban cultures, particularly the decline of Mumbai's pluralistic social identity and history. The 1980s and 1990s wrought havoc on working-class spaces and cultures as the city was reorganising through neoliberal economics and corporatism and the growing political influence of right-wing Hindutva groups. Historian Gyan Prakash captures the dystopic grimness of this period:

> A series of strikes, culminating in the crippling industrial action of 1982–83, brought Mumbai's textile industry to its knees. The collapse of the cotton mills tore apart the social fabric of Girangaon. As unemployment soared, the once thriving working-class neighborhoods became a landscape of despair and resentment (Prakash 2013).

In *Saacha* and *Irani Restaurant Instructions*, Monteiro and Jayasankar illustrate these fading instances of cultural pluralism by foregrounding the secular poetry of working-class poet Narayan Surve and their personal nostalgia for Mumbai's secular café culture. Grounded in the critique of identity construction through the limited possibilities of consumption and market economics, both films evoke personal and subjective history and memory as counter-narrative to grand historical writing. The filmmakers directly address contradictions around individual, collective and socially assigned identities in *Naata*. The film documents the secular community rebuilding efforts of Bhau Korde and Waqar Khan following instances of sectarian violence in Mumbai's Dharavi slum settlement. By foregrounding the functioning of a community-generated peace process, the narrative resonates with Arjun Appadurai's (2011) writings on 'vernacular cosmopolitanism'. This mode of cosmopolitanism, writes Appadurai, 'begins close to home and builds on the practices of the local, the everyday and the familiar' while circumventing the limits imposed by class, neighbourhood and mother tongue (2011).

Significantly, social critique forms the core of the filmmaker's practice which extends beyond documentary, forming more than a professional commitment. In collaboration with SMCS they have launched *Giran Mumbai*, a web-based archive of the cultural texts of the now-defunct Mumbai textile mill areas, as well as artistic works, research and photo collections about the space, its neighbourhoods and its communities. In these projects, the filmmakers once more raise problematic questions of historiography by bringing into the public sphere counter-narratives about urban resources, spaces, histories and cultures of Mumbai that challenge official claims.

Theory, art and politics

Consistent with Foucault's conceptualisation of dividing practices, the poststructuralist approach to subject construction is crucial to decipher the documentary politics of Monteiro and Jayasankar. Through the disciplinary practices of modern social institutions, states Foucault (1982), 'the subject is either divided inside himself or divided from others' (777). Foucault offers the examples of medicine and crime, which distribute persons into categories of the mad and the sane, the sick and the healthy, the criminal and the civic-minded. In their approach to film subjects, the filmmakers attempt to collapse discourses that establish a seperation between the subject of representation and the artist. For instance, in *Naata*, while discussing the fragmentation of identities amongst urban migrants the filmmakers devote considerable narrative space to their own identity issues as migrants to Mumbai and those resulting from their interfaith marriage. A review of another film *Our Family* reads, '*Our Family* subverts all ideas of the family whether they are patriarchal, biological or heterosexual, to give it new dimensions and dynamics.'[13] The film problematises the notion of the heteronormative family as a social construction anchored in a dividing practice between a heterosexual 'us' and transgender 'them'.

Expressively, the filmmakers attempt to transgress the conventional polemics of political documentary to instead chart a uniquely contemplative and artful documentary grammar. Cinematography for Jayasankar is a movement between an exterior sensory world and affect where images are tied up with intangible scales of private memory, association and pleasure. He draws inspiration from the visual poetics of Mani Kaul, whom Arun Khopkar describes as 'a superb craftsman. He treats his films like magic *mandalas*' (Khopkar 2011). In Anne Rutherford's (2006) description, the visual and symbolic poetry of *Saacha* created by Jayasankar, invokes 'moments of sensory experience' where the pace of the film creates moments of quietude to reflect upon the rhythm of the city (29). Jayasankar's deeply subjective relationship with image-making is filtered through the realm of personal meanings and accomplished by means of an enduring filmmaking partnership which assumes authority over conceptual and material aspects of the practice.

In these biographical accounts of the relation between cinematic expression and participation, a dynamic and reflective view of documentary can be identified. The possibilities extended by Monteiro and Jayasankar's engagement with cultural theory and art are undeniably of special significance in this equation, depicting a practice that is shaped not only by industry convention or contemporary notions of style but predominantly constituted through definite position-taking. Monteiro and Jayasankar's working methods reflect a practice generated through a deliberate process of inquiry and the testing and refining of ideas. The filmmakers often take years to develop an initial idea, allowing it to mature, grow and connect with wider contexts before launching into production. Admittedly, as independent filmmakers, their professional location within a large educational institution presents a conflict in terms of pure autonomy which reiterates the scholarly limitation of viewing independence through industry frameworks, and instead prompts us to consider alternate conceptualisations that take adaptation and agility into account, a discussion that continues in the next chapter.

Paromita Vohra

Biographically and in her cinema, Mumbai-based Paromita Vohra occupies a unique space amongst social documentary filmmakers in India. Unlike the foundational political exposure in the lives of many independent filmmakers, Vohra's relationship with documentary cinema is moored within her interest in cultural and artistic expression including cinematic arts, literature, and visual and performance arts. Initiating her film practice with *Annapurna / Goddess of Food* in 1995, Vohra's documentary practice intersects with narrative cinema, feature-writing and reality television projects. Drawing upon feminist film theory and postmodernism, the films are bestowed with unique subjective and individual dimension as objects that occupy a space of both knowledge and pleasure. From the perspective of independence, of greatest interest in Vohra's biography are the ways in which reflection and critique have mediated an idiosyncratic audiovisual grammar that produces singular authored works. The feminist axiom of 'the personal is political' frames Vohra's choice of subject matter as well as her documentary voice, to stand in contrast with the authoritative public address of social documentary. In a challenge to established realist documentary epistemologies, Vohra traverses a range of cultural and artistic influences, where each film combines elements of fiction, actuality, performance and drama that are rarely centred in verisimilitude or factuality alone.

In the Indian context, Vohra's journey to the documentary form is unconventional in its trajectory, objectives and outlook. Vohra's early years featured equally the pleasures of high art and popular culture that effortlessly fused an appreciation for Urdu poetry and commercial Hindi cinema. Acknowledging a talent for writing, Vohra studied English literature as an undergraduate at Delhi University, and upon completion in 1989 pursued postgraduate-level film studies at Sophia College in Mumbai. On the cusp of liberalisation, centralised broadcasting structures presented limited opportunities for independent documentary producers. Nevertheless, after graduating, Vohra elected to work with the documentary form. Unlike her filmmaking peers, Vohra's choice at this early stage was motivated by intuition and desire rather than determined political objectives.

Documentary film materialised as the creative terrain to express a wide range of political ideas as well as the freedom to cast an original cinematic vocabulary and style. Experimenting with the artistic possibilities offered by documentary, what has also evolved, is the strongly political dimension of Vohra's work, where rhetoric and aesthetic equally perform political critique and commentary. At the end of her filmmaking study, choosing to ignore the lure of the rapidly emerging television production houses and satellite television channels in a liberalising media economy, Vohra sought an apprenticeship with filmmaker Anand Patwardhan. Vohra's individual artistic expression took root, at once learning from but also critiquing the practice and rhetorics of Patwardhan's political cinema.

Vohra's internship with Anand Patwardhan extended to nearly three years between 1990 and 1993; a period that was one of Patwardhan's most prolific. In under three years, Vohra worked on *Ram ke Naam* (1992) and *Father, Son and Holy War* (1995), during a period of potent engagement with left-wing politics, as well as the world of radical films and filmmakers. The intellectual and political crossover between ideological politics, grassroots organisations and networks of citizens was, and continues to be, a crucial element of Patwardhan's film practice. Participation for Patwardhan extends to political action, a phenomenon to which Vohra was also drawn. The meaning of this experience is not lost to Vohra, and her first film *Annapurna* (1995) emerged from a meeting with trade unionist Datta Ishwarkar of the Girni Kamgar Sangharsh Samiti (Mill Workers Action Committee), who was at the forefront of the workers' agitation against the textile mill closures wrought by new economic policies.[14] The film is a portrait of the women's food cooperative Annapurna Mahila Mandal, which has supplied food to Mumbai's factory workers since 1975. This initial foray into the substantive and symbolic space of Mumbai's labour history and cultural politics has mutated into feminist urban critique in later films such as *Cosmopolis* (2004) and *Q2P* (2006).

A performative everyday

From a purely thematic reading Vohra's films appear in a continuum of feminist filmmaking but in fact, upon closer examination, they mount a critique of the convention-bound, issue-centric strand of Indian feminist documentary. Stylistically hybrid, Vohra's films sit uncomfortably with the historical purposes of consciousness-raising, propaganda or instruction for which feminist documentary is harnessed by social sector organisations. Indicative of an artisanal approach, Vohra attempts to make films with 'all the things she loves', a position where market or institutional demands are rendered peripheral and instead feminist thinking becomes a

Figure 2.2 Paromita Vohra dramatises the conflict around food practices by performing as Annapurna, Goddess of Food, in *Cosmopolis* (2004).

methodological and conceptual instrument.[15] The films bring together an unexpected kaleidoscope of visual and rhetorical modes including fiction, performance, found footage, interviews and observational material in complex narratives of everyday feminist struggles.

Expectedly, Vohra's views offer a rich source of theoretically informed ideas behind her uniquely reflective and provocative documentary practice. Vohra's interpretation of feminist politics implicates both the theory and practice of how Vohra mediates reality and her own subject position as artist:

> In every film I interrogate the notion of the political rather than dispense a notion of the political, which is what many filmmakers do. In these films, there's a politics and the films dispense a politics through an example of an event or a process. But for me the political process exists in everything at all moments and I am interested in discovering the nature of the political and this is why it's deliberately not in the moment of the crisis but in the moment that is not of the crisis but leads to the crisis.
>
> There are artists who feel they disengage to go into a world of trance to create art, the other kind of artistic practice engages heavily with the stimuli of the world. I see politics is all the time in the air, it's a daily occurrence that shapes the present and I

> am interested in catching that daily occurrence because that in feminist terms exists in the non-verbal, in the gesture, in the very tiny every day that is not privileged as being social process when they are in fact social process.[16]

The lived terrain of everyday life is central to the stability of political systems systemised through routine, repetitive and familiar practices. As Lefebvre (1991) states, everyday life assures 'non-revolution' through its practices that appear normative and self-evident (83). The conceptual dualism of tangible experience undergirded by a camouflaged set of power relations unfolds as a complex set of questions in Vohra's films.

To a large degree Vohra's postmodernist approach addresses the cultural conundrum through a simultaneously critical and referential film theory. Especially relevant is postmodernism's reaction against the established forms of high modernism, or the 'effacement in it of key boundaries or separations' between a distinct high culture and the so called mass or popular culture (Jameson 1992: 165). In documentary terms, the effacement of borders separating the 'sobriety' of social documentary and the pleasure of popular cultural forms can be seen in Vohra's narrative presence as a performative filmmaker and the use of fictionalised dramatic sequences. Performance, the 'experiencing, enacting and embodying of political activity', becomes a potent instrument in Vohra's bid to rearrange perception regimes as well as to foreground the constructedness of the quotidian in everyday life and in representation (Martin 1990: 9). In each of her films, Vohra is present in turn either as a fictionalised character, in *Cosmopolis* and *Unlimited Girls* (2002), or as a performative filmmaker making visible the process of film construction, in *Morality TV and the Loving Jehad* (2007) and *Partners in Crime* (2011). Making explicit the acts of staging, selection and assembly, Vohra's performance involves high theatricality realised through flamboyant costume, scripted dialogue and role-plays involving mythical or fictional characters. At other times, the filmmaker enacts herself, conducting interviews, commenting upon and evaluating the responses of her film subjects on camera, a relationship that contains ethical dimensions that I will explore more fully in Chapter 5. In *Partners in Crime*, a film that evaluates corporate ownership of culture, the raconteur is a sentimental lover whose commentary in the form of love letters laments copyright restrictions on artworks. The meticulously scripted and staged parts mobilise spectacle instead of the documentary conventions of sobriety to render political commentary and space for reflection.

To the extent that documentary film has occupied a space of intellectual thought, Vohra attacks the distinction between high and low culture in the diegetic blending of documentary inquiry with conventions of popular

Hindi cinema. With screenwriting credits for feature film *Khamosh Pani* (Sabiha Kumar, 2003) and directing credit for the reality show *Connected Hum Tum* (Zee TV, 2013), techniques of scripting, characterisation and dramatic narrative construction have flowed into Vohra's documentary projects. The transmission of creative elements into documentary films attacks the hierarchies of realist documentary convention. Documentary realism is, in Nichols's (1991) words, 'the buttress for rationalism' (167). In Vohra's films, the hegemony of realism is contested through a range of fictionalised dramatic sequences. Drama is an affective dimension of Vohra's aesthetic grammar. Drama comprises 'high stylization, expressionist methods, moral considerations, and affective engagement' to make vivid and sensate the realm of the ordinary and everyday (Vasudevan 2011: 21). Narrative techniques of Bollywood fiction cinema and television advertising expand Vohra's toolkit of representational devices. In *Unlimited Girls*, a film about contemporary Indian feminism, the ironic use of fictional advertisements mimics the gendered construction of television advertising while also dramatising the gestures through which patriarchal relations are normalised.

Figure 2.3 Digital duplication techniques visually illustrate the sameness of news in *Morality TV and the Loving Jehad*.

Digital technology and imagination

Digital video has fundamentally shifted the limits of Vohra's expressive realm to mediate the horizon of temporal and narrative linearity. 'Digital Video was made for people like me who are excessively restless, excessively curious, and look at everything at once,' says Vohra.[17] Vohra's reference to the multiple space–time relationship possibilities of digital video resonate with Homay King's (2007) conceptualisation of the digital as a database form that is 'a-temporal, synchronic or existing all at once', in contrast to narrative, which we understand as diachronic and temporally and spatially referential (424). In *Morality TV and the Loving Jehad*, we view the untethering of image from reference as the multilayered narrative against moral policing works across actuality footage, staged interludes and archives of television news. A range of postproduction techniques manipulate the temporal and spatial dimensions of the visual material. Split-screen, repetition, postproduction-animated visual effects and speed changes simultaneously make visible and critique, through exaggeration and juxtaposition, the sleazy and voyeuristic gaze of ratings-driven television news. In a recent initiative, *Agents of Ishq*, a web-based intervention in the area of sex and sexuality education and awareness, Vohra makes use of several web-based textual formats including blogs, listicles, tweets, gifs and embedded links to create an interactive repository of information hyperlinked with cultural forms like Bollywood drama, traditional performance arts and literary texts. Once again, technology becomes an active ingredient in the method and imagination of knowledge construction, not only its delivery.

The lateral movement across historical fact and imagination connects Vohra with earlier experimentalists or 'outliers' surprisingly from within the institutional structure of the Films Division (Sutoris 2016). In the films of Pramod Pati, S. N. S. Sastry and Sukhdev Sandhu, aesthetic experimentation ranges from the use of disjunctive sound in *Explorer* (Pramod Pati, 1968), formal reflexivity in *Flashback* (S. N. S. Sastry, 1974) and the presence of the narrator–filmmaker in *India '67* (S. Sandhu, 1967). Not dissimilar to the artistic imagination of institutional filmmakers, Vohra's reflexive impetus signifies a practice resistant to systemisation as it engages with the forces of history and institutional practices.

Artisanal Production

> By assuming several functions, the film maker in the end becomes omnipresent and his way of working that of a craftsman. (Shafik 2007: 38)

In her discussion of first-person filmmaking, Catherine Russell (1999) problematises the notion of an essential unified self to reconsider the formation of the subject through a 'staging of subjectivity', in a process in which the self is 'frequently played out amongst several cultural discourses' (276). It is my contention that the alternate positioning of the Self by independent filmmakers, in relation to society and cultural production, reveals an artisanal discourse of documentary film identified by the symbolically independent cultural producer whose work, although dependent upon a buyer, retains 'his own direction at all stages' (Williams 1981: 45). The reorganisation of moral authority is fundamental to an artisanal mode of production and I argue that in independent Indian documentary, we witness how this translates into a signifying practice where documentary is anchored in everyday social process which it interprets. The significance of an artisanal practice lies in providing an alternative theorisation of culture to neoliberal consumption-driven media representation and subject construction. Artisanal production evokes counter-narratives to consumerist aspirations and desires that have frequently been equated with neoliberalism and propelled through the medium of screen representation and media technology (Mankekar 1999: 47).

According to Ernest Mandel (1975), who historicised the post-World War II period as 'late capitalism', the distinctive characteristic of this period is the intrusion of the logic of work in all areas of life, resulting in an increasingly administered and disciplinary society. 'Mechanisation, standardisation, over specialisation, and parcellisation of labour', which in the past determined only the sphere of commodity production, in late capitalism cuts across all sectors of public life, writes Mandel (387). Under neoliberalism, the relationship between labour and capital is further hierarchised so that 'labor has become dispensable, disposable, and replaceable' in an 'extreme' form of late capitalism, producing more visible and identifiable outcomes (Ortner 2011). When applied to media industries, Mandel's conceptualisation of disciplinary work regimes becomes evident in the organisation of commercial television production, whose systemisation of process and content is what independent filmmakers position themselves against through practice and forms of expression. Specifically, as the home of network documentary, television is criticised for its 'factory nature', where creative labour is 'standardised, repetitive and anonymous', demanding consent from workers for an 'underlying culture of standardisation' (Ellis 2007: 277). Standardisation becomes the key prism to interpret Indian commercial television content where innovation is replaced by strategies to 'indigenize' global popular content and to promote popular formats of film and film music (Sinclair and Harrison 2004: 47).

In contrast, I contend that the key to artisanship is the repositioning of the buyer/spectator from a consumption relation of taste, choice and preference to different ethos and obligations between artefact, spectator and producer. The precise significance becomes clearer against the workings of the 'commodity image' or the systematic transfer of the profit motive onto cultural forms that favour exchange value over use value. By dismantling the connection between exchange value and cultural forms such as documentary film, the artisanal mode attempts to shift behaviour and patterns of perception that form around culture as commodity. Notably, Amudhan, Monteiro and Jayasankar and other filmmakers including Patwardhan, Saba Dewan, K. P. Sasi and Sanjay Kak choose to work outside the structuring confines of industrial media institutions and economies that formalise claims and accountabilities. Instead a range of working practices, aesthetics and forms of evaluation that typically resist the assumption of profit motive emerge in a practice that produces non-standardised, aesthetically unique artefacts available irrespective of monetary exchange. The overthrow of direct payment in exchange for cultural labour, I suggest, restores a greater degree of moral authority to the filmmakers. Furthermore, to the degree that the filmmakers identify themselves as artists, forms of systemisation such as network programming strands and evaluations through audience ratings exercise little direct control over the cinematic imagination. Marked awareness of the commoditised image relations produce a context against which filmmakers have actively resisted regulations like standardised content formatting, generic narrative structures and set programme duration. For instance, Amudhan's films range from five minutes to 124 minutes organised in multiple parts, as do Vohra's and those of Monteiro and Jayasankar, who furthermore employ critically valued narrative techniques such as performance, reflexivity, associative and non-indexical image–sound montage. In fact, when viewed as a body of work attached to individual filmmakers, the films invite readings as ethnographies of individual filmmakers' identities and subject positions negotiating the contemporary post-liberalised Indian society rather than media texts that submit to generic meanings and functions.

With the decentring of an economic motive and valuation, we must consider the alternate grounds where artisanal production formulates its logics and forms of valuation. I would argue that we consider artisanal mode not simply as a phenomenon predicated upon social privilege but as a practice that undermines discourses and hegemonies of professionalism, qualification and standardisation associated with media production (Atton 2002: 28). In Benjamin's (2008/1934) words,

> Only by transcending the specialization in the process of intellectual production – a specialization that, in the bourgeois view, constitutes its order – can one make this production politically useful; and the barriers imposed by specialization must be breached jointly by the productive that they were set up to divide (Benjamin 2008: 87).

The selected filmmakers and many others, including Anand Patwardhan, Sabeena Gadihoke, Sanjay Kak, Pankaj Rishi Kumar, Pankaj Butalia and Avijit Mukul Kishore, execute multiple roles of director, sound recordist, production manager, scriptwriter, cinematographer, editor, distributor and publicist, and often work with a repertoire of like-minded associates. In the process of deprofessionalisation or the 'collapse' of 'discrete roles' of manual and mental labour and technical, creative and editorial departments in film production, we witness a simultaneous collapse of industry discourses of specialisation with wider implications for media industries and the relations between capital and labour (Atton 2002: 5). Insofar as Mandel's observation regarding specialisation or 'parcellisation' explicates an industrial mode of mass cultural production, procedural actions determine the limits of what can be produced and who is authorised to act. In contrast, artisanal practice harnesses the possibilities of fluidity to move between artistic functions unrestricted by discourses of specialisation, presenting working models that mobilise against the dominance of capital in media production. Nevertheless, deprofessionalisation must not be perceived as a qualitative or critical horizon, and as the accounts make evident, filmmaking remains a function of knowledge, critique and artistic desire. Deprofessionalisation offers a productive consideration of the benefits of rebalancing relations between the disciplinary power of media industries and of the individual in society. As a counter-hegemonic position, the artisanal dimension contests discourses and industry logics of profit-making that act to reify relations of artist, audience, activist and performers.

The question of rewards brings into focus the alternate systems of valuation that comprise motivations for artisanal cultural producers. Documentary filmmaking that emerges from a private artistic goal as identified in the biographical accounts presents alternatives to the systemised structuring of rewards in quantitative (viewer numbers, economic returns) or qualitative (critical reviews) terms that estimate success at a specific node in the artistic process. The 'fixed' or composite system of rewards that ascertains value at the point of reception of media objects fundamentally fails to account for the ongoing developmental rewards associated with artistic process and individual growth. The acts of creative endeavour, intellectual and social process of research and idea construction, and opportunities to learn, experiment and design, produce a creative terrain where rewards are constituted in multiple ways as a function of artistic and critical advancement. Illustrated in the discussions of practice, filmmakers value the possibilities of artistic development, social collaborations and experimentation with new artistic techniques that contribute to notions of success. Nevertheless, cultural legitimacy or valuation cannot be discounted and the appreciation of artistic merit is equally significant to independent/autonomous art (Bourdieu, 1993). But once again, alternate measurements beyond critical and peer acclaim include functional valuation in terms of community use and endorsement by political movements and groups, a point I will return to in Chapter 5. For filmmakers like Amudhan Patwardhan and Sasi, who avowedly offer their films for purposes of mobilisation, consciousness-raising and even as evidentiary form, this is an especially significant criterion for defining legitimacy.

A Signifying Practice

In a sense if the abstraction of commodity relations is rendered peripheral, how might we conceptualise the relationship between independent documentary film and society? If independent documentary resists instrumental use as commodity form or as state speech towards production of social consensus, what meanings can it carry and what forms of knowledge does it produce? From the biographical accounts, it is clear that independent documentary filmmakers decentre the cultural location of documentary from its historical hierarchy as seemingly neutral communication to recognising it as a system of coded references that communicate and produce culture. In other words, in the symbolic struggle for meaning, culture is a signifying system in which cultural production and cultural practices are considered 'constitutive' of the social order and 'involved in all forms of social activity' (Williams 1981: 13). Independent documentary, I argue, as exemplified in the content examined, operates as a signifying practice that forms a system of references around contemporary social and cultural process. As networks of meaning, culture communicates, reproduces, embeds and organises the social order through everyday form and expression. The production and circulation of Indian independent documentary foregrounds its socially formulated nature, spatialised through exhibition in everyday spaces of classrooms, union halls, neighbourhoods and community halls, where it interprets the politics of social process, institutions and organisation.

Documentary's stake in social process forms around an alternative conceptualisation of participation that utilises cultural tools to sketch out an alternate system of meaning-making. Since 1991, this work is most evident in documentary's widespread disapproval of neoliberal dogme, its social instruments and uneven effects. In a public domain organised through institutions of democracy including a free press and an autonomous public broadcasting service, expectedly in 2013–14, nearly 800 cable television channels were registered with the Telecom Regulatory Authority of India (Annual Report, 8). Nonetheless, 'images and documents in favour of liberalisation' predominate emphasising familiar neoliberal dogmes of the accumulation of wealth and the market as a self-disciplining entity (Chowdhury 2011: 18). The market mediation of private subjectivity is a key site of intervention where the struggle for counter-narratives to neoliberalism has taken the form of powerful rhetorics including argumentation, case studies, visual documentation and testimonies to present knowledge alternative to the floating signifiers of growth, living standards and individual choice. This is marked most clearly in the films that translate abstract economic signifiers to observable signified referents. Films about entire communities facing exclusion, poverty and unemployment, like the Arundhatiyar shoemakers in *Seruppu*, the ritual Bhopa performers in *Of Bards and Beggars* (Yask Desai and Shweta Kishore, 2003), the handloom weavers of Sundar Nagri in *The City Beautiful* (Rahul Roy, 2003) and the Baiga in *Mahua Memoirs* (Vinod Raja, 2007) demonstrate the purchase of the concrete to interrogate concepts and claims of neoliberal economics.

The production and exchange of meaning through documentary form is a process whose success is contingent upon the making sense and cognitive interpretation of representational regimes. Undeniably, spectatorship is implicated in this process if signification is to shift relations between subject and society through viewing relations. We witness this effort in aesthetics frameworks that mobilise against direct relations of consumption between the spectator and screen by evoking more complex perceptive techniques. In their films, Monteiro and Jayasankar provoke slower perceptive regimes distinct from the genre-driven melodramatic conventions of television documentary, current affairs and popular narrative cinema. For example, in *So Heddan So Hoddan* (2011), Monteiro and Jayasankar use meditative long-duration shots in order to evoke the slower temporality of the desert setting. Each durational image is positioned as an audiovisual entity independent of expository or illustrative function and demands recalibrated perception and cognition that works against fragmented, commercially organised television viewing cultures.

Conclusion

In this chapter, I have identified an artisanal conceptualisation of independent documentary practice that asserts against standardised industrial media systems to make possible documentary's political reimagination as signification practice. Rooted in the social world, filmmakers formulate alternate references and vocabularies by drawing in forms of knowledge that are excluded and marginalised in official histories and narratives. A resistant practice promotes deprofessionalisation or collapse in the hegemony of specialisation and institutionally conferred status. Its significance lies in its potential to redistribute access to media production but also in disassembling a discourse of professional hierarchy that structures categories of mainstream and independent filmmaking. In the next chapter, I continue this discussion by taking into account the effects of institutional agreements upon independent film production and the ways in which filmmakers address the organising influence of institutional partnerships.

Notes

1. The biographical or subjectivist methodology employed in this chapter moves away from objectivist or positivist forms of social inquiry. Rooted in feminist research, it places great significance upon the individual subject. Specifically, the interests, competences, experiences and understanding of knowledge-producers produces a 'materialistic, but not a Marxist, theory of knowledge' (Stanley and Wise 1983: 191–2). It produces reflexive and localised forms of knowledge, historically situated, specific, concrete and observable. Personal interviews and observations become a key source of information.
2. According to V. Geetha, the anti-caste Self-Respect movement 'convulsed the Tamil country into eruptions of defiance, anger and subversion' between 1925 and 1939. It was led by E. V. Ramaswamy (Periyar), who would 'imprecate, rage, cajole and persuade' Adi Dravidas (original Dravidians) to fight an oppression which utilised their labour and cast them aside as untouchable.
3. All quotations are from personal interviews with Amudhan R. P., 3 May and 5 May 2013, Chennai.
4. Personal interview with Amudhan R. P., 5 May 2013, Chennai.
5. Ibid.
6. All quotations are from a personal interview with Rahul Roy, 6 April 2013, New Delhi.
7. Saba Dewan and Rahul Roy share a personal and professional partnership. Roy and Dewan were classmates at the MCRC and worked together as co-directors from 1987 until each pursued an individual practice from 1997 onwards. They continue to collaborate through numerous production inputs

into each other's work. Quotations are taken from a personal interview with Saba Dewan, 23 August 2013, New Delhi.

8. Personal interview with Rahul Roy, 7 October 2013, New Delhi.
9. Ibid.
10. Ibid.
11. The filmmakers' personal partnership is an example of Indian cultural syncreticism. Both are from different religious and linguistic backgrounds. The experience of an interfaith marriage in a society that dearly values kinship continuity produces deep sensitivity towards and critique of socially assigned forms of identity.
12. All quotations are taken from a personal interview with Monteiro and Jayasankar, 14 March 2013, Mumbai.
13. Chatterji, 'Fair Choice'.
14. Ishwarkar was one of seven workers who in October 1991 undertook an indefinite hunger strike against mill closures and the non-payment of worker dues, and sought permission to run mills on a cooperative basis. See news report, 'Textile Workers Withdraw Fast'.
15. Quotation taken from personal interviews conducted with Paromita Vohra, 5 September 2013, Mumbai.
16. Quotation taken from personal interviews conducted with Paromita Vohra, 4 January 2015, Mumbai.
17. Paromita Vohra, personal interview, 6 September 2013, Mumbai.

CHAPTER 3

Financing and Production

On 4 February 2014, the glamorous, celebrity-studded Good Pitch India arrived in downtown Mumbai. Jointly organised by the Indian Documentary Federation, founded by successful Bollywood film and television choreographer Javed Jaffrey in partnership with the Films Division of India, panelists at the event comprised sixty-eight corporate and civil society representatives, international documentary commissioning agents, film festival representatives and industry insiders from the international documentary community and Bollywood. With Bollywood film producer Kiran Rao as host, the event unfolded as a meticulously choreographed spectacle where each filmmaker used an allocated seven minutes to make a pitch for project funding and in-kind support to the pre-matched media, industry and civil society representatives. Smoothly rehearsed, the filmmakers called upon invited film protagonists to visibly amplify the emotional appeal of the pitch, the success of which rested upon a persuasive linkage between the project and the corporate social responsibility goals of participating organisations. Whilst highlighting these overlaps, filmmakers offered to take on board substantive editorial suggestions regarding certain lines of inquiry, choice of protagonists and storytelling techniques. Not surprisingly, a section of Indian filmmakers is deeply anxious about the strengthening correlation between financing and semiotics as international commissions and co-productions are fervently courted by middlemen and brokering institutions like IDF. While the global networks open up access to transnational institutional funding and circulation forums, veteran filmmakers like Anand Patwardhan take a political view and liken the position of the filmmaker to 'performing monkeys' in the service of a privileged Western spectator in these arrangements (cited in Korossi 2015). Pointing out semiotic issues, Jyotsna Kapur (2003) attributes the development of particular techniques such as the insertion of the Self within co-produced documentary narratives as a response to accommodate editorial pressure from abroad.

The nature of the relation between cultural producers, patrons and institutions fundamentally organises the creative remit and social relations of artists, mediated through the relative power and social authority of the commissioners or patrons of artefacts (Williams 1981: 38). Placing diverse levels of accountability upon artists with implications for autonomy, systems of patronage produce complex forms of social and institutional organisation and relations between artists, culture and society. This raises critical questions regarding artistic independence and the role and function of culture in society. For instance, where artefacts are commissioned specifically with the 'public as patron' and funded through taxation, artistic concerns are decentred and subordinated to the 'privileged situation of the patron', writes Williams (44). As patron, the public body 'derives its authority from the supposed general will of society', in which the maintenance and support of the arts is subordinated to measurable standards of public policy (43–4). The political economy of patronage highlights the analytical significance of institutional relations that not only bear upon textual properties but the wider cultural discourse of documentary and of the meaning and function of culture more broadly.

Particularly paradoxical, patronage-based financing evidently complicates the claims of 'independence' attached to a practice that strives to preserve artistic and political autonomy from regulations, norms and external obligations. From this outlook, my concern in this chapter is with the relation between documentary financing, production structures and practices and its implications for filmmakers in managing heteronomous institutional relationships and socio-economic rationalities not only to produce works of artistic autonomy but, importantly, to assign alternate values to cultural production, cultural producers and production processes in the Indian context. As suggested earlier, the selected filmmakers formulate their concerns through a critical understanding of historical power structures of class, caste, nation and state, and hence my focus is upon the practices and means through which individual filmmakers address the exercise of social and institutional agendas even as they are subjects produced through these systemic structures. I will argue that principles and procedures of negotiation and adaptation or 'tactical practice' transform institutional relationships into production opportunities. Primarily through a reworking of the importance of capital to the production process and the relative subordination of economic goals to artistic, social and cultural rationalities, the stage of production transforms into a space of ideological and cultural struggle between alternate cultural meanings insofar as artisanal production, personal expression and signification function identifies independent Indian documentary. Examining the formation of two primary modes of production in the post-reform era – NGO-sponsored and self-funded filmmaking – each reveals varying degrees of negotiation between an institutionally and socially constructed definition of 'use' that filmmakers must reinterpret both as radical text and, more broadly, as a radical relation between culture and society. Notably, being grounded in knowledge of practices, actions and texts, this inquiry works against the mythologising of independence in terms of political and artistic freedom, to instead argue for its relational positioning as a set of practices with social meaning.

In the first part of the chapter I outline the political questions around NGO-sponsored documentary, a modality that foregrounds issues of political and artistic independence and accountability against a strongly consensual NGO–state relationship in India. Next, I sketch specific methods and work practices of individual filmmakers particular to the NGO-sponsored and privately financed modes to outline how each is structured through accountabilities, claims and norms that in turn implicate material indices of work practices, interrelationships between filmmakers, semiotics of documentary representation and its relationship with the social order. I consider the claims and accountabilities particular to each arrangement, with an emphasis upon the implications for textual properties, particularly the range of issues explored, political perspectives and voice. In the final section of the chapter I argue that the practice of tactics must be viewed as a political response to circumvent, counter and minimise the disciplinary effects of the institutional and social contexts in which independent filmmaking occurs in contemporary India. As a tactical practice, I highlight its two main apparatus that entail decapitalisation of the production process and de-economisation of the cultural agenda, consistent with Michel de Certeau's (1988) proposal of 'minor practice' as an alternative to the social and ideological dominance of institutionally structured notions of culture and cultural instruments like documentary cinema (48).

NGOs and Useful Media

The general neglect of documentary by the Indian government's singular focus on fiction as the basis for 'quality cinema' during the 1970s and 1980s was matched by the industry's emphasis on popular cinema, television news and entertainment genres (Ganti 2004; Athique 2012).[1] An unlikely relation of dependence was thus forged between independent documentary and social sector non-government organisations. Amongst a wide range of opinions about the partnership, documentary filmmakers and critics categorise the institutionalisation of this relationship as an exercise of power or 'hegemony' in the service of a developmentalist agenda in which NGOs harness documentary as a 'vehicle to visualise an argument' (Dutta qtd in Sarkar and Wolf 2012a: 32; Wolf 2013: 929).[2] The agreements and contracts negotiated between individual filmmakers and domestic or international NGOs for the production of documentary films form what I nominate an *institutionally managed production mode*, where documentary film is located at the intersection of a compromise between institutional and artistic objectives. In these arrangements, filmmakers are accorded the symbolic authority of an artist to the degree that alongside individual artistic history, the political views and critical recognition of the filmmaker's 'name' are key considerations in commissioning decisions, relatedly raising questions regarding the fate of new and emerging filmmakers. Social sector NGOs have historically utilised cultural instruments including independent documentary for a variety of educational, instructional and advocacy functions, and particularly extended support for films and media that reinforce social discourses of development through the promotion of democracy and modern technologies. Whilst non-profit-oriented, NGO investments in documentary film are nevertheless strategic and outcome-oriented. Acland and Wasson (2011) conceptualise the cultural dimensions of non-theatrical screen media produced specifically by social sector organisations as 'useful cinema' employed to 'convey ideas, convince individuals, and produce subjects in the service of public and private aims' (3). Displaying overlaps with public service filmmaking, useful cultural forms like documentary function as institutional tools whose role may include the management of populations, capital and social hierarchies and the preservation of organisations themselves. The criteria of utility outline a form of patronage whose focus upon content, messaging, and effect pushes to the periphery questions of film aesthetics, representational politics and expression.

The longstanding NGO history of cultural participation in the field of audiovisual communication extends from the first television broadcast in India in 1959, viewed on forty-five television sets donated by UNESCO to the Indian government. In the present post-reform phase, the growing influence of NGOs in relation to the Indian state and society is accompanied by concerns about the implications of strengthening political and social consensus between both entities and the use of media as an ideological tool in this formation (Robinson 1997; Kamat 2004; Chandhoke 2003).[3] The rise of the NGO sector during the 1980s in India followed a renewed interest in a decentralised, participatory and indigenous model of development but whose progressively compliant relation with the state is a source of concern regarding the cultural investments made by NGOs. The principal criticism questions the ability of the non-governmental organisations to manage public functions of promoting and consolidating political change by making states more accountable and more democratic (Kamat 2004; Behar and Prakash 2004). Instead, by 'bailing out' government agencies and by 'plugging gaps in service delivery', NGOs have 'rescued and perhaps legitimized the non-performing state . . . [and] neutralized political dissent', argues Chandhoke (2003: 76). The agendas of Western donor agencies and global institutions involved in social development in the developing world is believed to coincide with the spread of Western forms of market capitalism to coalesce in the NGO model (Kothari 1986). A vital instrument to promote the penetration of developing economies, NGOs are particularly useful in accessing 'rural interiors', notes Kothari, where neither private industries nor government bureaucracies are generally successful (2178).

Critique of this mode of financing is further grounded in the ideological analysis of NGO structures and operations which are found to reinforce a form of democratic social reorganisation that coincides with neoliberal value systems (Kamat 2004). In the context of the nations of the Global South, the intention and actions of international NGOs, donor agencies and their local agencies are viewed as instruments to spearhead the spread of a neoliberal ethic of competitiveness and individual self-governance. Insofar as neoliberal states are condemned for the representation of private interests, NGOs have come to represent themselves as honest brokers of 'public interest', replacing other established associations such as trade unions, welfare associations and trade associations who traditionally advocate on behalf of specific social groups, states Kamat (157). Effective market economies require a restrained state that withdraws from social welfare to privatise the responsibilities for economic growth, employment and overall economic development. The three-way relay between the withdrawal of the state from functions of social welfare, the decline of collective societal organisation forms and the move towards an entrepreneurial self-governing modality is mediated amongst other mechanisms, through the functioning of NGOs. An example may be seen in the objective of 'empowerment' formulated by NGOs to advance the constituencies of the poor and marginalised. In strictly market terms, the World Bank Participation Sourcebook (1995) configures empowerment as a condition where the poor are 'capable of demanding and paying for goods and services from government and private sector agencies'. Founded upon increased capacity for consumption as a key value, the signification of the term discards socially formulated concerns with political empowerment, improved political representation, fairer distribution of resources and other means of building stronger social subjects.

Placing uncomfortable questions about the position of NGOs as institutions of democratic civil society, the claim becomes untenable on several grounds. First, the construction of 'constituencies' through means of categorisation and differentiation between marginalised groups based upon funding agendas and organisational priorities of donors privileges the interests of the particular over the interests of the general (Kamat 171). The notion of public good is reconceptualised in terms of a negotiation between specific interests rather than the strengthening of popular struggles for democracy by the socially marginalised. Relatedly, the reconceptualisation of public goods and services through a market discourse of economic capacity reduces the concept of public welfare to individual gains (169). The social democratic belief that public welfare and goods must be accessible to all irrespective of private interests and capacities is weakened by the individualising discourses of development and distribution. Kamat argues that both reformulations depoliticise the representative nature of democracy by privatising the public good to special interests, which take little account of the inherent structural marginalities that prevent groups from accessing public goods and public space (171). Reframed through a liberal discourse of individual self-determination, democracy which promotes the construction of public institutions and a public sphere to advocate for the voice and welfare of the collective is rendered unviable.

The deployment of media communication, including documentary film, by NGOs embodies a vital function to not only produce public approval for neoliberal social and economic values and policy, but in itself media consumption constitutes an indicator of socio-economic development grounded in 'developmental imitation' (Govil 2015: 43). According to Govil, mass communication theorist Daniel Lerner exemplified developmental imitation in a speech delivered in New Delhi in 1968 in which he insisted that modernisation could be achieved if the newly developing states 'imitated the West' in their consumption of media products (44). J. Vilanilam (2005) suggests that 'increased media use' was presented as the foundation for the economic and technological development of the West, and thus as a solution that could leapfrog developing nations into the modern twentieth-century 'stage of mass consumption' (156). Contemporary NGO-led media interventions are coded in the discourse of 'information', a set of seemingly neutral concepts and terminologies that is nonetheless based in objectives of capitalist modernisation. In this excerpt from the recommendations made by the UNESCO (India)

Participatory Content Creation for Development (2008), communication and information technologies are placed in hegemonic discourses of capitalist growth defined and codified with disregard for the history and struggles of particular societies.

> If introduced sensitively and appropriately, moreover, ICTs [information and communication technologies] can help some countries to leapfrog entire stages of economic growth through modernised production systems and increased competitiveness, similar to the Asian Tigers: Hong Kong, Taiwan, Singapore, Malaysia and South Korea. (UNESCO 2008: v)

The promotion of neoliberal values of individualism, self-interest and entrepreneurialism are staged and transmitted through NGO programmes that include partnerships with educational organisations, corporate entities and cultural organisations, and funding for contemporary media and information infrastructure, media organisations, media production and circulation. Insofar as NGOs have played an active role in the development of communication infrastructure and production, NGO support cannot be disassociated from the underpinning ideological frameworks. Critically, the cultures of neoliberalism emphasise performance measurement or audit culture through the production of seemingly objective criteria to measure complex social and individual phenomenon to create new forms of governmentality (Shore and Wright 2015). Against these utilitarian perspectives of culture in neoliberal frameworks, documentary films navigate the complex task of fulfilling institutional performance criteria while creating opportunities to realise alternative goals of imagination, independence of vision and artistic expression. The tension between artistic independence and institutional instrumentalism is played out at the site of documentary film, and the filmmaker as it were is faced with the struggle to modulate these concerns through arrangements of work practices and the construction of the film itself.

Institutionally Managed Practice

Amongst their extensive filmography, Rahul Roy's *When Four Friends Meet* (2000) and its sequel *Till We Meet Again* (2013) and Paromita Vohra's *Unlimited Girls* (2002) are financed by non-governmental organisations. In contrast to standardised or objectively framed protocols, the key to the association between the filmmakers and NGO sponsors lies in project specificity, to the extent that agreements are negotiated personally by the filmmakers rather than by professional mediators such as producers or production companies. Conducting a closer examination of Roy and

Vohra's negotiations discloses two interrelated sites where independence is organised. The first concerns the process of commissioning, and the second, the management of accountabilities and responsibilities wherein the filmmakers attempt to carve spaces for manoeuvring in order to realise artistic objectives. While films are commissioned in direct relation to the programmes and priorities of the sponsoring agency, artistic objectives are transfigured through a pragmatics that permits filmmakers to discharge multiple obligations and yet reclaim their position, albeit precarious, as independent filmmakers indirectly governed by the orders of commerce or institutional accountabilities.

Filmed twelve years after *When Four Friends Meet*, Rahul Roy's *Till We Meet Again* (*TWMA*) is one of four films making up the Let's Talk Men 2.0 project, a series that explores the social construction of masculinity and gender consciousness in contemporary South Asian societies. Completed on a budget of approximately A$30,000, the film was co-produced by Aakar, the joint cultural trust of Saba Dewan and Rahul Roy, and supported by a range of institutions including Partners for Prevention along with the International Planned Parenthood Foundation, UN Women, the Norwegian Embassy, Tróicare and Care. Located in a complex institutional ecology, *TWMA* is part of a toolkit of community education materials, along with a workshop facilitation guide and an outreach plan. Publicly positioned as pedagogy, the film aims to bring about a change in the 'attitudes and behaviour patterns' of boys and young men to minimise instances of gender violence (Aakar 2010: 5). For Roy, *TWMA* continues a relationship with the North Delhi settlement of Jahangirpuri and its working-class residents that began in 1997 when, as cinematographer for Saba Dewan's film *Barf/Snow* (1997), he filmed the Jahangirpuri residents who were to subsequently feature in his own extended two-film project.

A modified process

In the first instance, the decision to work with NGOs demonstrates a tactical choice to the extent that these partnerships are founded upon shared social concerns, and in contrast to formalised commissioning systems of arts funds and television broadcasters, these project-specific partnerships are privately negotiated. NGO financing is contingent upon distinct sets of factors which centralise the significance of individual networks, reputation and filmmaking profile. The Let's Talk Men partnership under whose umbrella both films were produced is a result of Roy's personal networking with a visiting UNICEF delegation at Film South Asia 1997 in Kathmandu, Nepal. Roy successfully pitched his documentary film concept and subsequently negotiated Let's Talk Men 1.0, a four-film project set in the South Asian nations of Bangladesh, Nepal, Pakistan and India. Vohra recalls a similar unplanned encounter with Naina Kapur (of the NGO Sakshi) that resulted in the commissioning of *Unlimited Girls*: 'It was a random personal encounter. Naina Kapur came for the screening of *A Woman's Place* (1999) and said that she thought I was the right person to make a film on feminism and equally on a whim I said yes,' states Vohra.[4]

Documented information about the commissioning of documentary by NGOs is scarcely available in the public domain. Hence interviews with institutional representatives like Action Aid's Abhilash Babu provide vital insights into the sponsoring process and underlying considerations.[5] Of primary concern for the organisation is the direct correlation between the subject matter of the film and the institution's programme priorities. Films are commissioned on the condition that they fit in with ongoing programmes and institutional outcomes. Next, a relation of consensual political positions is crucial to ensure that the film does not undermine existing institutional relationships and alliances. Finally, the organisation recommends that filmmakers cast a representative speaker from the organisation if the sponsorship amount exceeds a certain figure. Elaborating further, Ernest Norohna of the United Nations Development Programme (UNDP), active in India since 1951, states that along with artistic considerations the organisation evaluates the political positionality of the texts with respect to the prevailing policy environment.[6] He cites examples where the UNDP has supported film projects on the issues of human and LGBT rights, but rejected these same approved filmmakers when their projects challenged state policy positions on national security, terrorism and border disputes. In a recent interview, Cara Mertes – the director of the USA-based Ford Foundation's Just Films, an organisation that supports social-justice-focused independent film and digital projects worldwide – speaks of an organisational audit culture that emphasises monitoring and evaluation. Aiming to transfigure the documentary process, Mertes states, 'It's a measurement piece . . . Impact is a question you ask at the beginning of your film – it can benefit your funding and the telling of your film . . . we're looking to embed the questions of impact into the production process' (Renninger 2013). The emerging paradigm where NGOs are championing the overlay of corporate style performance evaluation upon documentary film is being closely monitored and addressed by filmmakers like Roy and Vohra.

For Roy, this means sidestepping the formality of the documentary pitch, a response to manage the formative effects of editorial intervention. 'I observed and thought, this is not for my temperament, I don't want to

Figure 3.1 Paromita Vohra with a Betacam camcorder in Bhuleshwar market in Mumbai, filming a scene from *A Woman's Place* in 1997.

be told how to make a film,' states Roy.[7] Hence both Roy and Vohra prefer to form private associations with social sector NGOs whose unfamiliarity with the documentary process translates into looser degrees of monitoring in contrast to standard broadcast environments. For instance, Roy was able to successfully pursue a reflexive inquiry, rarely found in instructional media formats: 'I pushed through a process-oriented project – where people are not told what to do and have ownership of how they do things. We were all male filmmakers and we began by questioning our own gender identity, which informed the project,' states Roy.[8] Paromita Vohra describes a similar process of negotiation with Sakshi, the producer of *Unlimited Girls*, where the narrative device of a virtual chat room is a creative solution to the youth target audience of the organisation and Vohra's personal interest in popular cultural practices.

Textual negotiation

The aesthetic translation of production relations expectedly implicates textual representation and formal aesthetics even as the processes of mediation and give and take between the filmmakers and the institutions confers a measure of elasticity to the film process. Principally, institutional functions of social communication organise the social domain into that of documentary value and that without, largely evident in the direct correlative mapping of documentary participants and institutional publics and constituencies. Historically, NGO constituencies are identified by their lack of capacity to participate fully in market systems and institutions of liberal democracy (Fisher 1997). Frequently people are organised as 'grassroots' groups or 'excluded and marginalised populations' who along with development programmes also receive media communication messages seeking to integrate them into a heterogeneously theorised market and systems of liberal democracy (Roy 2003: 83). In correlative relationships, the subjects of NGO-sponsored documentary films are primarily drawn from socially and economically marginalised, excluded or weaker sections of urban and rural society, a phenomenon that simultaneously conceals and distorts representational and social discourse. In the case of Roy specifically and social documentary more broadly, including, for instance, films like *The Hidden Story* (1995), *Sona Maati* (1995) and *The Women Betrayed* (1993), issues of patriarchy and gender discrimination are explored through the practices, experiences and beliefs of rurally situated women; which, importantly, addresses the issues in rural India, but culturally contributes to a biased spatial discourse of modernity and gender inequality. In response to my questions about his choice to delimit visual inquiry to the working-class residents of the semi-urban periphery of Jahangirpuri while overlooking the terrain amongst middle- and upper-income groups, Roy's response is reflexively candid. He explains:

> The documentary funding comes from the developed world and it dictates things to some extent. They are interested in populations that are disprivileged, so to begin with, it starts to be defined by the source of your funds.[9]

Suggesting more than mere causality between sponsor and textual aesthetic, Roy's analysis reflects ways of seeing transfigured through institutional prisms where the social body is fragmented and categorised. Fundamental questions arise about why NGOs consistently refuse to scrutinise the structural production of injustice and unequal access to resources. Within an institutionally constructed social horizon, to what extent do filmmakers subvert or reinforce the kinds of meanings and discourses through which NGOs define social concepts such as class, gender, labour and culture? Is it possible for filmmakers to create alternative narratives of social relations and social values through textual properties and work practices? These questions are critical if the filmmakers are to be viewed as independent artists defined by a critical and self-conscious standpoint.

Signifying an important index of artistic independence, in *TWMA*, the framing of Roy's rational social inquiry and representational schema are indicative of private concerns beyond mere institutionally defined obligations, perspectives and functions. Insofar as representations of gender violence and patriarchy in Indian documentary are concerned, Jyotsna Kapur identifies the operation of an overarching signifying framework of what she terms the 'fundamentalist project' (2006: 338). Taking the examples of Anand Patwardhan's *Father, Son and Holy War* (1995) and Lalit Vachani's *The Men in the Tree* (2002), Kapur outlines this project in terms of a shared focus on the 'public sphere' of right-wing Hindutva ideology as the productive grounds for an aggressive Indian masculinity. Roy nevertheless departs from this public ideological–cultural space of identity construction to turn towards the private domain of domestic relations and lived individual experiences of his protagonists. Thus, representationally, while the film draws upon the collective banal experience of middle age, uncertain employment and financial struggle, Roy's humanistic interest in the subjectivities accessed through the realm of the domestic and the personal renders each of the four protagonists, Bunty, Kamal, Sanjay and Sanju, in distinct terms. Processed through the prisms of individual life goals, flaws, habits and behaviours, the subjects exceed the normativising and binary governmentality that categorises persons as winners/losers, central/peripheral or oppressed/oppressors, to inhabit more complex subject territories. Metaphorically, intimate domestic spaces reflective of individual desire, aesthetics and economics and personal objects such as photo albums, computer games and mobile phones become the focus for symbolic expressions of individual subjectivities and personas.

Equally compelling, a discourse of contested Indian urban spatial relations figures in an underlying narrative concern when the distribution and claims on urban space are depicted as a function of class and social capital. Embedded through urban development and management policies, the arrangement of urban space according to Brosius (2012) is 'governed by the logic of segregation', which produces an inward-looking 'enclaved gaze' (33). The function of this gaze is to facilitate a 'caste system' of spatial arrangement in which condominiums, gated communities and clubs carve a private domain marked by the legitimate privilege to refuse entry to the 'other' or 'different' members of society (30). Relatedly, each of the four film protagonists is a second-generation migrant whose marginal position in the social hierarchy is reflected in the geographical location of their homes on the urban periphery, a former swamp reclaimed by the migrant families themselves in the 1980s when they were denied the legal right to exist within the established city limits. Thirty years later, neoliberal symbols in the form of malls, fast-food stores and corporate buildings have arrived, creating illusions of choice, upward mobility and narratives of luxury and high-class lifestyles through contact with shiny spaces of consumption. Nevertheless, as the film shows, access to the shimmering city is thwarted by the exclusionary 'enclaved gaze', and when the men visit a local shopping mall they are evidently outsiders memorialising the singularity of the visit through photographs. The production of subjectivities structured by the contestation between public and private space, the neoliberal privatisation of leisure spaces and the increasing regulation of public space through means of designation and rules of usage are enfolded into this narrative discourse. Evoking complex questions beyond an identified institutional concern with masculinities, the film embodies a continuation of Roy's artistic inquiry into the ideological production of cities and their forms of governmentality distributed across his recent filmography (*When Four Friends Meet*, *The City Beautiful*, *Till We Meet Again*).

Together with artistic expression, it is important that we focus on the context-specific adaptation of work practices through which Rahul Roy and Paromita Vohra interpret and subsequently attempt to de-systemise regulatory norms in order to render artistic objectives. This discussion will unfold later in the chapter, where I will use these materials to illustrate their potential as indicators and signifiers of a specific form of independence that asserts itself in institutionally funded Indian documentary film.

Self-managed Practice

A second and equally popular mode of private financing undertaken by independent filmmakers leads to what I nominate the *self-managed private production mode*. Covering a range of privately arranged forms of fundraising, this mode includes personal financial contributions, financial and in-kind donations, borrowed facilities and cooperative work arrangements, significantly identified by attempts to retain the right to self-manage the symbolic and substantive organisation of filmmaking practice and film content.

Private fundraising is organised through a variety of contingent and precarious arrangements without the formalised involvement of an NGO, corporate or state agency, and is increasingly commonplace amongst Indian independent filmmakers. Apart from what might be reasons of institution–project incompatibility, a majority of filmmakers frame this as an ethical and political choice that frees them from institutional obligation. The practice can be traced to the birth of independent documentary in India, marked by Anand Patwardhan's self-produced *Waves of Revolution* (1975) within a field dominated by the Films Division and its commissions. Financed through voluntary labour, in-kind donations and private financial contributions, the film offered an alternative model of economic and political independence. Forty years later, filmmakers like Anand Patwardhan, K. P. Sasi, Amudhan R. P., Surya Shankar Dash and Rakesh Sharma continue to shun institutional modes of finance, asserting their 'independence' in terms of creative and moral authority over all aspects of film practice and texts. Filmmaker Rakesh Sharma affirms the ideological basis of this practice:

> I have clarity that I am making films not to make money but to intervene, and the intervention has to be through a variety of networks that typically don't operate on a commercial basis. It makes no commercial sense for a classic producer–distributor to adopt this model (Sharma 2014).

The rejection of heteronomous claims on documentary texts reformulates independence as a political ethics of artistic autonomy where culture is considered incompatible with industrial production or patronal accountability. At the same time, Sharma's emphasis upon 'intervention' foregrounds transformation and change at the systemic level of social hierarchy and authority systems, raising the possibility of a 'real alternative' revolutionary cinema (Getino and Solanas 1976: 52). Hence, beyond an investment and return rationale, a variety of unique fundraising practices emerge besides standard presales or distribution deals, opening up new possibilities for alternate economies of documentary filmmaking. From investing personal funds and resources in documentary projects to alternate systems of social cooperation, the self-managed relationship establishes a range of non-commercial relations to access subsidised equipment and resources and in-kind collaborations with individuals and organisations. Of the many variations of private financing, Amudhan and Monteiro and Jayasankar's practice is predominantly self-financed and occasionally supported by various combinations of in-kind donations, voluntary contributions and informally arranged in-kind support from arts, educational and cultural institutions.

In particular, the decision to utilise privately owned means of filmmaking, including filmmaking apparatus, filmmaking skills and social capital, is indicative of a political economy that foregrounds an autonomous conceptualisation of culture removed from capitalist functions of income generation. Filmmakers Tapan Bose and Suhasini Mulay (1988, interview) attribute the production of their independent films *An Indian Story* (1981) and *Bhopal: Beyond Genocide* (1985) to the ownership of a camera and a cooperative team, both contributing factors in their ability to make films on a 'cheap budget' even with a high shooting ratio of 10:1 in *An Indian Story*. In combination with what Mulay (1988) describes as 'scraping money off the budgets of other films', both factors gave the filmmakers the advantage of producing films at approximately one-third the cost of larger NGOs and commercial production agencies (1988, interview). The private ownership of an Aaton camera, Nagra tape recorder and Steenbeck film editing system also facilitated Anand Patwardhan's independent practice. The production of *Bombay, Our City* (1985) was made possible by the filmmaker's personal ownership of a film camera and Nagra tape recorder (Korossi 2015). Private access to equipment was crucial for the production of *Leelavathi* (1996). Amudhan's first documentary project was tenuously filmed on VHS cameras borrowed from wedding videographers in Madurai, and edited manually using two consumer-grade VHS video cassette recorders.

More recently, private ownership of digital cameras and editing platforms is giving rise to new and advanced forms of mediatised political speech and participation, one that is clearly subversive, radical and largely outside the remit of institutional rationalities. Here the access to electronic recording is itself rendered a form of resistance against the closed hierarchies and technical discourses of organised media production. Media activist Surya Shankar Dash has lived in the eastern state of Odisha since 2005. Dash has worked with tribal communities in the region towards the creation of Madhyantar and Video Republic, both alternative non-funded cooperative models of digital media production. Through his support of local individual activists and organised people's movements against mining companies, notably Vedanta and Tata, Dash has built up a loyal community of media activists who use mobile phones and consumer-grade digital video cameras to capture and share recordings of local acts of community resistance on a regular basis. Dash edits and assembles these in the form of news magazines or as short documentaries for web-based exhibition on YouTube. According to Dash, alongside their function as an alternate record of public history, the video recordings made by untrained individuals issue a challenge to the conventional aesthetics of social documentary. Self-financing and independence not only take on political functions of the reorganisation of representational regimes but, through their forms of cooperative organisation, they challenge cultural notions of 'authorship', 'artistry' and 'genius'. Dash states that 'video is not about making pure films'; rather, it is a counter-weapon in the 'information war', where those who are not lettered can contribute through visual means.[10] At a political and historical level, the intimacy and immediacy afforded by digital video has allowed the community to record and bring into the public domain an alternative subaltern narrative of the historically propagandised issue of industry-led development.

Amudhan R. P.

Like his earlier films, Amudhan's *Seruppu* is produced through a mix of in-kind donations and self-financing, which evidently permitted the filmmaker to formulate site-specific work practices. In 2005, following an initial preproduction process of building trust relationships with the Arundhatiyar (ex-Dalit) community, Amudhan borrowed a Canon XL-AH1 camera from a local acquaintance in Madurai for a period of one month for the filming of *Seruppu*. A minimal rent of $200 was negotiated for the entire month, resulting in a total film budget of only $1,400, financed by Amudhan through personal contributions. What permits Amudhan to make this level of financial investment is an alternative source of livelihood. Amudhan makes commissioned films and conducts video training courses at educational and community organisations. He refers to commissioned films as '*coolie* films', a reference to the job of a porter hired to carry another's luggage, an allegory for his own position as a filmmaker/director hired to direct another's project like a 'coolie'. For Amudhan, the expression of aesthetics and politics conceptually demarcate his independent and commissioned film practice.

Figure 3.2 In Kodaikanal in 2008, Amudhan works single-handedly to record an interview for *Mercury in the Mist*.

Access to affordable camera equipment was crucial for Amudhan's filming methodology, which specifically concentrated on inquiry instead of pre-scripting and strict production scheduling. While Amudhan possessed a broader knowledge of the history and politics of caste relations in Tamil Nadu, he knew relatively little in relation to the history, issues and views of the local Arundhatiyar community at the heart of *Seruppu*. Uninterrupted access to the camera enabled Amudhan a continuous forty-day shooting schedule during which an ongoing process of inquiry through personal observations, questions and chance encounters shaped the video recordings. 'I kept on shooting and shooting. That was my method,' he says, 'People took me into their houses and I talked and talked. No assistant could have handled this and some may have anti-Dalit prejudice and hurt people through their body language, so I decided to work alone.'[11] The method of shooting solo outlined in Chapter 2, while partly a relationship of continuity with the politically revolutionary filmmakers that have shaped Amudhan's views of documentary, is also a tactic that allows Amudhan to develop intimacy and an insight into more latent community relationships and rhythms. According to Amudhan, 'The film evolved, I did not have premeditated ideas. After speaking to people I could understand their point of view, their aspirations and observations – all I had to do was listen to people. It's more of an observational film and so much was happening that I didn't need to plan the shoot'.[12] The aesthetic and rhetorical parameters of Amudhan's footage are generated through an uninterrupted process of observation, discovery and learning during a daily twelve-hour schedule of filming. In this inquiry-led project, the video footage is in a state of unexpected and continuous evolution, growing from the fluctuating encounter between the knowledgeable self of the filmmaker, the mechanical eye of the camera and the flux of the 'real' world.

Anjali Monteiro and K. P. Jayasankar

A spirit of inquiry permeates Monteiro and Jayasankar's engagement with historical sites and the documentary narrative emerges by contemplating the discovered, found and, often, yet to unfold. For Monteiro, films start as a 'process of documentation and the film emerges through watching, observing and recording over time'.[13] The attitude of patience towards temporality, of seeing time and events as durational and interlinked, enables the filmmakers to engage with history, protagonists and space in terms of interconnected patterns and cycles. *Naata* (2003), for instance, is filmed over a period of nearly five years, beginning with an initial month of documentation in Dharavi during 1998, after which the filmmakers returned to the film only in 2001, spurred by the events unfolding in the lives of its two central protagonists Waqar Khan and Bhau Korde. In 2002, sectarian violence in the neighbouring state of Gujarat prompted another return to the riot-prone Dharavi neighbourhood. This time, the narrative took shape around the community rebuilding efforts of the protagonists, while the earlier audiovisual materials were filmed with the intention of offering a counterpoint to the popular discourses of illegality surrounding urban slums. Both intermingle and yet retain their quintessence, in a fluent multilayered engagement with the cosmopolitan ecology of urban slum settlements.

Monteiro's description of their filmmaking method reveals an artistic perspective where the knowledge and affect produced during the process of making a documentary are considered equally as fulfilling as the finished object. A contemplative, patient and intellectually curious approach unsettles the economic logic of efficiency, cost rationale, professional role accountabilities and pre-scripting. Jayasankar explains:

> We spend a lot of time pre-shoot and post-shoot in the place building relationships. We hang out and try to become part of the furniture. We try to remain small and unobtrusive, so we shoot quietly and do everything ourselves except sound recording. Earlier we did this as we had no money but with time this has become our practice.[14]

Jayasankar's method appears to arise from the same visual toolkit as the fly-on-the-wall approach of direct cinema; however, the invisible filmmaker of direct cinema is immediately countered through the narrative inclusion of the self-reflexive filmmaker. In her analysis of Monteiro and Jayasankar's films *Naata* and *Saacha* (2001), Anne Rutherford notes that 'a challenge to indexicality' is fundamental to their practice (2006: 32). Therefore, even as the filmmakers claim an avowedly historical and public purpose to their film practice, this merges with their openness to the promise of contingency, accidentalness and surprise that underpins the documentary ethos.

During editing this quality configures the ways in which the narrative is organised in dialogue with avowed public objectives. The temporal and spatial arrangement of the narrative is drawn from the qualities of the raw materials, and the pulse of the film attempts to synchronise with the beat of the world being captured. Evident in *So Heddan So Hoddan/Like Here, Like There* (2011), a musical documentary about the Fakirani Jats and their ancient Sufi song traditions, the image and sound assembly follow a meditatively slow pace that seems to synchronise the visual image with the gradual temporal quality of the western Thar Desert. The natural

Figure 3.3 K. P. Jayasankar with sound recordist M. Harikumar filming in the village of Vagoth in Kutch for *So Heddan So Hoddan/Like Here, Like There* in 2010.

landscape is not simply the background setting, but is evoked through fewer edits that allow space and temporality to be durationally experienced. Shots of slow-moving windmills, bubbling streams and clouds floating above the stark white desertscape are held for no less than forty seconds; the duration is determined not by the urgency of rhetoric, but by the rhythm of the actions unfolding within the lived environment.

For Amudhan, Monteiro and Jayasankar, the efficiency-driven rationalities of industry production are rendered incompatible with an artisanal approach to filmmaking. Departing from rationalities of capital generation, the filmmakers aspire to alternate and diverse rewards that contour the ways in which their methods and authorial gaze are configured.

A Tactics of Practice

Insofar as the field of independent filmmaking seeks to maintain autonomy from aesthetic and rhetorical obligations to formalised institutional hierarchies, the development of a patronal relationship between NGOs and independent documentary overlays organisational discourses onto the documentary form, presenting a unique paradox in the Indian context. Moving from more generalised views of independence around its peripheral cultural status or as an intellectual and aesthetic alternative to mainstream cinemas, it becomes evident that independence assumes a tactical dimension through the modification of conventions and regulations placed by sponsors, to create the possibilities of artistic expression within social and institutional production structures. Taking advantage of Michel de Certeau's concepts of tactics and manipulation in *The Practice of Everyday Life* (1988), grounded in the practice theories of Pierre Bourdieu and Michel Foucault, my contention is that independence can be defined as a *tactical practice* comprising the reorganisation of the relation of capital to media production or decapitalisation, and the decentralising of an economics motive or de-economisation from cultural production. I suggest that the mechanism of a 'ruse' or subterfuge underpins this reorganised form of independent filmmaking, allowing it 'to escape capture by systems' and creating the possibilities of artistic expression within the systemic structures of social norms and institutions (xvi). The primary desire to escape confinement from governance is integral to resistance when seeking autonomy from within the very institutional system in which one is located, contends de Certeau (xviii). In contrast to strategies that create a defined relationship between a centre 'circumscribed as proper' (*propre*) and 'an exterior distinct from it', tactics allow resistance from within, through a collapse of these binaries, and therefore the subject 'insinuates itself into the other's place' to seize opportunities and turn them to its own ends (xix).

Decapitalisation

According to Raymond Williams (1981), the ownership of capital in the process of media production gives rise to a particular social relation that designates a media producer, or owner of skills and resources, and a media consumer who lacks specific capital and thus receives media artefacts. Industrial media production re-produces a social and political order that creates the necessary conditions for dominant market-centred ideologies and modes of production to continue by the means of culture. An alternative democratic conceptualisation of media that decentres its status as a discrete industry or cultural activity therefore requires the rebalancing of capital or decapitalisation such that the tools and materials of media production may be democratically reimagined and redistributed. Together with 'deprofessionalisation' and 'deinstitutionalisation', 'decapitalisation', or the evacuation of the capital factor from the production processes, is critical to the construction of an alternative democratic media sphere (Atton 2002: 4) In this respect, I argue that the reorganisation of documentary production by shifting the structural relation between capital and labour reveals a tactical choice to act from within the social system, but one that simultaneously acts to rearrange it by focalising interests and desires whose achievement is not delimited by the (un)availability of capital. The methods displace capital as a primary production factor where input of capital is tied to notions of quality, popularity, visibility and competitiveness, to create different modes of individual labour and social cooperation, artistic techniques, applications and uses of technology, and situated and specific work practices that signify a measure of resistance towards social and economic forms of cultural and economic ordering. The preference for decapitalisation becomes evident in individually crafted responses such as the preference for NGO sponsorship, a pragmatics where filmmakers balance smaller sums of finance with negotiable degrees of cultural autonomy.

Self-conscious identification of subject position becomes fundamental to the revision of capital in the artistic process, particularly under neoliberalism's idealisation of private enterprise and private property rights that organise cultural production into an enterprise and means of profit generation (Harvey 2005). Artistic self-identification, I suggest, constitutes the primary resistance to the social and cultural power relations that stabilise the market rationale while assigning fixed roles, functions and spaces to artists and to cultural production. Significantly, this self-conscious identity authorises filmmakers to invent and reinvent forms of action and decisions towards an idealised goal of artistic autonomy organised in semiotic and/or political terms. Responses of seizing chances 'on the wing', as it were, and shrewd actions that attempt to 'manipulate events in order to turn them into opportunities' become legitimate mechanisms for filmmakers who undertake a struggle to adapt the ordered schemas of NGOs into productive opportunities (de Certeau, xix). We witness this in Roy's commissioning contract for *TWMA*, for instance, which covers epistemological approaches to the issue of gender violence and masculinity and its social discourse but, crucially, omits guidelines round aesthetic or formal criteria such as narrative treatment and structure, sound design, visual treatment or indeed, film duration. Hence the filmmaker notably explores cultural and representational issues that critique documentary representation and functionalist discourse, allowing the film to occupy multiple critical–textual territories beyond simply performing instrumental functions.

The tactical rearrangement of capital is made apparent in adaptations to methodology and work practices that bring into effect adapted context-specific solutions, often as alternatives to established conventions and ways of operating. For instance, specifically in the expressive understanding of their films, the filmmakers discussed in this chapter largely eschew the technical expertise of industry professionals, industry-standard equipment or orthodox workflows and instead formulate work practices that respond to available resources, filming conditions and artistic goals. Amudhan and Monteiro and Jayasankar's inquiry-based video methods and Roy's refusal to participate in competitive documentary pitching illustrate localised solutions to circumvent heteronomous claims of accountability and the standardisation of technique. In the decision to opt for an inquiry-driven approach to narrative construction, the filmmakers offer us another dimension of resistance towards being 'captured by systems'. The documentary script, according to Alan Rosenthal (2007), is one of the necessary requirements for successful television commissions, and nearly 80 per cent of documentary films for television are fully scripted before setting out to film (15). In contrast, the unscripted, uncontrolled shooting or partial variations thereof outlined in this chapter, the processes and ways of 'making' outlined by Amudhan, Monteiro and Jayasankar, proceed from individual responses to the real world, to the extent that scripting is replaced by research questions that structure the method, design and direction of inquiry. Regarding the assembly of audiovisual material, in the absence of precisely pre-scripted narrative structures, sequences and storylines, filmmakers like Rahul Roy assemble narratives principally by a process of reviewing the issues that emerge during shooting, and through repeated close viewing of the filmed footage. Roy, for instance, assembles narrative tracks as separate sequences that come together in multiple tentative permutations during the rough cut. The rough cut is frequently twice as long as the final version and is edited down through a process of reviewing, consultation and feedback from peers and experts. This reflective period of fine cutting and mixing may extend to three or four months. Hence, for the self-conscious artist who seeks artistic and intellectual satisfaction, the non-market NGO offers a symbolic symmetry with their goals of social participation through art. Not only do the films offer a representational critique of the function of capital and power in the structuring of social relations, resource distribution, spatial relations, gender relations and commodity relations, but the production process and practices are indicative of ways in which the decentring of capital produces possibilities for alternative social relations, means of expression and social critique.

De-economisation

Neoliberal socio-economic thinking represents an epistemic move towards beliefs that all social agents are calculatively rational and calculably responsive towards monetary incentives (Adaman and Madra 2014).

Figure 3.4 'Free Entry' – all Vikalp screenings at Prithvi Theatre, Mumbai are free and open to members of the public.

The displacement of calculable economic incentive as recompense for intellectual and artistic labour involved in documentary-making accomplishes a tactical solution to the constraining political and semiotic effects of contemporary economies of cultural production. At the outset, both institutionally managed and private self-managed modes share structural similarities that reorganise the distinctive and historically specific possibilities of artistic autonomy achievable in these modes. Industrially, in relation to the wider field of screen production – including the narrative cinema industry, advertising, broadcast television and multiple types of video-based promotional films, instructional videos and others – both modes are based on alternative revenue models where films themselves are not exchanged as commodities. Screenings are free, open to members of the public and arranged through communication between filmmakers and audience representatives rather than predefined industrial territories, market relationships or theatrical infrastructure. Unlike generic classifications (e.g. human interest, nature, environmental, biography, etc.), which function to segment and categorise network documentary and audience tastes, Indian independent documentary filmmakers have resisted these discursive and market-focused forms of organisation that render documentary interchangeable with or reducible to formally comparable screen forms. In this formation, independent documentary asks us to view it as an object of 'cultural value' or one that acquires value not through economic valuation but through the rules that Pierre Bourdieu (1993) terms 'cultural legitimacy' or approval upon its own artistic terms (113). Discernible from the consumption economies of commercial cinema, screenings at specialist film festivals including the International Association of Women in Radio and Television (IAWRT) and Mumbai International Film Festival (MIFF), cultural centres such as Prithvi Theatres in Mumbai, the India International Centre in New Delhi, educational and cultural events such as International Women's Day and specialist critical reviews generate knowing, familiar and experienced spectators who connect with films and filmmakers upon multiple epistemological and critical levels.

Tactics are the dispersed and creative ways in which individuals within disciplinary systems fragmentarily and clandestinely reappropriate space and power, suggests de Certeau (38). In regulatory and accountability-driven institutional arrangements, the process of creating independent spaces originates with the conscious modifications in artistic practice as a response to the hierarchies of income generation in a tightly organised and taste-driven field of industrial cultural production. For Bourdieu (1993), organisational relations in the field of cultural production are a reflection of relative power and capital which determines the structure of available positions and forms of cultural legitimacy and authority. Of consequence is the fact that independent Indian filmmakers are in a fundamental position to disavow an economic motive fully or partially, reflecting a self-determining class and economic position which enables the choice to perform aesthetic and intellectual labour in flexible arrangements across paid and unpaid sectors. The choice to untie economic goals from artistic expression creates a plane of positions authorising relations of solidarity with a coalition of socially conscious and intellectual art-making communities, towards further affirmation of a conscious, independent artist self. This economic rebalancing is fundamental to the assumption of a moral authority where, despite patronal obligations, filmmakers struggle to avowedly assert and emphasise stylistic and rhetorical concerns.

Sidelining capitalist commodity relations, de-economisation makes evident a range of economies formed around beliefs and practices that documentary filmmaker Michael Rabiger (2004) describes as a joint enterprise: 'A documentary is the sum of relationships during a period of shared action and living, composition made from the sparks generated during a meeting of hearts and minds' (33). A flourishing network of individuals and organisations supports the possibility of independent cultural production grounded in shared ideologies or a belief in the social importance of particular films. Unlike the exchange-based logic of an institutional relationship or direct patronage obligations, these one-off, short- or long-term partnerships form around diverse private, political and historical considerations.

These partnerships extend to crucial modifications within institutional systems of patronage, often by recruiting individuals who employ subterfuge to support independent filmmakers. While referring to their films as 'by-products' rather than the focus of commercial and economically viable activity, filmmakers Suhasini Mulay and Tapan Bose reveal a relationship of creative interdependence with a wider community of individuals, friends and institutions. Bose explains, 'Our friends in government and private agencies are keen to help and they understand that the funds will be used for another project' (1988, interview). In a similar vein, for the members of the Mediastorm Collective, the initial private financing for the production of *In Secular India* (1986) took the form of donations collected from like-minded individuals together with editing facilities donated by the educational institution Mass Communication Research Centre, as well as wildlife filmmaker Mike Pandey's New Delhi-based Riverbank studios.

Decentralising monetary exchange authorises various scales of cooperation between filmmakers and organisations through the means of in-kind support in the form of intellectual, cultural and infrastructure resources. Amongst others, this includes support through field knowledge and access to community interlocutors, access to archives and knowledge collections, and field support in the form of transport, accommodation and, often, experts and guides. Many of the organisations themselves run on models of collectivism and voluntarism. Founded in 2001, the Bangalore-based Pedestrian Pictures (PP) is one such organisation, identifying itself as 'media activist' involved with struggles for Dalit rights, women's rights, Adivasi [tribal] rights, sexuality minority rights, class struggles and issues of environment and displacement, among several others (Pedpics 2007). A collective financed through a combination of public donations, screening fees, equipment rental fee and film sales, PP's cultural activities also extend to a public access library of approximately 200 political documentary films. Providing valuable knowledge support to filmmakers, film libraries facilitate the exchange, transfer and flow of knowledge and culture between global and local film cultures.[15] PP's organisational model echoes the revolutionary film production and circulation models of the Kerala-based Odessa Film Society of John Abraham (f. 1984), a film collective funded entirely through public donations that produced and screened art-house cinema across regional Kerala.

To the extent that the artistic goal of self-expression motivates tactical adaptations, it is important to evaluate the ways in which these modifications permit textual expression outside the frameworks of instrumental valuation. On a representational level the independent films that I examine in this book are clearly distinguishable from a 'spokesperson'

NGO documentary through the degree of creativity and creative disorder present in the narrative. Constructed through processes of experimentation, flux, trial and error, creative disorder, in my contention, signifies the contested presence of non-instrumental or 'non-useful' elements in objects of institutional communication. I view this as a form of resistance to a culture of assessment and audit, through a formulation of accountability encompassing a deeper ontology of the term beyond 'procedural validation' (Giri 2003: 173). Creative disorder depicts a form of accountability that encompasses an ethic of responsibility to self-growth and to the creation of dignified relations in society. For example, Vohra's ludic dramatic performances and associational narrative structures in *Partners in Crime* (2011) and *Unlimited Girls* (2002) testify to the filmmaker's critical concerns and resistance towards the sponsor's primary goal of messaging. In *Till We Meet Again*, Roy's concern with the politics of representation finds similar expression in his pointed and often incredulous responses to the statements and actions of his protagonists. Finally, glimpses of his own performative presence, which reveal his persona as a filmmaker in the narrative, offer a contrast to the invisibilising of the filmmaker's subject position in NGO-sponsored films.

Conclusion

In this chapter I have presented ways to theorise independence through a close consideration of the organisation of the production practices of selected independent filmmakers. Criticism and theory have positioned independent documentary in relation to its ideological political standpoint of dissent and its commitment to the representation of marginalised voices and issues. Yet in the contemporary Indian social, technological and cultural realities, independence is far from a textually or politically homogeneous practice and is instead related to both the private and public concerns of filmmakers. At the same time, its industrial location cuts across public and private institutions and, as I demonstrate in this chapter, it is often produced in partnership with NGOs, which as a sector have attracted criticisms of advancing neoliberalism in the developing world in coalition with governments. These contending and conflicting factors complicate the definition of independence in textual or industrial terms. Hence, in this chapter, I have explored the problem through the prism of production-level decisions, actions, arrangements and modifications that demonstrate the ways in which filmmakers resist overarching forms of general and localised systemic rationalities through a tactical approach towards social orders and industry production practices.

Approaching independence through the direction of practice, I have proposed the concept of tactical practice; a reflective, context-specific adaptation of both organisational and industry conventions, norms and regulations founded on decapitalisation and de-economisation, with the purpose of asserting the artist's self. The application of tactical practice, I have argued, renders possible the goals of inquiry-driven filmmaking as well as the private artistic and cultural concerns of commissioned filmmakers. From within regulated institutional environments, tactical practice attempts to offer resistance to the subordination of documentary and, indeed, cultural production to a utilitarian discourse of 'useful' or institutionally defined episteme of communication. It permits the exercise of non-instrumental and individual aesthetic expression that is central to the independent vision of filmmakers.

Documentary circulation forms the next part of the equation. When organisations finance documentary films, the success of the films is evaluated through exhibition and public presentation. It is the regulated public space of cultural circulation where documentary films perform the simultaneously rational and threatening functions that I will examine in the next chapter.

Notes

1. Quality cinema emerged from Satyajit Ray's criticism of the hybridity of the all India movie. See Athique (2012) for a discussion of the development of this policy initiative and its institutional implementation. See *Annual Report 1982–1983: Ministry of Information and Broadcasting* for primary information about policy steps taken to promote quality cinema.
2. In this discussion I exclude organisations operating primarily within the fields of art and documentary financing, due to their limited presence in India and their governing criteria and outlook, which are framed through different viewpoints. My discussion in this chapter refers predominantly to social development sector NGOs prominently operating in the field of poverty reduction, health, education, gender equality and so forth.
3. The 2009 Asian Development Bank Report on civil society organisations in India states that nearly 1.5 million organisations were active in 2009 in India. The NGO sector was formally recognised in 1953 with the establishment of the Central Social Welfare Board by the Government of India, and assigned the primary objective of promoting public participation and social welfare activities. The 1980s witnessed an explicit acknowledgement of the cooperative relationship between the state and NGOs, and greater recognition of NGOs as development partners with the state. The state–NGO relationship was further strengthened in 2007 following the new National Policy on the

Voluntary Sector, which creates a policy framework to enable NGOs to contribute to the 'advancement of the people of India' ('National Policy on the Voluntary Sector', 2007). Amongst its four objectives, the policy strives to 'create an enabling environment for NGOs', and a partnership model of association that begins with an identification of the 'systems by which the government may work together' with the organisations.

4. Personal interview with Paromita Vohra, 12 March 2013, Mumbai.
5. Action Aid India was founded in 1972. Since 1993, the organisation has taken a rights-based approach instead of a project-based approach to facilitate the empowerment of the poor in the process of social development. See Akerkar (2005) for details about the organisation's history and projects operating in India. Personal interview with Abhilash Babu, 10 November 2014, New Delhi.
6. Personal interview with Ernest Noronha, 27 November 2014, New Delhi.
7. Personal interview with Rahul Roy, 6 April 2013, New Delhi.
8. Ibid.
9. Ibid.
10. Personal interview with Surya Shankar Dash, 10 August 2013, New Delhi.
11. Personal interview with Amudhan R. P., 5 May 2013, Chennai.
12. Ibid.
13. Personal interview with Anjali Monteiro and K. P. Jayasankar, 10 June 2013, Mumbai.
14. Ibid.
15. The small but select PP library includes films produced by radical filmmaking collectives such as the New York-based Big Noise Media, and the West Bank-based Balata Film Collective of young Palestinian filmmakers.

CHAPTER 4

Circulation and Exhibition

> I would like my films to make a difference in the real world. I'm not content to make a film and let it sit idle or let it go only to some film festival or museum and be appreciated by a tiny fraction of well-to-do people. I want the films to be in the mainstream and do as much as I can to get into that mainstream, so that they have an impact in the real world. (Patwardhan 2013)

How might circulation regulate the visibility and perception of independent documentary film? Though possibly unusual, the question speaks to the constitutive role played by the structures and practices of circulation in the differentiation, classification and ordering of documentary film insofar as regulating its prominence and perception in the public domain is concerned. From a cultural point of view, the 'specific social history' and 'social relationships' of media forms, according to Raymond Williams, are critical to meaning-making, suggesting a materialist mode of analysis beyond the radical possibilities offered by subject matter or authorship (1977: 163). If cultural analysis and criticism are to take into account social history as constitutive of meaning, the dialectics of circulation become central to the discussions. Inasmuch as circulation itself is a product of ideology, it also produces ideologies through its mode of presentation and the meanings that it imparts or suppresses in works of art. In *Contemporary Cultures of Display*, Grunenberg (1999) provides potent insights into the ways that the exhibition of artworks and cultural forms is shaped through ideologies and also produces perceptual regimes and viewpoints that politicise the act of viewing. The dominant mode of art display, for instance – the modernist white cube of the modern art museum – conceals its ideological construction, a surface designed for 'the apparent exclusion of all reference to the wider world beyond the domain of pure form', writes Grunenberg (31). The subordination of the original context and content made possible by the white cube results in an 'effacement' of the struggles and religious, political and personal features particular to artworks and their contexts of production. This neutralisation of history transforms functional objects into museum objects of 'aesthetic appreciation' (31). Therefore, beyond the specific site of viewing and subject production, structures, practices and modes of documentary circulation acquire political significance as constituent factors in the production of particular types of meanings, documentary publics and discourses of documentary film.

Independent filmmakers like Anand Patwardhan, Amudhan R. P., K. P. Sasi and others take a political view of circulation and have reiterated their commitment to an expanded documentary public by going beyond the limits of critical and aesthetic appreciation that materialise in spaces like film festivals and cultural institutions. In the context of film and video, in addition to representation, these public ambitions sketch an interventionist agenda traversing new social and geographical territories as a response to political and institutional authority forms that shape the circuits and modes of circulation. Hence by focusing upon practices of circulation and bringing into discussion wider sociological arrangements of infrastructure, labour, public policy, institutions and technology, I am concerned with how circulation may be repositioned as 'mediator' (Latour 2005: 39) that not only determines access but contains the possibilities for the transformation of social relations and perception of documentary itself.

My focus in this chapter is on the responses and practices developed by filmmakers to manage and counter two historical regulatory forces that restrict the mainstream circulation of documentary and its access to an idealised public realm where it can 'alter the world' itself (Nichols 1991: 3). With the gradual retreat of the Indian state from the function of social welfare, as discussed in the previous chapter, NGOs have assumed a partnership with the state for the delivery of social policy and development initiatives. Since the 1980s, the use of documentary by this sector predominantly for functions of social communication has continued to strengthen, with an emphasis upon objectives of documentation, messaging and knowledge transmission (Wolf 2013: 929). Undoubtedly institutional usage has expanded the general visibility, geographical and social dispersal of documentary but the formation provokes critical questions about the nature and scope of documentary authorised in these arrangements once functions of utility and proclamation become interlinked with the very identity of documentary film (Monteiro and Jayasankar 2015). A second regulatory force of official state censorship and an emergent, predominantly aggressive form of unofficial censorship enforced by pressure groups with clashing notions of public interest has arisen to regulate the circulation of cultural forms including documentary cinema considered 'dangerous' or 'disrespectful'.

From this position, I argue that structures and practices of circulation that form around independent Indian documentary extend its 'tactical' nature by deploying new media technologies, citizen participation and historical practices of organising to theorise and mobilise new forms of resistance against a regulated public domain. This is critical if filmmakers are to challenge key modes of regulation, including official and unofficial censorship and the discourses of social utility that map organisational functions upon documentary films. What emerges is a politically formulated praxis marked by the operation of 'tactical media' practices (Garcia and Lovink 1997) that contests the subordination of cultural production to market and institutional rationality of 'utility' not only through textual representation but also through alternative models of cultural circulation. Notably, these circulation practices make evident the significance of frontal challenge to social authority but simultaneously underline the discrete 'minor practices' through which filmmakers and citizens transform the reified categories of media producer and viewer. For documentary, these practices hark towards an alternative episteme of effects beyond the site of spectatorship.

The Regulated Public Domain

Official and unofficial censorship

The modern public domain, cautions Lyotard, is beset with constraining rules that filter discursive potentials to privilege certain norms of statements while restricting the flow of counter-meanings.

> The constraints function to filter discursive potentials, interrupting possible connections in the communication networks: there are things that should not be said. They also privilege certain classes of statements (sometimes only one) whose predominance characterizes the discourse of the particular institution: there are things that should be said, and there are ways of saying them. (Lyotard 1984: 17)

Along with 'tenuous' funding and 'unorganised' distribution, the state authority to censor documentary content produces one of the three 'challenges and obstacles' faced by independent Indian documentary (Pendakur 1995). The public exhibition or theatrical release of films in India is subject to certification by the Central Bureau of Film Certification (CBFC) in accordance with the Cinematograph Act 1952, the Cinematograph (certification) Rules 1983, and the guidelines issued by the central government under section 5(b) in 1991. Insofar as the ideology of censorship is concerned, Mazzarella (2013) concludes that a particularly paternalistic 'pissing man' view of the masses founded on assumptions of an 'underdeveloped political rationality' and 'excessive permeability to affective appeals' is inherent in state actions (12). The CBFC's evaluation of the criteria of public interest offers a case in point where restrictions to the free flow of cultural meanings seek to shield the general public from counter-information and, more importantly, alternative semiotic orders. The CBFC can either grant an 'adult only' (A) certificate, subject to demand for cuts in order to render a film eligible for 'unrestricted' (U) public exhibition, a necessary condition for television broadcast; or it can ban the film outright under Article 19 (2), based upon perceptions of threat to the public order. Consequently, in structural terms, by restricting circulation to private groups either through an outright ban on film exhibition or by granting an 'adult only' certificate, censorship fragments the public domain as a strategy of containment.

As discourse, censorship operates by constructing and modifying rules, evolving boundaries of debate, categories and subjects to not only restrict the flow of 'threatening' material, but to manage the terminologies and terms through which ideas and concepts are defined (Bhowmick 2002: 3151). At a semiotic level, censorship enshrines the state as the primary actor in the staging of public interest, and often grounded in Western industrial modernity, artworks are categorised and their exhibition regulated using state-nominated value-based concepts like 'antiscientific', 'antinational' and 'obscurantist' amongst others (cbfc.in). To the extent that the terminology reflects symbolic judgement, in practice, the interpretation of these categories by state-appointed functionaries is selective and targeted. In 2004, the CBFC refused to grant a censor clearance certificate (2004) under Section 5(b) 1 of the Cinematograph Act 1952 to Rakesh Sharma's *The Final Solution* (2003), an investigative account of state complicity in the sectarian violence against the Muslim community of Ahmedabad, Gujarat in 2002 that left many thousands dead. Denying the certificate for public exhibition, the Board noted that the film 'attacks the basic concept of our Republic i.e. National Integrity and Unity', with the additional fear of endangering 'public order' (Sharma 2004). While the film won the Wolfgang Staudte award at the Berlin International Film Festival and the Humanitarian Award for Outstanding Documentary at the Hong Kong International Film Festival, domestically it was consigned to private circulation. This action follows several earlier instances of similar rulings aimed at invisibilising particular films in the public domain. In 1981, following complaints by the police department, the CBFC banned *An Indian Story* (1981), a searing investigation into police brutality against prisoners under trial. While the film was eventually granted an 'A' or adult rating, it failed to attract theatrical distribution and remained invisible in the wider public domain.[1] With eight of his films subjected to the CBFC's demand for cuts, Anand Patwardhan is the most visible and vocal opponent of censorship of independent documentary alongside others including Shubradeep Chakravarty and Meera Chaudhry, Pankaj Butalia, Tapan Bose and Suhasini Mulay (this is by no means a comprehensive list), who choose a constitutionally authorised frontal approach to confront the marginalisation of documentary to the periphery of the public arena. In a determined exercise of individual constitutional rights, filmmakers have judicially challenged the decisions of the CBFC and in many cases secured significant victories through the Film Certification Appellate Tribunal and the higher courts.[2]

Equally as restrictive as statutory tools were the actions of emergent vigilante groups in the 1990s who sought to censor images of women's sexuality and sexual freedom seen as 'inimical to Indian culture', which later extended to artistic representations of religion, caste, language and other cultural symbols (Seshu 2016: 251). In their analysis of this paradoxical threat to free expression wielded by citizens themselves, Kaur and Mazzarella (2009) interpret it as a consequence of the fragmentation of postcolonial notions of a national identity contiguous with the rise of consumerist desire and regional chauvinism. Propelled by the cultural effects of economic liberalisation, these shifts have fundamentally implicated citizenship by displacing the grand nation-building schemes of the Nehru years. Seen as 'coming from below' instead of the Nehruvian 'commanding heights of the Planning Commission' the fragmented assertions of identity-based citizenship have attained a new image of authenticity in the post-reform phase (19). Ideologically distinct from the nationhood frameworks of state censorship, the claims and counter-claims are focused on issues of regional, linguistic, religious and caste-based local self-interest. A paradoxical disregard for national institutions is indicated by the choice to bypass constitutional channels in a bid to directly check the circulation of counter or alternative narratives. 'Such extra-legal censorship is the bane of our lives,' declares filmmaker Rakesh Sharma (2014). The unauthorised, primarily religious identity-based groups restrict cultural performance and circulation through corporeal means and political intimidation directed towards producers, institutions and publics.[3]

As a community of cultural producers whose appeals are directed towards the vast non-producer public rather than centralising the peer or critic, independent filmmakers have formulated both frontal responses and an inventive repertoire of 'minor practices' to summon publics through texts and radical methods of circulation. Confrontation with censorship requires filmmakers to formulate action beyond representation which embodies transformative potential in ways that the achievement of artistic objectives becomes tied with social and political resistance. In an interesting parallel, Shiva Rahbaran (2016) argues that for Iranian filmmakers, acts of resistance to censorship are events where engagé artists transform into political and intellectual figures. Recognition of their own existential continuity with society has motivated Iranian filmmakers to engage deeply with social realities, albeit by creating new experimental forms that can survive the scrutiny of censorship. In India, the public arena is a site of cultural struggle in which filmmakers use constitutional instruments of public speech, petitions, public action and judicial trial as well as a host of small-scale, non-systematised tools that confront its organising terms and rules.

The criteria of organisational utility

While the tensions between broadcast documentary and television industry practices are well documented (Chapman 2009; Corner and Rosenthal 2005; Kilborn and Izod 1997), in India, NGOs have taken a frontline role in the circulation and exhibition of documentary film but escaped substantive cultural analysis. Documentary is deployed by social sector NGOs for a variety of internal and external communication purposes including training, advocacy, institutional publicity, public awareness-building and knowledge-sharing connected to specific programmes and campaigns. At a fundamental level, the possession of knowledge by NGOs in a social context marked by uneven access to instruments and institutions of knowledge production produces social consequences. Access to a powerful cultural tool like documentary film reinforces the hierarchy of social class relations allowing NGOs to maintain their status as 'developer' in relation to the subordinate position of public as the subject of development (Jakimow 2012: 35).

But in fact, the relation between cultural circulation and the production of meanings deserves deeper examination, particularly as NGO sponsorship translates into specific rules and criteria that aim to intervene in public discourse and reshape public culture. In addition to the compromising effect of sponsorship on editorial independence in sponsored media production, circulation operates as the flip side of the same coin by acting to control meanings at the point of reception. In India, involvement with documentary circulation may occur at the micro level, where NGOs undertake to exhibit one-off films amongst their constituencies, or at a macro scale through the sponsorship of public events like film festivals, cultural festivals, educational seminars and workshops. Importantly, the relations between events and sponsors are anchored in the strong continuity of values, beliefs and public image, between both entities. The political economy of these partnerships, whilst often concealed in discourses of public good, is nevertheless grounded in concrete objectives that will bring short-, medium- or long-term benefits to the sponsor.

In his analysis of the production of neoliberal public culture, Jim Mcguigan (2016) has argued that philanthropic and corporate sponsorship, which has come to occupy the gap in public cultural funding, produces a problematic blurring between meaning and money and culture and commerce. While sponsorship is promoted as merely disinterested patronage of good causes, the sponsoring organisations are quite clear that it is not just a tool for communication but that it purposefully aims at the 'seduction of public opinion' (192). Contrary to its popular understanding as an act of generosity, the sponsorship of public-funds-starved cultural initiatives like film festivals and literary events realises concrete goals of building positive connotation, positive community attention and self-promotion. For sponsors, the opportunity to build specific narratives and meanings in a message-saturated public domain is seen in terms of symbolic capital, which is expected to bring indirect benefits; for example, allowing the entities to 'conceal certain kinds of actions' (Bourdieu and Haacke 1995: 18). Arundhati Roy's sharp observations regarding cultural sponsorship in India clearly identify such a function:

> 'Of late, the main mining conglomerates have embraced the arts – film, art installations and the rush of literary festivals that have replaced the 1990s obsession with beauty contests.'[26] At the Jaipur Literature Festival in 2012, there was controversy over opposition to Salman Rushdie's right to speak. Yet, there was no controversy over sponsorship of the festival by Tata Steel and Rio Tinto Zinc. (Qtd in McGuigan 2016: 194)

According to Wragg (1994), sponsorship is always a business transaction aimed at tangible benefits and thus in its selection of events, the sponsor targets particular population groups that may not be accessible to other forms of advertising (11). McGuigan (2010) identifies two types of sponsorship: 'associative sponsorship', in which an organisation benefits by association with a prestigious event, in contrast to 'deep sponsorship', where the sponsor develops a culture entirely for its own benefit (51). In my on-site research with New Delhi-based non-governmental organisations, a complex constellation of institutional and technical factors appears to structure the relations between NGOs and documentary circulation which collapse the distinction between associative and deep sponsorship.

Documentary film is a key audiovisual component of Action Aid India's (AAI) communication strategy. AAI is involved with regular documentary film screenings, partnership with documentary film festivals, a YouTube channel and the circulation of DVDs through its 278 nationwide regional partners. An active participant in the area of poverty reduction and social justice, AAI's direct constituency of 5,025,915 individuals in 2012, spread across twenty-four Indian states and one union territory, comprises socio-economically marginalised sections of the urban and regional population. Owing to its social development focus, AAI seeks to engage upper-class urban publics as a way to initiate change not only from below but also by creating coalitions with decision-makers and policy-makers. Amongst others, this authorises support for several documentary film festivals and while in principle AAI does not intercede in curation, its support is contingent upon broader political consensus between the curated films and the political positions of the institution.[4] 'We are very choosy and considerate of the political landscape, as we don't want to court controversy,' states AAI communications director Abhilash Babu, outlining a strategic standpoint governed by institutional pragmatics.[5] Thus, at the Mumbai chapter of the 2014 IAWRT Film Festival, which was partially sponsored by AAI, Babu informed me that AAI declined to 'link' with Amudhan's pointedly critical *Radiation Stories* (2010–12) while supporting screenings of *Shit* (2003), which is a political examination of social injustice but one that does not take direct issue with the state, individuals or political parties. The standpoint indicates the potential of associative sponsorship to exert 'subtle pressure' on editorial decision-making and programme selection, a phenomenon concealed by an optics of arm's-length involvement, necessary to preserve an official image of cultural integrity. Most significantly, McGuigan (2010) argues that as sponsorship becomes naturalised in the cultural sphere, associative sponsorship may slip into deep sponsorship and/or subtle pressure may be rendered in more concrete effects (16).

The deeper stake in shaping documentary cultures and publics becomes evident in the way AAI manages the circulation of one-off documentary films. The public performance of documentary is valued through the criteria of organisational utility that translates into a pragmatics of organisationally specific forms of evaluation. Not dissimilar to the formatting function exercised by commissioning agents, distributors and network producers, the circulation of documentary alongside print, performance and audiovisual campaign materials is subject to criteria that operationalise as a form of cultural gatekeeping organised through three rules. Documentary circulation is systemised around campaign specificity, constituency relevance and political consensus between the organisation and the documentary film. In 2013, AAI curated a DVD compilation of five films on the subject of gender relations as part of an overall campaign strategy that embraces documentaries to promote participatory social action and gender activism and awareness (Action Aid India website). The direct correlation between the organisation's operational goals and film exhibition can be considered through the selection of *Immoral Daughters in the Land of Honour/ Izzatnagar Ki Asabhya Betiyaan* (Nakul S. Sawhney, 2012), a hard-hitting portrait of orthodox patriarchal practices in the northern state of Haryana. The film is contiguous with AAI's *Beti Zindabad* (*Long Live the Daughter*) campaign in terms of subject matter, argument, geographical scope and the featured communities and cultural practices. Tangible cultural specificity is a further filter, and the organisation supports films that contain symbols of perceptible significance to target audiences. Madhu Bala from feminist training organisation Jagori, which works amongst working-class groups in non-metropolitan and urban circuits, emphasises that successful films contain substantive cultural symbols like music, language, iconography and known individuals that address audiences directly.[6] Moreover, film duration is a critical factor, and for campaign-related use Bala selects short and medium-length films as opposed to feature-length productions that could disrupt daily routines. Notwithstanding the cultural value of the documentary exhibition platforms provided by NGOs, I am concerned with how the process of filtering centred in institutional criteria produces particular discourses of documentary film, publics and culture, equally through the films selected and the films discarded.

With the blurring between documentary and media communication, at stake are questions of artistic autonomy and documentary's capacity to summon dynamic publics and perform meaningful functions of social organising. In the post-reform period, marked by the unequal distribution of media and communication technology, the systemisation of media functions, and the strengthening discourse that attributes 'property rights' to cultural artefacts, the key question is: how do independent documentary filmmakers mobilise alternative meanings to produce counter-narratives of independent cultural production through circulation practice? In the next section of this chapter I turn to examine the extent to which these considerations translate into individual circulation practices, and the ways in which these produce a dialectics of meaning by means of text and context.

From Information to Emotion

How do filmmakers take a political view of circulation to dispute the socially utilitarian framing of documentary film in a discourse of 'useful' communication by institutional sponsors? In this section I am concerned with this question and the ways in which filmmakers like Rahul Roy and Paromita Vohra unseat the epistemic standardisation of documentary film enshrined in institutional communication to seek alternate affective relations between the screen and spectator.

Rahul Roy

On a humid evening in September 2013, Roy premiered *Till We Meet Again* (*TWMA*) at the plush South Delhi India Islamic Cultural Centre. The audience in the unusually packed 300-seat state-of-the-art auditorium included the film crew, family, filmmaking fraternity, scholars, 1997 Booker Prize winner Arundhati Roy, and Bunty and Sanju, two of the film's four protagonists. Insofar as screenings on this scale are extremely rare in India, nevertheless, the gathering is suggestive of the culturally experienced documentary cinema audiences particular to urban exhibition forums. In cities, *TWMA*, along with Roy's other documentaries, is most frequently screen on campus and at film festivals, film societies, and special interest events.

For Roy, equally significant as contributions to critical and scholarly debate are the affective relation between the individual spectator and screen protagonists that form around the delicately observed lives of individuals in the films. Hence, in contrast to information transmission, the visual inquiry and diegesis in *TWMA* is framed by this objective to probe individual expressions of masculinity from private vantage points of domestic relations and everyday life. Expectedly, this treatment is specific and intimate and less widely translatable across diverse cultural and geographical terrains, and has consequently diminished the value of the film in its primary function as gender training material. Bearing directly upon institutional utility, at least Jagori did not include this film as training resource in its regional gender training courses in 2014. Of particular interest then is Roy's attempt to create different documentary publics and its implication for textual properties, and more importantly, its bearing upon reorganising of relations between documentary, institutional authority and society.

Expressing a desire to construct publics through processes of primary identification between screen subjects and spectators, Roy states, 'I am interested in moments of catharsis and identification . . . where the audience starts reworking or reflecting on their own life . . . In that moment are you able to identify or empathise with the "other"?'[7] Speaking to the 'othering' concerns raised by Monteiro and Jayasankar, Roy's aim to invoke relations of identification through catharsis reveals a view of documentary that is contrary to its epistemic deployment for 'domination', 'power' and 'knowledge' (Nichols 1991: 4). Notably, catharsis is traditionally associated with television drama. According to the uses and gratification theories, spectators deploy active processes to put screen images to use in daily lives (Kilborn 1992). By building individual relationships with screen characters, catharsis allows viewers to 'cleanse the soul' in an Aristotelian sense by 'empathetically experiencing the suffering of others' (Chamorro-Premuzic and Kallias 2014: 99). Catharsis in Roy's films encompasses the opportunity for affective assembly between documentary spectators and protagonists mediated by means of universal human emotions of 'love, anxiety, fear and failure'.[8] At odds with the detached gaze of 'epistephilia' – knowledge through looking – catharsis indicates the variety of subjective functions to which spectators may put the documentary form.

Textually, what distinguishes this approach from rhetorics of factual persuasion is the drawing together of a shared private realm between individual subject and spectator. Frequently outside the largely public horizon of social issue filmmaking, this is an impressionistic space of unspoken thoughts, minor gestures and banal observations. Thus, subjects are often filmed indulging in intimate acts like dressing, sleeping and eating. Family members, including husbands and wives, separately take the filmmaker into their confidence, constructing multilayered portrayals of domestic gender relations. Roy psychologically probes the subjects' hidden vulnerabilities. For instance, in *Till We Meet Again*, we witness the despair of Kamal's professional failure and the contemptuous attitude of his family. We view several wide shots of him watching daytime television in bed. 'I'm not able to figure out anything,' he utters as an audiovisual fragment of a visibly younger Kamal from twelve years earlier is superimposed to highlight a stagnant life trajectory. Underscoring more than mere social representativeness, the emphasis on individual vulnerability creates possibilities for subjective forms of identification, a response tied to the 'particulars of situation and character' (Nichols 156). The film asserts distinctive relations between screen and spectator to overcome an institutional horizon that foregrounds relations of pedagogy, communication and advocacy. Rather, the diegetic private realm is indicative not only of Roy's aesthetic critique of social documentary's historical construction of social archetypes, but a similar critique of grouping produced by systemised institutional documentary circulation.

Paromita Vohra

> *Partners in Crime* is true to her vision; it is used as a vehicle to disseminate her ideas about the sometimes competing concepts of copyright, creativity and capitalism, but it never commands a fix-all solution . . . And the fast-paced, lively, and sometimes humorous tone of the film makes the 94-minute viewing experience immensely enjoyable. (Duggal 2013)

Vohra's *Partners in Crime* was commissioned by the Magic Lantern Foundation under a Ford Foundation grant for the production of audio-visual educational materials on the subject of intellectual property rights. Like her other films, it features an English-language commentary and circulates predominantly amongst English-speaking, urban audiences. What is of interest to me are the ways in which Vohra's films potentially reconfigure geographies of circulation to expand documentary publics. Vohra's complex staging of aesthetic which sits uneasily with narrowly defined institutional functions serves important functions in this process. This objective is predicated upon a shift in the historical perception of social documentary, and consequently a far more speculative and asymptomatic symbolic regime emerges to attack an institutionally imagined documentary audience formulated as needy recipients of notionally useful knowledge.

At the outset, Vohra decries the Griersonian sobriety that has 'shaped the ideas and practices of Indian documentary', which she identifies in terms of an evacuation of creativity, accompanied by the dislike of fictional elements, that together harden documentary as a discourse of sobriety (Rajagopal and Vohra 2012: 9) Insisting that these legacies continue to structure contemporary social documentary, feminist filmmakers like Madhusree Dutta and Paromita Vohra mount resistance through their refusal to institutionally categorise audiences via issues, geographies and vocabularies. Picking up on themes I introduced in Chapter 1, Vohra's documentary narratives partake of feminist documentary positions that defiantly blur the boundary between documentary and fiction to problematise the ideological construction of the 'real' in history and in signification systems (Johnston 1985; Kaplan 1983). It is manifestly apparent that transformation in subject position for Vohra centralises a critical perspective towards the certitude of knowledge. In other words, rather than effective persuasion prosecuted by indisputable facts or logical proofs, the films invite a critical and evaluative relation with history and knowledge. Marked most clearly in *Partners in Crime*, Vohra's narrative performance is akin to a *bahurupiya*, adapted from what Emigh and Emigh (2003) have termed the 'wild card' trickster-narrator of Rajasthani popular theatre. As the provocative *bahurupiya*, Vohra attempts to dismantle the historically conferred authority of the filmmaker and the truth claims of the documentary medium (163). Vohra performs multiple on- and off-screen roles: a lovelorn artist-narrator, by turns an incredulous, curious and occasionally defiant interviewer, and always a quick-switch trickster shifting angles and standpoints to interrupt the singularly fixed and passive position of spectator-receiver.

Notably, a shift becomes evident in the way spectators view Vohra's films. Surpassing content-based assessment of representational accuracy and political position-taking in independent documentary, spectators frequently identify and critique formal criteria like 'touches of humour', 'humorous tone' and 'beautiful soundtrack', hinting at phenomenological modes of engagement with the films (Khan 2004; Duggal 2013; Mohanty 2011). This can be seen as an affirmative step towards the creation of new publics. The recuperation of pleasure creates an opening for documentary to inhabit an everyday cultural landscape and attack its public perception as 'emergency communication' connected to social crisis (Rajagopal and Vohra 2012: 11). By foregrounding the capacities of pleasurable ludic aesthetics and performative elements like drama, music and poetic language to carry political meaning, documentary salutes the affective and sensory virtues of its viewers.

Between Participant and Audience

For most of the 1980s, the socially emancipatory discourse of participatory communication subtended a utopian imagination of video and formed a basis for independent media producers to trial democratic production and circulation practices. Amudhan and Anjali Monteiro initiated their documentary practice during this idealistic phase and continue to work through varying degrees of community embeddedness and cooperation. Focusing upon film participants as first audience, the filmmakers build upon the horizontal communication potential of small-scale media and adopt localised, atypical methods of circulation.

Amudhan R. P.

Amudhan's *Seruppu* (2006) is an intimately observed study of the social and economic discrimination faced by the formerly Dalit Arundhatiyar leatherworkers of Tamil Nadu. Prominently featured in themed festivals, the film has had screenings at the Jeevika South Asian Film Festival on Livelihood (2007, New Delhi), the One Billion Eyes Documentary Film

Festival on the theme of caste (2007, Chennai), and at the Indian School of Folklore (2006, Chennai). Unfortunately, beyond issue-focused forums, the film is likely to be shrugged off as yet another 'victim' narrative, critically denounced for constructing a socially predictable 'other'. Brian Winston traces these legacies to Griersonian documentary representations that valorise 'heroic' proletariat figures but whom the spectator often derisively views as 'poor, suffering characters' (1991: 40). In contrast to canonical readings of documentary representation, the textual elements of *Seruppu* reveal new meanings when historicised against circulation practices and the methodology of audience participation intrinsic to the aesthetic and rhetorical construction of the film. Amudhan's *Radiation Stories* (2010–12) and *Seruppu* have circulated extensively amongst audiences related socially, culturally or politically with the communities represented in each film. Socially proximate groups are of major interest to Amudhan, more so than critical acclaim. 'I don't make films for festivals,' he states, a fact verified by Amudhan's individual screening tours to regional schools, trade unions, factories, colleges and community groups, arranged in cooperation with social activists, teachers and community organisers.[9] My concern in this account is with the nature and organisation of this specific form of circulation and the management of demands that it creates upon film text, working methods and the artistic autonomy of the filmmaker. As will become apparent, circulation has a primary bearing upon key textual choices grounded in a constitutive view of audiences and viewing cultures.

Circulation as constitutive dialogue

Amudhan's film *Shit* (2003), an observational study of manual scavenging, is notably successful. However, for the filmmaker it marks a key shift towards an audience-oriented practice that frequently collapses processes of production and circulation. Amongst its successes, *Shit* is used by Adhi Tamilar Pervai (ATP), the political movement of the Arundhatiyar community, proving instrumental in changing the living conditions of its lone protagonist Mariyammal, who no longer works as a manual sanitation worker. But surprisingly, the singular portrayal of Mariyammal met with disapproval amongst participant and related communities on the grounds that the film lacked social representativeness and hence public validity. *Shit* is the first film in Amudhan's caste trilogy, and in later films, *Seruppu* and *Notes from the Crematorium* (2005), which address the same social terrain, a gradual textual transformation becomes evident in response to the audience critique of *Shit*. It is important to bear in mind that the choice of documentary interlocutors reflects both artistic and social ambition – often chosen for their eloquence, those who can 'argue well' and 'tell stories well', the individual speakers are the ones most likely to help realise the goals of filmmakers (Ghosh 2009: 61). Nonetheless, Amudhan's later films modify storytelling technique and include collective 'talking groups' to not only implicate aesthetics but the ways in which the filmmaker perceives, selects and translates the complexity of the historical profilmic into filmic narrative (Waugh 2011: 246). In *Seruppu*, for instance, the narrative focus is upon an entire community, allowing the filmmaker to draw from a larger social and historical canvas with several interlocutors who articulate diverse personal standpoints.

Amudhan's pursuit of creating 'involved' audiences extends to the reframing of working methods, since audiences symbolically enter the project at an earlier stage instead of receiving a finished media artefact. At a structural level, Amudhan has personally built grassroots networks with socially conscious individuals, activists and groups who facilitate screenings amongst communities connected by caste, histories and forms of livelihood. For instance, the ATP movement has screened *Seruppu* in the Arundhatiyar-dominated villages and cobbler tenements across Erode, Coimbatore, Salem and Tiruppur in Tamil Nadu. Methodologically, an immediate and direct feedback loop between an attendant filmmaker, text and audiences comes into being at the local screenings. Audience members pose questions and for Amudhan an editing roadmap emerges if his explanations and arguments are refuted by audiences: 'I wouldn't dismiss their objection by claiming my point of view,' he states.[10] Significantly, in the case of *Seruppu*, the negotiation between aesthetic and social function finds favour amongst audiences to the extent that social activist and screening facilitator Revathi reports 'deep identification with characters', a rare phenomenon, 'which never happens with documentary'.[11] To examine the mechanics of this 'undeniable emotion' noted by Revathi, I will outline the nature of cultural negotiations that unfolds at these events. Foremost, the post-production assembly process transforms into a work in progress mediated through the cultural habits and practices of the viewers to thus forego the call of critical or market appreciation. Embodied in the very architecture of *Seruppu* are community viewing cultures; for instance, a modified duration of 74 minutes extracted from an initial 120-minute film responds to the work routines and patterns of everyday activity as identified by audiences. Further, in consideration of the linear structures of mythological storytelling popular in the local region, Amudhan reassembled *Seruppu* from an initial non-linear and associational form to three precise parts structured around key issues of livelihood collapse, social and religion-based discrimination, and financial and economic discrimination, each a complete argument in itself.

From a critical perspective, the film is arguably problematic in the collapse between audience and text which complicates auteurist notions of authorship. But I would argue that although Amudhan sidelines critical approval, the film performs an organising function in the context of documentary representation and its truth claims. Organising function is the formal capacity of cultural forms to alter and rearrange the historical hierarchies of the means of production through the shifting of subject position. Benjamin (1970) gives the example of 'interruption' in Brechtian epic theatre to describe its organising function as a device that disrupts responses of catharsis and instead obliges the spectator to take a position towards the action (94). Punctured by moments of awkwardness that characterise the filmmaker–film participant encounter, these extra-diegetic moments in *Seruppu* distinguish it from the smooth form of informational media communication. Disrupting singular readings of film protagonists as victims or survivors, these moments produce reflective considerations of artist–protagonist relations and the construction of media representation.

K. P. Jayasankar and Anjali Monteiro

Naata (2003) is Monteiro and Jayasankar's most exhibited film, with screenings across cultural and educational settings ranging from colleges, film festivals, international art galleries and television broadcast to community screenings organised by amity and rights groups. The circulation of *Naata* is particularly instructive, for it reveals a social formulation of documentary as a form that embodies multiple purposes and objectives and responds to the viewing practices and properties of its potential audiences. This is not to argue that the filmmakers decentre artistic motives, but is indicative of the ways in which the goal of creating active publics is a function interconnected with critical reflection, artistic goals and non-standard work practices.

As a symbolic system of references, *Naata* not only questions the popular representation of the urban slum as an instance of the breakdown of social authority but, through a self-reflexive narrative, disrupts the historically 'safe' viewing position occupied by the experienced documentary spectator. Representationally, *Naata* weighs against the urban redevelopment viewpoints suggestive of 'contemporary gentrification' that are symbolised by capital-led development and subsequent marginalisation of original residents, according to David Harvey (2008: 178). The film enunciates a critique of urbanisms in the cities of the Global South, where complex structural iniquities propel slum gentrification that often includes 'slum removal' altogether (Lees 2014: 514). On a representational scale *Naata* takes on a vast body of films such as Sudhir Misra's *Dharavi* (1992) that deploy popular signifying tropes of promiscuous women, mafia and violence to signify Dharavi, to instead foreground its alternatively cosmopolitan and quotidian urban economy.

However, extending beyond representational critique, *Naata* also makes evident a textual response to the vexed issue of the benign but ultimately non-self-indicting gaze of the archetypal Indian documentary spectator. Discomfort with a historically systemised documentary viewing culture has motivated the filmmakers to turn towards reflexive storytelling (*So Heddan So Hoddan* 2011; *She Write* 2005). In *Naata*, for example, autobiographical elements undo a fundamental 'othering' or the symbolic self-positioning by spectators in a hierarchy with an imagined 'addressee' or subject of lack, reminiscent of the instructional relations of public service documentary. *Naata's* first-person narration is visually staged as basic stop-motion animation by means of ubiquitous domestic objects (toothbrush, comb, toys) contextualised through personal significance to the filmmakers. Disrupting the narrative focus on Dharavi's residents, the recurring brief one-to-two-minute sequences perceptively displace cathartic and affirmatory readings of the protagonists as the noble subaltern but ultimately the 'other'. Markedly, the interjections create a diegetic plane of interpretation where meaning is mediated through suggestions of shared histories and provocative questions about identity and its expression.

But within and outside of bourgeois cultural circuits, in constituencies where the film also functions as lateral means of communication, an interesting conjecture opens up to touch the core of artistic autonomy as a visible tension between artistic and social goals. Exhibition in educational and activist spaces predominantly draws on documentary's knowledge functions of information, representation and evidence. The film is widely used by community amity and education groups interested in themes of secularism. One such group, Avaaz-e-Niswaan, conducts education and skill-building programmes for Muslim women from the marginalised communities of Kurla and Mumbra in Western Mumbai.[12] An intern at the organisation describes the discursive framing of a particular screening of *Naata* to introduce the women to perspectives of neighbouring Hindu communities with whom they ordinarily have little or no communication. In this and similar settings, the unconventional reflexive elements are frequently called into question, prompting the filmmakers to retract the particular sequences and remaster *Naata* under the alternate title *Ham Sab* (*We All*). Nevertheless, acknowledging the constructed nature of meaning, the filmmakers have re-inserted these elements into *Naata*, removing *Ham Sab* from their catalogue in subsequent years. In its present form *Naata* is widely screened in Dharavi and elsewhere across India, where the reflexive narrative raises stimulating debate.

When examined together, the perspectives of Amudhan and Jayasankar and Monteiro bring into focus a reconceptualisation of circulation from a one-dimensional notion of dissemination towards multidirectional functions of dialogue laterally amongst publics and between publics and filmmakers. For these filmmakers, circulation practices built on a localised and historically situated view of audiences centralise cultural specificities and needs rather than abstracting viewers into broad categories. Thus, in contrast to mass circulation, the attention to particularity and dialogue, I would suggest, is pivotal to the discourse of independent documentary as a process aimed at reconfiguring audiences into participants in a shared goal of social transformation.

A Tactics of Circulation

Can circulation practices produce an alternative relation between culture and subject positions and, prominently, can documentary step beyond its institutionally approved functions of knowledge transmission to perform an organising function? Independent documentary filmmakers have responded to this significant question by modifying work practices and textual strategies in attempts to assign alternate meanings to culture, circulation and the relation between artist and audience. Importantly, by expanding this discussion to take into account broader structural and ideological questions that form around documentary circulation, what becomes apparent is a 'shadow zone' located within and in the interstices of formal and regulated cultural circulation and exhibition. Drawing upon ideas sketched by Ramon Lobato (2012) about 'shadow economies of cinema' or alternate economies of informal film circulation that lie beyond the reach of 'regulated, measured' forms of state and corporate governance, I am interested in identifying the ideological and epistemological foundations of this space that permits the circulation of radical content through radical and alternative means (4). Importantly however, while Lobato is interested in examining its significance to audiovisual culture and commerce, I am interested in the political significance of the prominently non-economic structures and practices of this zone. In other words, I am concerned with a shadow zone in relation to independent Indian documentary and its radical meaning for reorganised structures of social relations and media functions in a scenario where documentary circulation is proscribed, culturally marginalised and institutionally regulated. Chief amongst these, I will argue, is the development of 'tactical circulation' across a virtual and historical terrain that adapts and redefines technologies and norms, including those of 'copyright' and 'piracy', in order to mobilise not merely 'informed' publics but 'involved' publics (Atton 2002: 25).

Lobato's emphasis on questions of structure underscores the analytic significance of examining concrete circulation practices, which in India are grounded in a culture of small-scale, one-off screenings across metropolitan and non-metropolitan circuits, based in cooperative networks of people, institutions and venues. Against the near absence of organised distribution, alternative rationalities like exchange, participation, community-building and solidarity produce a historical culture of free-to-attend screenings and hand-to-hand circulation of documentary film. I would suggest that the pivotal attention to public performance by independent filmmakers underpins these channels and the broader practice of 'tactical circulation'. Extending Michel de Certeau's 'tactics of practice' in radical and contemporary directions, I identify tactical circulation as a subversion of the regulatory logic of gatekeeping that draws ordinary people into significant relationships with documentary film and wider documentary cultures through adaptive usage of available resources and technology. I will outline the principles and practices through which filmmakers, consistent with Garcia and Lovink's 'typical heroes', take advantage of available and non-specific resources to construct the adaptive phenomenon of 'tactical circulation' (Garcia and Lovink 1997). From this premise, I draw its two key principles; the construction of 'participant publics' and the redefinition of 'copyright' and 'piracy' that together attempt structural as well as symbolic reorganisation.

Participant publics

Seeking to address the 'crisis' of the dominant system, for Lovink 'tactical media' is a distinctly political response by groups and individuals who 'feel aggrieved by or excluded from' the mainstream culture (Garcia and Lovink 1997). Comprising dexterous production and circulation, tactical media come into being when 'the cheap "do it yourself" media', made possible by the revolution in consumer electronics, interlocks with 'expanded forms of distribution', from community access cable to the internet (ibid.). Founded upon media and communication technologies that comprise much of the present structures of cultural production and circulation through which societies create and assign meaning, the reconceptualisation of audiences and intellectual property rights authorise filmmakers' use of technologies in this specific manner rather than for primary uses focusing upon consumption and profit generation.

An optimistic conceptualisation of viewers is critical to the re-evaluation of circulation in a political framework. Audiences participate in tactical circulation in concrete and diverse ways that permit a shift in subject position, in contrast to the subject produced primarily through processes of viewing or media consumption. Independent filmmakers have shown that they view the audience as evaluative, selective subjects of agency and circulation itself as a site of meaningful cognitive exchange and dialogue that leads to an embodied publics. A material concern for building embodied publics is embedded within an overall artistic goal for filmmakers like Anand Patwardhan, Rakesh Sharma and Amudhan, who are not content merely with representing politics but seek to expand the domain of documentary and transform audiences into social participants by redefining circulation as a public forum. For instance, the filmmakers' longstanding emphasis upon direct interaction with audiences in a spectrum of international, metropolitan and mofussil spaces is indicative of attempts to expand documentary publics and moreover, through rational public dialogue and debate, dissolve the hierarchy of speaker and listener with far-reaching consequences for political change.[13] In a more radical reworking of circulation as dialogic exchange, as shown by Amudhan, audiences become intrinsically meaningful to the creative process. Attacking market frameworks that categorise audiences qualitatively (e.g. opinions, tastes) and quantitatively (e.g. income, spending), filmmakers interpret historical–cultural specificities as context and constraint, crucial to meaning creation. In *Seruppu*, this involves the modification of the narrative structure, duration and methods of storytelling in consultation with audiences who may collectively deploy the film themselves to effect social transformation. Notably, this speaks to issues about the dominant voice of the filmmaker in documentary films by showing methods through which a range of heterogeneous cultural positions and voices may form part of the diegesis and further, on a connotative level, it publicly exposes the functions of power and selection intrinsic to the construction of media messages.

In structural ways, democratic collaborations between filmmakers and concerned citizens are giving rise to 'expanded' meanings of circulation. By expanded, I refer to a form of circulation that decentres a narrow industrial discourse of media circulation to self-consciously perceive itself as a phenomenon embedded within histories, practices and discourses of power, cultural flows and the circulation of meanings. Beyond addressing the problems associated with uneven distribution of technology or the digital divide in India, expanded circulation networks mobilise means to bring about a shift in the ideologies that have organised media circulation in India around categories of urban–regional, educated–illiterate, centre–periphery, cultured–vernacular and digital–analogue.[14] Jan Sanskriti Manch (JSM) is one such voluntary initiative comprising individuals from a range of social classes, professional groupings and geographical locations that initiates tactical solutions to 'participate' in events 'rather than report them', a crucial factor that separates tactical from mainstream media (Garcia and Lovink 1997). Founded in 1985 by progressive artists and social activists, JSM produces innovative technological and organisational solutions to address historical cultural inequalities and regulatory mechanisms. Convening a free-to-attend flagship Cinema of Resistance (COR) film festival series, JSM has constructed an ingeniously simple organisational model of temporary, event-specific coalitions between geographically dispersed cultural groups and a core festival organising committee. Contesting the artificial blankness of the White Cube, place-based methods of festivals like COR emphasise the standpoint of local and locality that takes into consideration specific cultural histories, infrastructure and forms of social organisation.

Organising between seven and ten festivals a year in districts, towns, blocks and villages, each COR event is undergirded by principles of site specificity, decapitalisation and participatory production. By examining the place-based considerations of COR, we witness the production of a tactical response to essentialist discourses of nation and national that frame official concepts of public or national interest. Specific to place, each curation is site-specific and accomplished jointly by the local organising committee and the core festival committee, drawing local artistic expression,

Figure 4.1 Secondary school hall repurposed as screening venue for the Cinema of Resistance Film Festival at Salempur 2013.

social concerns and cultural producers into a positive relation with a representative public domain. Publicity, for instance, takes into account locally available infrastructure that varies from a blend of social media, local small-media to rickshaw-mounted public address systems, handbills and word-of-mouth methods. Moreover, the low-cost decentralised model of screening mobilises on-site available technologies; for example, DVD donations from filmmakers, laptops for DVD playback, generator sets for powering of equipment and the repurposing of infrastructures such as high school halls, factory buildings and auditoriums into screening spaces (Kishore 2017). The property of mobility and portability has encouraged involvement from geographically and socially marginalised groups hitherto categorised by ideologically structured cultural circulation practices (Ganti 2004).[15] Arranged by commercial distributors according to notions of taste, ethnicity, linguistic markers and geography, a 'class/mass' binary perceives audiences from regional towns to be unsophisticated, a phenomenon that an expanded view of circulation addresses and counters. In a broader sense, the collaborations symbolise new modes of participatory

Figure 4.2 Banner in Hindi advertising the Cinema of Resistance Film Festival at a busy street crossing in Salempur in 2013.

Figure 4.3 Not only films; film-based literature, posters and pamphlets accompany the screening programme at Cinema of Resistance in Salempur.

circulation that involve the possibility of shifts in subject positions and a greater investment in collective building in contrast to individualist, self-focused subjectivities produced through neoliberal institutions and cultural practices.

Decomposition of copyright

The tactical reconceptualisation of circulation rests on foundations that dispute the 'creative economy' view of cultural production where an economic logic confers the status of enterprise upon cultural production and entrepreneur or 'wealth creator' upon the producer (McGuigan 2016: 22). The valuation of cultural artefacts as property forms the basis of intellectual property rights. By criminalising unauthorised exchange or piracy, copyright laws claim to 'create social and economic conditions conducive to creative intellectual activity' and the promotion of cultural enterprise in modern economies (Fisher 2001: 171). The need to commercialise the expressive value of cultural artefacts through regimes of copyright, patents and trademark is evident in the equation between cultural value and economic value through seemingly objective monetary measurements of dollars and cents. At the level of selfhood, McGuigan (2016) argues that the symbolic meanings produced through neoliberal practices such as those of copyright and intellectual property laws contribute to a *neoliberal structure of feeling* which is inscribed by means of routine practices governing everyday life and experiences in semiconscious ways (22). Cultural production, when governed by the rationality of copyright, reinforces an entrepreneurial self-formation insofar as culture is no longer primarily about a mode of self-expression or disinterested social contribution but tied to notions of investment, career and self-maximisation.

Conversely, the ideologies embedded in institutionalised cultural property rights are destabilised when filmmakers or authors place value not only upon economic ownership or enterprise but on the social potential released from the free flow, exchange and performance of artworks. Speaking equally to questions of 'authorship', authority and originality as raised by Roland Barthes in *The Death of the Author* (1978), the re-conceptualisation asserts against positivistic ideas and terminologies drawn from the domains of economics, law and industrial media that endorse the aggregation of power by extending ownership to cultural artefacts. To the extent that the subordination of a copyright and property discourse is reflected in a developing ethic and practice of cooperative relations between filmmakers, ordinary citizens and netizens, it also acts as a counter-instrument against a public domain fragmented by rules and practices of cultural circulation.

In 2004, following the CBFC ban on the release of *The Final Solution*, Rakesh Sharma formulated an innovative distribution strategy, displacing the discourse of economic valuation to the periphery of his artistic concerns. Sharma commenced a 'Pirate-and-Circulate Campaign' wherein he distributed free-of-cost video CDs to members of the public on the proviso that they pirate and circulate forward at least five copies of the film. By February 2007, the *Hindustan Times* estimates that 14,000 video CDs and 4,000 DVDs were in circulation (Zachariah 2007). In addition, Sharma reports, 'I allowed people to hold screenings without my permission' (qtd in Nagpaul 2015). By October 2015, the film had been freely uploaded to YouTube by user Irshaad86 and had attracted nearly 80,000 views. Another related incident occurred eight years later. During January 2015, bowing to right-wing pressure, the students of Indian Law Society College Pune called off a screening of Anand Patwardhan's *Raam ke Naam* (1992). Within a fortnight, the director uploaded the entire film on YouTube free from password restrictions, in what he states was a response to the 'hostility on the ground from right-wing elements' (qtd in 'Video: After Screening'). By June 2017, the film had over 169,000 views, exponentially greater than a single campus screening. In June 2017, following the official non-certification of three documentaries at the International Documentary and Short Film Festival Kerala, the filmmakers responded by sharing the films online and enlisting the support of citizens, news sites and commentators to not only expand but potentially create new circuits of circulation.[16] The 'free spaces in the media' that continuously appear due to the speed of technology are the sites from where filmmakers create a radical circulation praxis of independent documentary that contests the ascribed meaning of cultural circulation and consumption (Garcia and Lovink 1997).

The critical evaluation of copyright legislation opens up new possibilities for 'expanded' sites of spectatorship with fewer constraints of time and space and possibilities for the reunification of films and social context. Free web-based film streaming addresses some of the criticisms associated with the 'black box of the theatre' and the 'white cube of the gallery' that determine the conditions under which films are viewed to institutionally and ideologically fix subjects in particular viewing positions (Uroskie 2014: 8). On the other hand, viewed on platforms such as blogs, websites and free streaming sites, film uploads are embedded alongside a variety of hyperlinks, text and information, creating an impetus for participatory narrative navigation, interactive viewing and expanded associational readings. Amudhan's blog, Amudhan R. P. (<http://amudhanrp.blogspot.com.au>), comprises extensive journal entries of screening tours, photographs, observations, interviews, news items and reports from film festivals which function as paratext whose notations and images expand, extend and create multiple layers of meanings to link films to local histories, movements and social actors. We witness a gesture that foreshadows future transformations in the viewing culture of documentary towards a more participatory, socially dialogic and embedded form of viewing as a social affordance of the internet.

The political significance of the public visibility of alternative narratives, voices and histories in relation to institutional forces of cultural dominance and regulation cannot be underestimated. Tactical media are media of 'crisis, criticism and opposition', a public position strengthened through COR's political stance against economic and institutional dependence which sanctions frontal responses towards gatekeeping and cultural suppression (Garcia and Lovink 1997). In 2015 the JSM's Nainital Film Festival took an oppositional stance against the Ministry of Information and Broadcasting's ban on *Caste on the Menu Card* (Ananya Gaur and Anurup Khillare, 2015), a film about the social exclusion of beef-eating populations. Denied certification on grounds of 'communal' and 'provocative' content, even as other festivals dropped the film, the Nainital Film Festival demonstrated an alternative definition of 'public interest' and screened the film.[17] Festival convenor Sanjay Joshi stated, 'This festival is dedicated to the cinema of resistance and this film will be screened despite all odds to signify that message' (Upadhyay 2015). Signifying the enormous implications for the public domain, the filtration function of gatekeeping is destabilised through the alternative 'spaces, channels and platforms' formed through adaptation and cooperation, where temporary reversals in the flow of cultural meanings can take place (Garcia and Lovink 1997).

Conclusion

The public circulation of independent films in India must contend with official and unwritten institutional and political rationalities that regulate the gathering of documentary publics. Central amongst these are censorship and the gatekeeping functions of NGO sponsors, who privilege instrumental applications of documentary communication while also dividing the social collective into normative audience groupings. What I have tried to illustrate here through the examination of a variety of contemporary circulation practices of documentary cinema is the development of context-specific, reflexive media practices whose tactical nature is marked by the historical awareness of the structuring functions of ideology and capital in media systems. The analytical responses outlined are crucial to the meaning and assertion of independence, for they are robust verification of the signifying role of documentary in the public domain through representation and notably as alternative set of media practices in relation to participation, capital use and organisation.

In this chapter, I have concluded that the examined circulation practices signify localised elements of tactical media whose reorganised production and circulation methods produce political subjectivities and ways of being in the world. Garcia and Lovink's conceptualisation of a politics of tactical media is grounded in a pragmatics of repurposing non-specific resources to construct temporary, targeted and low-cost media interventions. I identify two forms of tactical responses, one of which adapts consumer-grade media and communication technologies to redefine the legislated meaning of piracy and copyright laws. The tactical redefinition of piracy evident in the physical and web-based circulation initiatives of Rakesh Sharma, Patwardhan, Amudhan, Monteiro and Jayasankar signals their commitment to a public domain open to national and transnational flows of culture and plurality of cultural meanings. Second, a tactical response emerges in the cooperative citizen associations that respond to site-specific infrastructure constraints through decentralised and scalable models of circulation. Once again, by repurposing low-cost locally available resources, a do-it-yourself model of film festivals, the Cinema of Resistance presents new arguments for considerations of site specificity, the importance of place and coalition-building to cultural circulation.

This chapter is a companion piece to the previous chapter, where the tactical reorganisation of practice is shown to carve out spaces for the exercise of artistic sovereignty. However, beyond the creation of documentary publics, documentary filmmakers work with real subjects, and predominantly it is the weaker and disempowered individuals and groups who are subjects of representation. My next chapter picks up on this thread and continues to engage with the question of how documentary filmmakers interpret the norms of social hierarchies that position filmmakers and social participants as social and film subjects.

Notes

1. Other films to face the CBFC's disapproval in this phase include *A Time to Rise* (Anand Patwardhan, 1981), *Bombay Our City* (1984) and *Bhopal: Beyond Genocide* (1986).
2. A selection of films that have successfully challenged the CBFC include *The Textures of Loss* (Pankaj Butalia, 2013), in whose favour the Delhi High Court recommended the grant of a U certificate, *En Dino Muzaffarnagar* (Shubhradeep Chakravorty and Meera Chaudhary, 2014), which was recommended an A certificate in January 2015 by a judicial order of the Delhi High Court, and *An Insignificant Man* (2017), which was cleared by the Film Certification Appellate Tribunal after the filmmakers successfully challenged the CBFC direction to seek 'No Objection Certificates' from the politicians featured in the film to avail of a Censor Certificate.
3. Vigilante right-wing groups disrupted the screening of the film *Ocean of Tears* on 14 February 2014 at the VIBGYOR Film Festival in Thrissur, Kerala. On the same day, they also vandalised the offices of the organising committee of the festival. For more information, see Aarefa Johari's (2014) report on the attacks. Ten months later, right-wing Rashtriya Swayam Sevak (RSS) vigilantes publicly burnt copies of Perumal Murugan's book *Madhorubagan in Tamil Nadu*, prompting the writer to give up writing. See Soutik Biswas's (2015) report on the factors leading upto Murugan's decision.
4. AAI partnered with VIBGYOR International Film Festival (2009), the International Association of Women in Radio and Television (IAWRT) Film Festival (2013, 2014) and the Shehernama Film Festival (Chronicles of the City 2014).
5. Personal interview with Abhilash Babu, 10 November 2014, New Delhi.

6. Personal interview with Madhu Bala, 21 November 2014, New Delhi.
7. Personal interview with Rahul Roy, 7 October 2013, New Delhi.
8. Ibid.
9. Personal interview with Amudhan R. P., 5 May 2013, Chennai.
10. Ibid.
11. Personal interview with Revathi, 6 May 2013, Chennai.
12. The suburb of Mumbra in the Thane district of Greater Mumbai has the lowest monthly average income in the Navi Mumbai (New Mumbai) area. For more information see Jain (2014), *Mumbra: A Status Report*, for a baseline survey of the development deficits in the area.
13. According to the OED, mofussil originally referred to those parts of India outside the three Presidency capitals of the East India Company (Bombay, Calcutta, and Madras). In contemporary usage, it refers to areas that lie outside any of the large cities, rural and provincial localities in India.
14. India has low internet penetration, with the World Bank reporting that in 2016, 29.55% of individuals were using the internet in India consistent with lower middle income countries where 29.85% of individuals had access to the internet. See <https://data.worldbank.org/indicator>, accessed 19 April 2018.
15. New and existing regional cultural groups including the Udaipur Film Society, People's Film Collective (Kolkata), Hirawal (Patna), Azamgarh Film Society and Sankalp (Ballia) have collaborated on festival organisation and curation, with many launching related offshoots.
16. The three films banned by IDSSFK include *In the Shade of Fallen Chinar* (2016), uploaded by Drokpa Films, 13 August 2016, <https://www.youtube.com/watch?v=JBUwW5z6aNo> (accessed 14 April 2018); *The Unbearable Being of Lightness* (2016), uploaded by Ramachandra P. N., October 2016, <https://vimeo.com/181043555> (accessed 14 April 2018); and *March March March* (2017), uploaded by Kathu Lukose, 14 June 2017, <https://youtu.be/_KupWieLwH0> (accessed 14 April 2018).
17. The New Delhi-based Jeevika Film Festival 2015 decided to remove the film from its programme following the decision by the Ministry of Information and Broadcasting.

CHAPTER 5

People and Documentary

In December 2015 I watched the private video recordings of Anand Patwardhan's screening tour of *Jai Bhim Comrade* (2012) in Dalit (ex-untouchable)-dominated settlements of Mumbai including Ramabai Nagar, whose bloody events the film documents. These extraordinary recordings captured a series of enormously emotional encounters consisting of visceral spectator responses that reflected an existential fusion between the screen protagonists and audience members. Embodied expressions of grief stirred by the witnessing of individual suffering erupted alongside lived narratives of trauma and political arousal. The revolutionary music of the Dalit musicians of the Kabir Kala Manch featured in the documentary generated complex embodied affect of pleasure and sorrow. Above all, these post-screening forums made tangible the subjective ways in which spectators derive meaning from films. The corporeal response evoked a terrain that Gaines describes as the production of 'political mimesis', an embodied phenomenon that connects subjects and audiences through bodily responses or mimesis (Gaines 1999: 85). Some years earlier, Meghnath, founder of Jharkhand-based film collective Akhra, had noted mimetic audience response to *Voices from Baliapal* (1988), a documentation of nonviolent protests by 70,000 fishermen and farmers from the coastal state of Odisha:

> People in a struggle always identify with their counterparts elsewhere and learn from them very fast . . . after seeing the film, women of the Auranga dam agitation emulated the experiences of Baliapal and stopped forest department officials from felling the trees. (Meghnath 1997)

In these settings, films seem to exceed their ontology as media objects to not only mediate symbolic solidarity between the on- and off-screen communities but to invoke the formation of a publics produced equally through shared experience and affect.

As major participants in the construction of documentary texts and subsequently documentary publics, documentary participants and spectators have been somewhat marginalised in documentary studies.[1] Viewed through the 'real vs representation' debate, spectatorship studies focus on critical textual analysis of documentary's representational systems to draw conclusions about documentary's construction of screen subjects, narrative address and forms of spectator subjectification. On the other hand, the documentary participant is largely a site of anxiety, viewed through the discourse of documentary image ethics and its construction of moral obligations between filmmaker and film participant (Gross, Katz and Ruby 1991). In neither framework does analysis surpass the horizon of the text to encompass alternative methods, voices and standpoints in order to determine the social meaning or nature of these relations. As a documentary scholar primarily interested in the relation between documentary, ideology and social conditions, the embodied responses outlined earlier illustrate the vast possibilities of historical reorganisation incipient in the concrete practices of independent documentary. The paradoxical coexistence of diversity and site-specificity of independent documentary complicates the purely interpretative and the equally rigid image ethics frameworks of understanding subject relations, not least as individuals engage at various stages of production and circulation for a variety of motivations. My focus on documentary practice rather than mere reception or effects is underpinned by a belief that documentary 'publics' are created not only through viewing but also through material contact with the documentary process. I am interested in the meanings this contact generates for filmmakers who work independently, and for participants who come into contact with this art practice. In other words, do these types of 'contact' have the potential to transform social relations within and across documentary by producing alternate meanings and subject positions associated with producer and participant? Particularly in the context of the NGO-dominated production and distribution environments marked by institutional hierarchies and subject positions, these relationships function as a lens to bring into focus the reorganisational scope of independent documentary practice and its potential to challenge socially assigned identities and functions.

The limitations of current studies with regard to the sociality of documentary are being recognised with calls for an expanded consideration of documentary impact, from 'individualistic models' that evaluate the impact of finished films to a revised 'coalition model' (Whiteman 2004: 54). Extending beyond the cognitive site of viewership, a coalition model conceptualises documentary as part of a 'larger process' that includes production and distribution to the extent that impact is viewed in the 'larger political context' in which films connect with the social body and social process (54). Besides obligation, a variety of affinities and correspondence underpins documentary production and circulation which rests on cooperation between filmmakers, socially and culturally diverse film crews, scholars, activists, communities and individuals. Examining documentary from this epistemological standpoint allows us to reposition the form in an expanded discourse of 'social practice' that implicates community formation amongst groups with diverse levels of cultural and economic capital (Williams 1977: 158). This method significantly opens up another standpoint to examine documentary's relation with the social collective and widen the signified meaning of documentary's social 'function'. From a consideration of the voices and practices of filmmakers and film participants, in this chapter I will argue that independent documentary can be identified through an emergent 'interdependent' reconceptualisation of filmmaking that places its functionaries in mutualistic relations. I will outline how common goal formulation recognises filmmakers and participants as co-functionaries formulated through practices like 'negotiated consent' based upon the recognition of individual needs and motivations of all those who participate in documentary production.

In documentary studies, the off-screen and on-screen relation between filmmakers, participants and viewers is analysed and managed through the moral parameters of documentary image ethics discourse. While the ethical approach focalises the wellbeing of documentary participant and subsequently the represented subject, the documentary subject is also a social subject whose subjectivity is mediated through discourse. Contiguously the overlap between documentary subject and social subject brings into focus the operation of NGO governmentality that intervenes in the ordering of subject relations in the historical world and when involved with documentary, the represented world. The construction of subject position through image ethics and the institutional governmentality of NGOs function to produce subject hierarchies against which I will identify and critique the social relations that form around and through independent documentary practices. Methodologically, heeding Gross, Katz and Ruby's (1991) call for 'rooting deliberations in actual events', I draw upon a range of voices, most notably those of documentary participants who provide us with 'insider' accounts of the give and take, negotiation and compromise that constitutes the documentary encounter (7).

The Subject: Institutions and Representation

People in documentary; self/other

In documentary studies, the discharge of obligation between filmmakers and social subjects including spectators and participants are seen as areas fraught with moral and legal questions. Documentary claims a relation with both journalism and art which produces three types of ethical obligations of filmmakers: to their subject, to their audience, and to their sponsors and their own vision (Gross, Katz, and Ruby 1991: 6). Documentary has developed rules and conventions that authorise degrees of mediation between the real and its representation, a condition which creates consequences for represented participants. This leads Brian Winston (2000) to argue that filmmakers have a primary obligation to treat participants in an ethical manner, while for viewers he advises a healthy attitude of skepticism towards screen representation. Nichols (1991) argues that the responsibility for ethical conduct lies with the filmmaker on account of the imbalance of power between filmmakers and participants arising from the consequences of representation. Demonstrating a need for greater concern for the participant, Gross, Katz and Ruby (1991) list four categories of invasion performed by documentary filmmakers: intrusion, embarrassment, false light and appropriation. The requirement of informed consent forms one of the key ethical safeguards against the exploitation of participants, guaranteeing a notion of voluntary rather than coercive participation. Nevertheless, the notion of informed consent itself is a contested one. For Pryluck (1976: 22), the method of obtaining participants' consent is 'stacked' in the filmmaker's favour where the subject is given little choice and is persuasively coerced by the presence of the film crew into consenting, a position confirmed by Winston (1995: 224). Whilst not entirely representative of documentary's diverse social arrangements, these fears have led to calls for safeguards against coercion, with protocols such as consent and privacy agreements coming into focus as the legal and enforceable proof of ethical relationships between filmmakers and film participants. An essential industry practice, the successful securing of formal agreements between filmmakers and film participants is increasingly embedded in the formal protocol of documentary film production.[2]

The critique of the image ethics paradigm emphasises its narrow construction of filmmaker–participant relations within a horizon of moderate social concern, resting upon a presumption of an unequal relation of power between filmmaker and participant. Patently focusing upon a narrow band of social documentary, critics argue that image ethics contrasts participants with an 'empowered self of the filmmaker', to effectively reinforce a hierarchy of knowledge and agency (Waldman and Walker 1999). Harking back to a journalistic perspective of documentary, concerns to 'safeguard' and discharge 'obligation' to ethical representation is systemised into procedures and protocols, a doubtful solution to the diversity of documentary's associations with participants. Against this, feminist film movements beginning in the 1970s have provided substantial evidence of the diverse motivations, stakes and relations that underpin documentary filmmaking, prompting a rethink of the discrete categories of filmmaker and film participant (Lesage 1984; Juhasz 1999). Collaborative forms of filmmaking arising from a meeting of minds and objectives produce different subject positions and render change possible, not only representationally but through material practices of the process of filmmaking. Particularly in the Indian context of non-industrial documentary production, the image ethics discourse typically has limited applicability. The prevalence of sponsored and private fund raising diminishes the instance and utility of systemised ethics protocols and in effect transfers the responsibility of ethical conduct onto individual filmmakers. Insofar as relationships are constituted between individuals, reflecting documentary's relationship with the world and persons, the consideration of heteronomous and unsystematic frameworks like private values, objectives and social capital expands the conceptualisation of ethics by bringing into consideration the diverse meanings and contexts that signify morality.

The institution and the subject

Civil society institutions function as a site where discourses of social relations are produced equally through the implied and stated order of social initiatives, institutional and public communication and sponsored documentary production that collectively assign social roles of producer, viewer, expert and subject. Not only must we examine the site from the perspective of the agencies' dominant influence upon regimes of documentary representation, but also the social relations produced and authorised between filmmakers, participants and institutions themselves. The key question for independent documentary-makers in this context is whether they acquiesce to institutional arrangement of social relations, or whether through film practice they contest these fixed orders and provide space for shifts in subject positions.

As constituents of civil society, non-state and non-market institutions, according to Foucault, function as mechanisms of governmentality or the 'concrete ensemble' within which populations are organised for purposes of social management (qtd in Burchell et al. 1991: 23). The teleology embedded in the production and management of subjects is achieved through the assemblage of institutions, procedures and tools which in a liberal democratic nation like India include systems of education, criminal justice, industrial relations, electoral politics, public infrastructure, generation of data and statistics, to name a few. In a close analysis of social development NGOs working in the economically marginalised regions of northern India, Shiv Ganesh (2010) finds that NGOs operate as part of the concrete ensemble of neoliberal governmentality following, amongst others, principles of entrepreneurialism. The operations of the examined organisations position it as an 'expert' on the subject of the 'rural poor', who are cast as clientele to be enterprised as 'potential consumers' by means of increased market participation (24).

Despite idealising the market, historical hierarchies of nationalist development persist in categorising organisations and institutional representatives like filmmakers as bearers of authority or experts in relation to a clientele or the subject of nationalist development. In this disocurse the human subject of development is frequently cast as the 'primitive' or the premodern, which in India include tribal groups, peasants and the rural and urban poor (Skaria 2003: 232). Produced through the function of management, the work of highly bureaucratised development professionals and procedures, the ordinary subjects rarely proceed into decision-making and knowledge-generation roles within NGOs or the society in general (Chandhoke 2009: 10). Although outside the scope of the present inquiry, institutional policies, language, organisational structures and specialisation function as systems of signification that deserve further examination in ways that they reproduce what Kaviraj terms 'bourgeois developmental perspectives' in conjunction with the institutions of state planning (Kaviraj 2010: 105).

Evidently both discourses implicate representational and practical considerations including the selection of subjects, framing and construction of rhetoric. Expectedly, analysis of the representational politics of the 1980s and 90s NGO-financed documentary films reveals a 'top down' schema of representational relations where the aporia of developmentalism and modernity transforms people into homogenised, 'essentialised victims' (Monteiro and Jayasankar 2015: 61). Reflecting institutional perspectives, in many of these films the filmmakers' own viewpoint remains outside the scope of filmic inquiry to symbolically reinforce the top-down relation between documentary participants and NGO, state and elite social groups.

Artist, Meanings, Obligation

Jay Ruby (2005) observes a 'cultural confusion' within the discourse of documentary ethics regarding the status of the filmmaker; is he/she to be viewed as an 'artist' who is appreciated for his/her mastery of the form, or a 'technician' who reflects the world to itself? (213). In the practice of Rahul Roy and Paromita Vohra, ethics is a space of tension formulated through artistic desire and contending obligations to participants, organisations and stakeholders. Even as both filmmakers work in partnership with NGOs and their systematised procedures of monitoring and evaluation, both filmmakers attempt to organise competing ethical obligations by taking into account site-specific political, cultural, social and intersubjective relations unique to each film.

Rahul Roy

Meanings and obligations

The contract between Rahul Roy and the NGO funding partners of the Let's Talk Men 1.0 and 2.0 projects highlights the pedagogy function of the films as 'vehicles for reflection and change' targeted towards an audience of 'young people and policy makers' (4). Remarkably, the thirty-three-page contract of LTM 2.0 makes no mention of the wellbeing of participants, informed consent or dispute resolution processes. The absence highlights an evident paradox between the sponsoring institution's stated goals and modes of actions with regard to the concern for vulnerable members of society. Hence, Roy's relationship with film participants is not subject to official verification or inspection bringing into discussion alternate sites like intersubjective relations, motivations and relative authority that configure the ethical parameters of the partnership.

Roy's methods draw upon David MacDougall's (1970) practice of ethnographic filmmaking, in which the filmmaker seeks to 'increase' the 'number of meanings' conveyed through filmed materials (16). This requires the filmmaker to welcome the tonalities that reveal the 'texture of human life on a variety of levels', a feature critics appreciate in Roy's films (27). In *Caravan*, Trisha Gupta (2013) describes Roy's style in *Till We Meet Again* (*TWMA*) thusly: 'What makes Roy's films remarkable is the non-judgmental space he creates, leaving his male protagonists free to express opinions that might diverge from his own.' This absence of judgement is part of a bigger artistic project to break through the representational coding of documentary's 'tradition of the victim', considering that Roy's film subjects frequently belong to the working classes located on the periphery of urban space and power structures.

Nevertheless, if individual lives are to be opened up for counter-readings, a tension between accountabilities to the artistic or an objective ethnographic self and to the wellbeing of the participants must be considered. The question is, how does the filmmaker reconcile a commitment to disentangle a multiplicity of meanings while acting ethically towards the subject, which entails taking care to avoid intrusion of privacy or causing of public embarrassment? The contending obligations are illustrated in the following sequence from *TWMA*, wherein the filmmaker performs a symbolic double move to simultaneously project and delimit a conflicting range of meanings.

Relaxing in the company of his male friends, we see Bunty, a married father of two, indulging in a sexually suggestive mobile phone call with an unidentified woman. Part of the conversation is transcribed below:

Woman (on telephone):	You are bad because you've been avoiding me.
Bunty:	From where am I bad?
Woman:	Ummm . . . I am not speaking to you.
Bunty:	You are not opening? First tell me from where am I bad? Am I bad even there? (*TWMA*)

Throughout the nearly one-minute phone call, the camera stays on Bunty, and the woman whose voice is heard on the speakerphone is never identified. Later designating it as a 'friendship', Bunty admits he has no intention of bringing the relationship from the virtual world to that of physical actuality. Displaying an ambivalence around moral conscience, Bunty does not intend to split up their respective families, as he says, 'God is watching'. From an image ethics perspective, the scene appears to be an invasion of privacy in addition to potentially placing Bunty and his wife in positions of embarrassment and personal distress. Moreover, given the secrecy and discretion surrounding extramarital affairs, this video documentation is particularly provocative, begging questions about the depth of the relationship between the filmmaker and participant that allows consent for the recording and dissemination of this volatile information.

It is instructive to provide a brief history of the relationship between Roy and the film subjects, for it is both duration and density that may provide answers. *TWMA* is the result of a lengthy thirteen-year relationship that extends beyond the professional horizon of the film project. In November 2014 in New Delhi's outer suburb of Jahangirpuri, when I met Sanju, one of the four male film subjects, he spoke of Roy with easy familiarity. 'We often go and watch films together in cinema theatres,' he said, and emphasised a personal friendship: 'I can visit Rahul at his house whenever I want.'[3] The filmmaker first met the men in 1999 through Action India, a women's organisation active in the field of gender justice and education in Jahangirpuri. During research for *When Four Friends Meet* (2000), the female social workers at the organisation introduced Roy to their young sons, on the threshold of confronting youthful formulations of gendered identity and sexuality. Selecting a group of about twenty young men, Roy spent six months leading fortnightly discussions on various private topics like family relationships, education, career goals and sexuality. Sanju, Bunty, Sanjay and Kamal were four friends selected from this initial group as protagonists for *When Four Friends Meet*, a group that Roy returns to twelve years later in *Till We Meet Again*. During this period, Roy kept in contact with the men and aware of events in their private lives. The trust relationship between the filmmaker and the subjects was evident when Bunty and Sanju accompanied Roy to the podium for the post-screening discussion at the film's premiere in September 2013.

Figure 5.1 Bunty teaches his son to read while Rahul Roy records the scene in *Till We Meet Again* (2013).

Admittedly, for Roy, the treatment of Bunty's suggestive phone call was the most 'difficult dilemma' during the editing of the film, and one he managed analytically. As Roy states,

> To me the question was of disconnect that is an important aspect of the majority of marriages in the area and outside. It is something important to hint towards and excavate – how do people still survive and somehow seek some kind of romance and pleasure in their lives? To me it was very important that this aspect is there as each of those marriages is very different and that is how marriages are.[4]

At this juncture it becomes difficult to map a clear terrain of ethical obligations – the ethnographic project inevitably rubs up against the filmmaker's intimate knowledge, trust relations and self-defined obligations to the individual protagonists. We witness a double move whereby the filmmaker manages contending obligations by simultaneously releasing and delimiting multiple meanings through the instrument of sequencing techniques. Immediately following Bunty's suggestive phone conversation, we see a shot of a morally suspect husband returning home from late-night shift work. Bunty handholds the digital camera as we see the city through his perspective, a dark, alienating metropolis against which he narrates a series of personal tragedies including the death of his first wife from a freak accident. About his phone affair, he explains, 'It feels good talking to her, she talks about herself and her husband who beats her. I would tell her about my tensions and troubles' (*TWMA*). Through the juxtaposition of the two sides of the protagonist, the filmmaker attempts to subordinate multiple meanings, perhaps even the 'voyeuristic, freak show quality' of this material, to a relationship of empathy within the overall diegesis, which is admittedly problematic (Winston 2008: 251). The question it raises concerns the role of the filmmaker/film as an intervention in this matter; does documentary representation add to the injustice, or does the filmmaker have an obligation to intervene beyond documentation? Nevertheless, I would argue that the issue marks a site where in the absence of systematisation, obligations are managed through negotiation between diverse considerations during filming and subsequently in the edit room. From the perspective of participant wellbeing, it would appear that the participants view the film as pure visual documentation irrespective of editorial intervention: 'Rahul has captured it how it is, this is how our life is,' states Sanju.[5]

'I' consent

For film participant Sanju, consent is a matter over which he believes he has considerable agency. 'The access is up to me,' he states. 'I have to allow the filmmaker to get close.'[6] Importantly, this means that consent is not given freely, and factors that are evaluated include disruption of everyday life and privacy concerns, both of which Sanju considers before stating: 'Nothing is hidden, Rahul knows what is going on in our houses.' Moreover, he appreciates that Roy 'just works around us, we do not have to make any adjustments for the film'.[7] Sanju's statements reveal a degree of critical evaluation of the consequences of participation insofar as private lives are made public and the 'extended and perhaps indefinite' life of documentary films exacerbates the consequences of participation (Winston 251). Having participated in the initial film twelve years previously, Sanju and the others have first-hand experience of the extended temporal existence of these audiovisual documents. Ironically, they lament that 'nothing changed for us', perhaps expecting more concrete rewards from documentary participation (*TWMA*). Despite this view, they agree to participate in the sequel, indicating that rewards are not singularly constituted in a linear relation with participation, and perhaps their personal association with the filmmaker and individual motivations associated with media representation cannot be underestimated. A more psychologically framed analysis would undoubtedly reveal distinct individual desires and viewpoints that invite further consideration of consent and its diverse determinants.

Paromita Vohra

In Vohra's view, the obligation of a filmmaker towards their art practice takes precedence: 'your duty is to your film, I cannot say or pretend it's to something else', she states.[8] Unpacking the frameworks of ethics and obligations in Vohra's films and film practice is a complex and slippery task. Ethics is not simply a matter of representational accuracy or judiciously obtained informed consent, but a critical proposition about an ethics of documentary authorship and documentary viewing. Concerning participants, Vohra sketches project-based partnerships grounded in an ethics of transparency and a defined framework of roles and obligations limited to the duration of the actual association. Central to the moral underpinnings of the definition is Vohra's assessment of her filmmaking as an art practice and of her own subject positioning as an autonomous artist.

Vohra's films refer to elements of feminist 'theory film' that attacks ideology and its reproduction by proposing an alternative language of critical cinema and means of subject positioning (Kaplan 1983: 58). Even though Vohra continues to draw materials from the historical world, the filmmaker no longer privileges interviews, words or testimony for an intrinsic meaning as 'fragment of truth'. Instead, individual participants are one of many actual, archival and fantastical raw materials assembled in multilayered narratives. The moral force attached to truth is decentred by Vohra's acknowledgement of performance as a mode of communication and being in the world. Content to engage with individuals' performative personae instead of pursuing an essentialist notion of subjectivity, participants are provided with a space of choice to modulate performance and the range of information they wish to divulge to the camera. Hence Vohra issues an upfront caution: 'Please don't tell me anything that you don't want me to use. No filmmaker is honourable, I want to be honourable but if you don't want me to put it in the film, don't say it' (int). In a reversal of image ethics, where filmmakers aim to cement trust relationships, Vohra unseats the quest for historical truth by foregrounding her dual subject position as objective researcher and subjective artist. The disavowal of deep trust relationships forecloses journeys into interior life-worlds or private realms, and questions of artistic style, method and voice take centre stage in the way that the actuality is mediated and framed in audiovisual form.

Formally, this produces an essayistic mode comprising an expanded arrangement of imagined, constructed and performed techniques that invite conceptual engagement. Artistic manipulation of actuality material is the foundation of the essay film, which 'no longer binds the filmmaker to the rules and parameters of the traditional documentary practice' (Alter 2002: 7). As an organisational form, the essay film is 'digressive, playful, contradictory, and political', each an apt descriptor for diegetic relations in Vohra's films (7). In *Partners in Crime*, Vohra includes a sequence where Osama the street-pirated DVD seller requests Vohra to film his face: 'I want to to become famous,' he laughs. These moments of performance digress from pure functions of rhetoric, creating a spectatorship of pleasure derived from intersubjective relations of playfulness and spontaneity.

Interventional gaze

The analysis of 'gaze' in documentary allows us to apprehend the ethos of Vohra's relations with participants and spectators. Axiographics is the way in which an ethics of representation comes to be 'known and experienced through space' (Nichols 1991: 77). Space in documentary film is created through dimensions of time (e.g. narrative and exposition) and those of space (e.g. changes in distance, place and perspective) that together produce the filmmaker's 'gaze' through which the historical world is represented (77). In *Partners in Crime*, the discursive framing of subjects through audiovisual techniques and rhetorical means allows the spectator to 'read' Vohra's attitude towards the individuals. Of great interest from the perspective of ethics is the fact that the film subjects too are able to read the filmmaker's attitude through the ways in which each encounter is staged. By keeping these encounters intact to a large degree, each opens out as a site where in addition to rhetoric, additional forms of information are encoded and made available for analysis.

According to Nichols (1991), the ways in which the filmmaker's presence is encoded in the text serves as an 'index' of their own relationship to the people and problems in the historical world (79). The gaze of the filmmaker towards the film subject therefore reveals the measure of his/her personal attitude and feelings towards this human subject. I would suggest that Vohra's gaze is 'interventional' rather than neutral, a representational mode that abandons the 'precondition of distance' to transform personal detachment into the 'involvement of a look' (Nichols 85). Disavowing the objectivity claims of observational image-making, the viewer is deliberately positioned to view the subject through the filmmaker's personal values and politics, which creates discourses of approval/disapproval or trust/distrust.

In on-camera conversations with film subjects, Vohra frequently includes her questions, interjections and remarks that combine with vocabulary, verbal tone, the spatial components of composition and editing to form a paratext that creates complex moral discourse. Beyond functions of reflexivity, these sites are tangential to thematic concerns but nonetheless signify an interventional or evaluative gaze where the filmmaker takes an evident position with respect to the world. With Osama, we witness this gaze sonically in Vohra's playful and equanimous conversational tone, which acquiesces to his demands to shoot after business hours and to film his face. Vohra even adds a warm pink tint to the images to evoke a dreamy, romantic effect. In contrast, in the encounter with anti-piracy vigilante M. M. Satish, Vohra makes her position of disagreement clear through a disapproving vocal tone and argumentative questioning. For instance, Vohra puts to Satish, 'Eventually the only people who are harmed are private corporates and they are linking it to terrorism to make the government fight their cause. Why should the government protect them now?' (*Partners in Crime*). The provocative and frontal nature of her questions leaves little doubt as to Vohra's disagreement with the subject's positions. Significantly, the retention of the performative persona creates a multilayered text in which semiotics and 'gaze' visualise an interlocked ethics relation between filmmaker, participant and viewer. After all, the spectator must evaluate not only representation but also the concrete evidence of the relation between filmmaker and participant captured in these fragments.

Speaking with the Subject

Amudhan and Monteiro and Jayasankar's view of filmmaking invokes a practice of historical transformation and expresses itself in a primary concern for the existential conditions and needs of the participant. With the perception of the film participant as the subject of history, the obligation to wellbeing enfolds a larger social proposition wherein the practice of documentary filmmaking enacts an organising function resulting from its social relationships with persons. Amudhan's films *Serruppu* (2006) and *Radiation Stories Part II* (2012) and Monteiro and Jayasankar's *Naata* (2003) and *YCP 1997* (1997) allow us to consider the role of shared beliefs and political solidarity between filmmakers and film subjects in the construction of representation, and in the social relations mobilised during film production and circulation. Rubbing up against what Gross, Katz and Ruby (1991) have termed the 'outsiders' and 'observers' relation between filmmakers and participants formulated through fundamental belief in documentary objectivity, the selected filmmakers make a choice to *speak with* rather than *speak about* the film subject (16).

Amudhan R. P.

Amudhan first entered the Dharamanathapuram-located community of ex-Dalit Arundhatiyars in 2005 to make a film commissioned by the local Catholic diocese. Soon afterwards, he decided to make an independent film about the social injustice faced by the residents. The materials that follow provide an enlightening account of how two particular areas, informed consent and embarrassment, are negotiated and managed by the filmmaker through paradigms alternative to image ethics, and the subsequent textual implications of his decisions.

Obtaining consent

Gaining consent from the evidently marginalised community followed complex negotiations. Wary of being represented in condescending terms, in an obvious demonstration of agency, members of the community asked Amudhan to prove his 'credentials and motivation' for making the film.[9] Amudhan responded by organising a public screening of *Shit* (2003), an empathetic portrait of Dalit sanitation worker Mariyammal, for the residents. Evidence of the filmmaker's avowedly activist position against caste discrimination was crucial to a favourable decision, and Amudhan was subsequently given the 'freedom' tempered with a 'responsibility to represent the community's aspirations', he states. In undertaking the moral responsibility to represent the community's political goals, Amudhan places himself firmly on the side of an involved, rather than a detached bystander-filmmaker.

This step has important implications in a discourse where informed consent is frequently dismissed as a 'myth' and a 'notion' against the values of artistic autonomy (Anderson and Benson 1991). As a key example, Fred Wiseman's observational film *Titicut Follies* (1967) is notable for foregrounding the problematics of informed consent due to the filmmaker's insistence upon 'editorial independence', particularly as he has consistently chosen to reject 'collaborationist cinema' (Anderson and Benson 1991: 84). In the ethnographically inflected method of filmmakers such as Wiseman and Amudhan, where films are produced in close and extended proximity with participants, 'complete collaboration' is vital (Pryluck 1976: 27). While complete collaboration remains a loosely defined concept, a standpoint opens up when Amudhan outlines his filmmaking goals not only in aesthetic–critical terms but historically related to the function of the film to influence the achievement of the community's objectives. Therefore, collaborative editing processes appear as a solution and, as discussed in Chapter 4, Amudhan takes the rough cut to community meetings, where views and opinions are assimilated to promote the effectiveness of the film. Crucially, Amudhan measures the success of the film in terms of use-value for purposes of community mobilisation by community-based organisations. *Serruppu*'s continued use by Aathi Thamizhar Peravai and Rural Education and Action Development are evidence of the ways in which the filmmaker is able to reconcile his artistic and social concerns with the representational and ethical parameters placed by these forms of use.

Embarrassment

During the filming of *Serruppu*, Amudhan was confronted by a moral dilemma. In the absence of piped water supply, women in the settlements bathed in public view at communal taps, periodically concealing themselves from passing strangers. Over time, as familiarity between the women and the filmmaker strengthened, they continued bathing in Amudhan's presence, acts that Amudhan recorded but decided to exclude from the final version of the film. An understanding of this decision is critical to establish the distinction between the public and private self of the filmmaker and how it implicates ethics in relation to documentary participants.

With only 36.4 per cent of the Indian population able to access private and safe toilet facilities according to the 2011 census figures, slum-dwelling women face 'shame, humiliation and embarrassment' each time they venture in search of an open toilet or bathing facility (Chant and McIlwaine 2015: 105). In addition to the threat of sexual abuse, embarrassment from conducting intimate private acts in public makes women particularly aware of and protective against the presence of men during these bodily acts. Nevertheless, images of women and children conducting these functions in public have come to function as iconic media symbols of poverty, homelessness, poor infrastructure, and even religiosity, seemingly beyond the coverage of discourses of privacy, sexualisation and consent. For the documentary filmmaker, it represents a familiar predicament when confronted directly with individual suffering and injustice; the dilemma of whether to represent the compelling evidence, or to conduct a private assessment of the harms associated with the dissemination of the information amongst the immediate and wider communities.

Amudhan's decision to reject the material conveys an ethos cognisant of the contending claims brought by the historical position of the participant as an individual with life outside the documentary, against his own editorial authority as a filmmaker. In the absence of binding agreements, we witness the filmmaker's application of a personal value system that centralises an ethics over editorial goals. Insofar as Amudhan has undertaken to visualise the community in a compelling and urgent light, this decision runs counter to the evidence-based epistemology of journalistic inquiry founded upon the public's right to know. However, if analysed against Waugh's (1991) four categories of ethical accountabilities of documentary filmmakers – to their selves, their constituencies, their audience and their subjects – Amudhan's decision to not transgress into a taboo space foregrounds his accountability to his subjects. Instead of a systemised approach to documentary, the decision discloses a case-specific evaluation of filmmaking contexts and of representation as an act of power and historiography.

Anjali Monteiro and K. P. Jayasankar

In December 2014, I met with seventy-year-old former schoolteacher Bhau Korde in Mumbai. Bhau is a grassroots community leader with the Dharavi-based unit of the Mohalla Committee Movement (MCM, Neighbourhood Committee Movement) and, together with Dharavi resident and community activist Waqar Khan, figures as the protagonist whose community regeneration activities are documented in *Naata*. My conversations with Bhau reveal an evaluative approach towards consent and the rewards associated with documentary participation. As well as bringing a vital participant perspective, this section discusses a socially constituted ethos of documentary filmmaking which organises the relationship between filmmakers Monteiro and Jayasankar and film participants.

Information and consent

Bhau Korde is a veteran but interrogative documentary participant.[10] Ambivalent about what he interprets as unethical documentary practices, Korde's consent is informed not only by the pleas of filmmakers but by personal experience and knowledge of documentary participation. Bhau's dissatisfaction arises primarily from the media stereotype of Dharavi as a space infested by poverty, filth and crime. 'Seventy per cent of Dharavi is middle class and only a minority of the population lives below the poverty line,' he points out otherwise.[11] Korde is especially scathing of filmmakers who fail to reciprocate participants' trust and emotional investment in documentary productions. His experience confirms that participants are cast aside after filming: 'We cannot even enter the places where the films are screened,' he states, referring to the exclusive urban circuits of documentary exhibition. In response, Bhau refers to a growing culture of paid participation centred on monetary rewards rather than trust relationships. The residents of Dharavi 'are not interested in films, except when they get money immediately', he rues. Korde disapproves, choosing to participate in projects that he believes contain genuine methods for community engagement. Prior to giving consent, Bhau primarily discusses methodology. 'My first question is, "Are you going to discuss with the common people or just interview people like me?" If so, I am not interested,' he declares. Bhau's critical–analytical approach towards consent testifies to located awareness of the cultural politics of documentary representation where the filmmaker becomes one of many informants in the decision-making process.

In contrast to run-and-gun current news and affairs reporting, *Naata* is anchored in a durable four-decade-old relationship between Monteiro and Korde where all share an objective to foreground the creativity, vigour and enterprise of Dharavi in order to counter mainstream media narratives. The longevity of the relationship is constantly renewed through informal social and intellectual encounters, and cooperative short film and video projects in Dharavi and beyond.[12] Since the launch of MCM in 1994, the filmmakers have taken an active interest in Bhau's experiences with the Dharavi-based initiative.[13] In 2001, Bhau introduced garment manufacturer, community leader and amateur film producer Waqar Khan to the filmmakers whose Bollywood-inspired community-building methods are documented in *Naata*. Post-Godhra, the grassroots community rebuilding efforts of both documentary protagonists are not only contiguous with the filmmakers' personal belief in secular cooperation, but highlight the shared optimistic belief in projecting these narratives into the wider national space.[14]

Naata brings to the fore an alternative mutualistic paradigm where documentary filmmaking embodies the expression of overlapping individual objectives. For Monteiro and Jayasankar, the film is a further chapter in the examination of Mumbai's social history, vernacular forms of secularism and subaltern narratives. On the other hand, Bhau desires a 'documentary record' of the unique community-generated MCM initiative, 'run without funding or NGOs'. For Bhau, the value of participation is realised in the exhibition of the film in Dharavi, its use for purposes of awareness-building and the historical recording of the success of the unique initiative.

Participant wellbeing

Monteiro and Jayasankar's *YCP 1997* (1997) is a 43-minute medium-length documentary about five prisoners incarcerated in Pune's Yerawada Central Prison, four of whom write poetry while the fifth is a classical musician. A crucial decision by the filmmakers with respect to ethical obligations makes it abundantly clear that participant wellbeing is a tangible determinant of textual representation.

> Prison exists only in the mind. Who isn't in prison? It's only a matter of a larger prison or a smaller prison (Harrison Cudjoe, *YCP 1997*).

By focusing on the philosophical truths in Cudjoe's above quote, *YCP 1997* resists dominant tropes of prison documentaries whose sensationalist narratives highlight 'extreme institutions and the most violent inmates' (Cecil and Leitner 2009: 184). In contrast, as much as a form of creative expression, documentary filmmaking is equally an exercise of deep ethical judgement where both filmmakers take decisions that acknowledge the relay between representation and individual wellbeing. Hence, far from sensationalising, the filmmakers refuse to even reveal the case histories of the represented subjects and equally reject the insistent fact-based appeal of journalism and infotainment. For a film whose subjects are framed through their identity as prisoners, this omission reflects the exercise of moral judgement process. Jayasankar explains:

> We decided not to ask anyone about their crime and many viewers still ask us why we didn't include this information. They suggest that we should have put it next to their names. Our answer is, we all commit crimes – for instance we don't want to be known as tax evaders or digital pirates.[15]

To the extent that the decision makes apparent an alternative ethics paradigm, the film subject rather than the viewer is enshrined as the focus of concern, at the risk of closing off particular modes of affective relations or identification between screen and spectator. Choosing to delimit the possibility of an undesirable relation of judgement, voyeurism or stereotyping between the spectator and the participant, the decision speaks to the filmmaker's efforts to address 'dividing practices' which organise subjects and identities in society. Consequently, the narrative explores emotional and sensory realms, private anxieties, personal memory and artistic expression to humanistically recuperate each individual as an everyday and ordinary human being.

Independent: Interdependent and Negotiated Consent Practice

From a sociological perspective, the relational modalities of filmmakers, participants and viewers extending outside semiotic horizons produce a site of vital significance in the evaluation of documentary's relations with society. Remembering that neoliberal and institutional subject positioning enacts the context for documentary to bring about shifts in subject position, it is my contention that the particular independent filmmakers I studied function in and construct an interdependent relation reflective of associational relations between filmmakers and social public. According to Johnson and Johnson (2006), social interdependence exists when the 'outcomes of individuals are affected by each other's actions' (287). Positive interdependence is a situation when the actions of individuals promote the achievement of joint goals (287). Defined in terms of a correlative relationship between the goals of diverse groups and individuals, positive social interdependence is a construction where individuals develop cooperative, rather than competitive, solutions to address structural forces. Against the individualist underpinnings of modern forms of socio-political organisation, interdependence validates a new politics and possesses the capacity to produce counter-subjectivities and new subject positions. Relatedly, interdependence adds additional considerations that transform individuals into relational agents, rather than detaching them from systematic considerations as independent identities (Alexander 2001: 319). I will highlight how 'common goals', a primary foundation of interdependence, based in an assemblage of localised considerations, contextual knowledge and personal obligations explicates the moral dimensions of the social relations fostered by documentary practice (Johnson 936; Alexander 315). Furthermore, once the inquiry is opened up to the wider histories and practices of independent documentary cinema in India, the social, historical and cultural contexts of independent filmmaking brings localised formulations of ethics practices into focus. Most significantly, the unsystematised and discrete management of informed consent outlined in the practitioner narratives reflects the way documentary practice has developed in response to pragmatics outside network spaces with few of the usual industry protocols and governing hierarchies of regulatory checks and balances. This has given rise to what I argue is a *negotiated-consent practice*, particular to small-scale artisanal filmmaking setups, characterised by personal knowledge, flexibility, long-duration filming and often an observational style of filmmaking where rhetoric and argument construction are as much a function of editing as predetermined thesis. For documentary studies, this is a site which provides a different model of managing consent that addresses the exhaustion of informed consent as a set of defined practices.

Common goals

The formulation of a goal structure determines the nature of social relations according to social interdependence theorists who argue that positive interdependence exists when 'individuals' identify that they can accomplish their goals 'if and only if the other individuals with whom they are cooperatively linked attain their goals' (Johnson and Johnson, 288). Group members are made interdependent through the formulation of common goals and efforts to facilitate the goal attainment of others (292). The construction of common goals can be understood to underpin the conceptual basis of early feminist 'shared-goal filmmaking', founded upon 'convictions held jointly' between filmmakers and participants (Waldman and Walker 1999: 17). A distinct strand of the 'committed documentary', shared-goal filmmaking aims to 'intervene' through representation; however, common goal formulation invests further political potential in documentary filmmaking as a cooperative form of action against localised issues.

There is little doubt that the social minorities who are the subjects of independent films like those made by Amudhan, Monteiro and Jayasankar and others lie outside the arc of media visibility in India. In 2006 a staggering 88 per cent of all media decision-making positions in mainstream Indian media were found to be occupied by Hindu upper castes, with not even one of the 315 senior journalists surveyed belonging to the Dalit castes (Loynd 2008: 71). The background against which filmmakers and participants frame their common goals includes a dominant developmentalist discourse of 'lack', a crisis of invisibility and misrepresentation. For participants, the opportunity for documentary participation can be seen as a move towards addressing the structural obstructions that restrict access to media representation and production.

Interaction is defined as individuals' simultaneous or sequential actions that affect the immediate and future outcomes of other individuals involved in the situation. As the key to effective interdependence, interaction is based upon the perception of social context and determined by an individual's representation of the world with which they assume they are contending (Johnson and Johnson 288). The cooperative nature of interaction, whether direct (oral, written, electronic) or indirect (individual acts that affect the success of goal achievement) promotes the achievement of joint goals, unlike in a competitive relation where interaction may be directly oppositional (Johnson and Johnson 292). In the actions of certain filmmakers, we witness a critical evaluation not only of historical conditions but of documentary filmmaking itself, evaluated in terms of its effectiveness and historical contributions, a function that promotes cooperative interaction. Brian Winston (2000) is unequivocal in his belief that despite the best intentions of documentary filmmakers and publics, documentary films at best contribute to gradual changes in public opinion and accomplish very little (151). Undoubtedly open to debate, the actual instances of documentary films leading to visible shifts in general attitudes, perceptions and social policy are admittedly minimal and moreover, gesture towards an 'impact' discourse actively resisted by filmmakers. Patently, restricted by virtue of limited circulation and marginal cultural location, in empirical terms, change in concrete life conditions of the participants remains an indirect and unlikely goal of documentary film. Whilst an uncomfortable fact to confront, I would suggest that in the way many of the examined filmmakers frame joint goals, their interactions acknowledge the inherent ambiguity of representational tools together with an analysis of close contexts particular to individuals, families and communities. The active consideration of differential and often hierchical social contexts frames the meaning of personal obligation, demonstrating that at the core of interdependent filmmaking is a narrative that runs counter to the neoliberal emphasis upon self-optimisation and its standpoint of the individual as an autonomous agent.

Monteiro and Jayasankar work with socially marginalised individuals and groups whose vulnerability arises from, amongst other factors, a lack of social and economic capital. Beyond the perceived rewards associated with representation, a small but significant action by the filmmakers reflects the way awareness of historical and intimate contexts bestows a materialist meaning to the framing of 'obligation'. Following the production and screening of *YCP 1997*, one of the participants, Harrison Cudjoe, approached the filmmakers with a request for assistance with his legal defence. Cudjoe had served eleven years at Yeravada Central Prison in Pune without conviction while under trial, and hoped to involve the socially connected filmmakers in mounting a new legal defence. The filmmakers agreed and successfully arranged for legal representation for Cudjoe, who was acquitted in January 1998 of an offence for which he had been under trial since 1986.[16] More recently, Anand Patwardhan helped establish the Kabir Kala Manch Defense Committee to support the legal representation of the jailed members of Kabir Kala Manch, co-protagonists of *Jai Bhim Comrade*. Patwardhan's donation of Rs. 51,000 prize money, awarded to *Jai Bhim Comrade* by the state government of Maharashtra, contributed to the establishment of the committee, whose work he continues to support through public and private means.

As the accounts make evident, filmmakers acknowledge the unverifiable benefits of representation and by taking into account the inequitable distribution of social and economic capital, effectively mobilise their social capital in a historically formulated notion of 'committed' documentary. In terms of goal formation, we can see these concrete actions as a move beyond individualistic self-interest towards a formulation that reinvests in the ethic and practice of the collective as a means of social reorganisation. For the social realm, interdependent practice paves the way for alternative coalitions inaugurated in spaces across and between existing systems of social organisation including labour, consumption, education, religion, caste, language and geography. Groups such as Jan Sanskriti Manch, discussed elsewhere, initiate alliances between filmmakers and ordinary citizens relaying examples of associations founded upon mutual political and cultural goals that seek representation, legitimation and mobilisation. From a historical and representational perspective, these alternative gatherings pose new questions about the way documentary practice may create opportunities for a shift in subject positions and social relations as well as posing new frameworks for the analysis of power, ethics and obligation in documentary studies.

I would like to draw attention to the symbolic function of interdependence, a phenomenon that foregrounds the multiple positions occupied by participants in relation to the cultural objectives of documentary filmmakers. I would suggest that while filmmakers share the socially transformative objectives of the participants in social terms, in tangible ways participants ensure the symbolic success of filmmaking as a personal and cultural project undertaken by cultural actors, by bestowing specific forms of 'consecration' or cultural valuation (Bourdieu 1993). While for participants, participating in documentary projects may result in phenomena like greater visibility, self-affirmation or public projection, the goals of cultural production also include an affirmation of the artistic claim of cultural legitimacy. Autonomous art addressed towards an audience of peers and critics achieves this cultural value through critical appreciation and I would argue in social framed projects, participants occupy this position to perform similar functions of providing specific forms of consecration through their agreement with and approval of the film and filmmaker. Underscoring the significance of symbolic legitimacy, the political position of the filmmaker is affirmed once the participant privately or publicly endorses the film and acknowledges its utility and representational value. While less of a function of formal recognition through awards or reviews, legitimisation nonetheless occurs through acts such as public screenings supported by community groups, inclusion of films/filmmakers in public manifestos and use of the film as evidentiary form. These forms of endorsement create a type of symbolic capital where filmmakers are acknowledged in terms of political conscience or contributions, and thus elevated above a generally indifferent upper-class public. The forms of legitimation in the practice of interdependent filmmaking identify key power positions and specific forms of authority and norms of valuation. Recognising participants as agents allows us to move beyond a benefactor/beneficiary framing of the functionaries of interdependent filmmaking to disclose the operation of wide-ranging transactions and forms of reciprocity that organise the site.

Negotiated consent practice

My analysis of the accounts captures the subtle shift in the way consent is understood and managed, which generates a different set of possible relations between filmmakers and film participants and with the film project itself. Addressing the shortcomings of informed consent, a negotiated consent practice, I suggest, sketches a primary distinction in the way that information is understood and treated and subsequently, the management of decision-making, which is opened out to all concerned groups. Speaking to relations of interdependence where agency forms the background to an ethical relation, negotiated consent practice indicate how the acknowledgment of agency foregrounds the process of interaction that leads to consent. The simple model of informed consent has three main conditions: information, competence and voluntariness (Faden and Beauchamp 1986: 274). According to consent theory and practice, only when someone has pertinent information can they provide genuine consent (or refusal) (O'Shea 2011: 19). In documentary practice, write Barbash and Taylor (1997), the nature and scope of information shared in informed consent protocols is understood to be determined by the filmmaker and associated producers with the ostensible objective of minimising future litigation and disputes, a position that resonates with what Beuchamp and Faden (1986) term the 'legal vision of informed consent' that focuses on financial compensation for unfortunate outcomes (3). Frequently asymmetrical distribution of information between professional filmmakers and participants results in disparities and hierarchies of information not dissimilar to other specialised professions where experts bear claims to authority through access to information. The theory and ethics of informed consent is paramount to professions like medicine, where the relation between understanding, intentionality and authorisation ideally govern what is considered the autonomous approval of consent (Faden and Beauchamp 1986: 299). In these discourses informed consent is structured through a wide set of technical and moral criteria that signify and classify what counts as information. Describing two levels of information, the discourse suggests that the professionals disclose a core set of information, or 'core disclosure', while indicating willingness to enable participants to determine and evaluate other information based on their values, needs and interests. Core disclosure forms the springboard from where participants may initiate further dialogue necessary for substantial understanding (308). Here I would like to consider the episteme of information as a basis of critique of informed consent where the discourse of information is rarely interrogated or disentangled to determine its meaning for the documentary participant. Drawing attention to the grounds of information as signifier, in documentary, information marks a different terrain of concepts, conjunctures and projections in contrast to the defined verifiability of precedents, objective modelling, scientific data and case studies that constitute information in fields of law and medicine. The documentary participant, unlike the medical subject with a pre-defined need and treatment goal, possesses different forms of agency and frames his or her objectives through diverse social and personal stakes. In contrast with the patient–doctor or litigant–lawyer relationship, the nature of the documentary participant and filmmaker relationship relies less on the bulwark of objective data, compelling it to embrace speculation, conjecture and uncertainty in building a shared understanding of the importance of the project.

Interaction, I suggest, constitutes the critical departure in negotiated consent practice, marked by a shift in the focal point of decision-making from agreement or disagreement with set criteria to a process of dialogue between filmmaker and participant that acts to determine the scope and terms of the project for both parties. The practice emphasises the significance of 'interaction', a process that is critical to the building of interdependent social relations and includes variables like 'exchange of needed resources', 'effective communication', 'trust, and constructive management of conflict' (Johnson and Johnson 292). Hence agreements over the nature of physical and symbolic access to persons, spaces and events are determined through a process of interaction which becomes an active consideration in navigating how the inquiry is designed and conducted. Effective 'communication' is central to the exchange of ideas and the way meaning is inferred. While communication underpins informed consent discourse, in negotiated consent practice, communication is recast beyond procedural probity as an active mechanism which encourages comprehension of diverse cultural contexts and conceptual associations (Faden and Beauchamp 1986: 316). Negotiated consent practices, as we have witnessed with Amudhan and others, rely on communication to appraise and respond to the specific informational needs and interests of the participant in written, verbal or audiovisual formats that are accessible and relevant to locally framed purposes. Varying with site and circumstance, in certain instances, these needs may be filtered through atypical contextual factors such as past experience, social standing, personal circumstances, perceptions and cultural norms, made evident through communication, factors generally inaccessible to generic informed consent protocols. The signified and connoted meanings of words and concepts may indicate vastly different phenomena to the parties based upon cultural and historical perceptions and assumptions, and thus effective communication requires an attentiveness to the cultural contexts which govern the production of meaning. Insofar as negotiated consent presents an alternative to the conceptual hierarchy of knowledge between filmmaker and film participant, by acknowledging the agency of participants, it also opens for debate the signified meaning of 'consent' and 'information'.

When considering the constitutive elements of negotiated consent, admittedly Pryluck's insistence on complete factual accuracy holds moral validity; nevertheless, contemporary media-saturated environments signal the changing profile of participants' needs, suggesting further interrogation regarding the position of the filmmaker as the locus of information (25). The availability of mobile technologies of video recording and internet and user-generated content practices have fundamentally blurred the identities of producer and consumer, a problematic that is currently beyond the epistemic purview of image ethics. Assa Doron and Robin Jeffrey (2013) provide a wide-ranging account of the public and private practices inaugurated by the pervasiveness of mobile phones in India. New practices of governance such as sting operations and surveillance, for instance, encourage citizens to 'record or even video their exchange with an official' for the exposure of corrupt and illegal actions (8). Widespread ownership of mobile phones leaves the authors in no doubt that new forms of agency and social participation are inaugurated through a greater knowledge of the techniques, tools and effects of recording technologies. And as participants in *Naata* and *Seruppu* make evident, facts are determined through secondary means which include social networks, personal knowledge and cultural experience, to the extent that the filmmaker is one amongst many informants who provide the facts that lead to decision-making. Information in this context assumes distinctive and particular rather than generic meanings for the participant who is media-literate and possesses the tools to select, construct, and disseminate media content, communicate with others and participate in society.

Particular to the conceptualisation of negotiated consent, there is a need to examine the way films are produced and function, and in particular I suggest that negotiated consent works within a horizon of social conscience filmmaking. Deriving from the repositioning of the filmmaker and participant in varying degrees of cooperation rather than the 'abstraction of materials for processing, production, and selling', negotiated consent supports an interdependent ethics of documentary practice (Berry 2003: 140). Interdependence foregrounds the interconnection between a range of social agents and documentary practice to the extent that the distinct boundary between film participants and audiences often collapses. Thus films are evaluated on substantive empirical and historical grounds of fair representation, honesty and effectiveness by specific social audience groups rather than 'disinterested' critics. In other words, while informed consent might function as an abstract issue of legal protocol in network or institutional documentary, the proximity and frequent overlap between participants and audiences places direct and explicit accountabilities upon filmmakers. Negotiated consent provides the ethical framework for both filmmakers and participants to view the film as an artefact embodying mutual investment for the realisation of particular purposes. Nevertheless, in relation to the formulation of artistic autonomy, I would like to draw attention to a number of conceptual issues regarding negotiated consent practice that require further investigation: To what degree does negotiated consent centralise transparency as the ethos of the film process? Who draws the line between artistic discourse and historical representation? And what does this level of specificity mean for documentary impact, wider audience appeal and circulation?

Conclusion

In this chapter, I have discussed the extent to which independent documentary in India is the product of negotiation between filmmakers, social agents and their diverse goals. Documentary ethics has understood the documentary subject fundamentally through the politics of representation that reproduces a discourse of power with the filmmaker assuming responsibility for the wellbeing of the participant. In documentary studies, concern for the participant does not extend to the incorporation of participant voice in consideration of documentary ethics, effectively enshrining the filmmaker as the locus of power and the film subject as the object of both representation and discourse. In this way, documentary criticism echoes developmentalist paradigms that deny agency to documentary's traditional 'victim', and whose subjectivity remains bound in discourses of lack. The position of the documentary filmmaker, the government bureaucrat and NGO expert represented as figure of public authority and expert knowledge, remains unchanged in both discourses.

The situated analysis of the production and circulation practices of independent documentary filmmakers, nevertheless, reveals diverse methods of operation that are organised through complex processes of dialogue and negotiation. At the level of text, the mutualistic approach shapes representation, narrative inquiry, political standpoint and aesthetic expression. At the social level, associations between filmmakers and participants are governed through practices of common goal formulation action that run counter to the individualistic narratives of neoliberal modernity. Representation alone presents an indirect method to realise transformative ideals and therefore interdependence examines injustice as a structural issue to formulate embodied forms of action.

Independent film reflects the desire to form alternate relations of viewing. In contrast to the public authority of the Griersonian state documentary and NGO spokesperson film, critical-reflexive filmmakers question hierarchies of knowledge that structure media forms leading to the personal disavowal of this status. Unlike the smooth surfaces of instructional, advocacy or human interest documentary, devices like an interventionist gaze permit the 'reading' of the filmmaker's personal standpoint to provoke critical spectatorship of documentary and, extending beyond, of media representation. In this respect, independent filmmakers focalise an ethics of viewing and transformation through the construction of a media-literate and critical publics.

Ultimately, of special significance is the fact that despite the neglect of safeguarding procedures and protocols in institutional documentary partnerships, filmmakers have attempted to evolve ethical means of operation. I have argued that negotiated consent indicates one such localised response to an analysis of social and media power structures within which filmmakers and participants come together to make films. Acting to a large extent in defiance of the exploitative and self-interested logics of competitiveness and authoritative claim-making, negotiated consent requires the willingness to become accountable as evident in the sharing of editorial control and the extending of material support beyond the documentary film project. Together with production and circulation, these arrangements testify to the organisation of independent documentary as a practice that resists the systemisation of identity and function attached to culture, cultural producers and cultural production under neoliberal forms of governance.

Notes

1. I draw a distinction between the entities of subject and participant on the grounds of representation. By 'participant' I refer to individuals who take part in documentary films as potential subjects of representation, while 'subject' refers to the participant as represented in the film through the apparatus and conventions of documentary filmmaking.
2. Jerry Rothwell (2012) argues that such negotiations are the 'key' to both 'producing and directing' (193). In *Directing the Documentary*, Michael Rabiger includes a sample personal release form and lists this document as a necessary element of the documentary preproduction toolkit.
3. Quotations taken from personal interview with Sanju, 26 November 2014, New Delhi.
4. Quotation taken from personal interview with Rahul Roy, 14 January 2015, New Delhi.
5. Quotations taken from personal interview with Sanju, 26 November 2014, New Delhi.
6. Ibid.
7. Ibid.
8. Quotations taken from personal interview with Paromita Vohra, 4 January 2015, Mumbai.
9. All quotations from a personal interview with Amudhan R. P., 3 May 2013, Chennai.
10. Bhau Korde is cast as the key representative of the residents of Dharavi in *Dharavi: Slum For Sale* (Lutz Konermann and Rod Appleby, 2010).
11. All quotations from a personal interview with Bhau Korde, 17 December 2014, Mumbai.
12. Korde assisted the filmmakers during research and filming for *Tanda* (1988), accompanying them in their travels to the rural areas of Maharashtra and Rajasthan.

13. A community-building initiative launched by social activists and Maharashtra Police, the MCM was founded in 1994 in the wake of violent sectarian riots in Mumbai.
14. On 28 February 2002, religious clashes began in Gujarat, western India, leaving more than 1,000 people dead, mainly Muslims. Dibyesh Anand (2011) contends that these clashes were not spontaneous and were characterised by 'state complicity' through police inaction, frequent police participation in anti-Muslim violence and hate speeches by members of the state government (144).
15. Quotations from personal interview with Anjali Monteiro and K. P. Jayasankar, 19 December 2014, Mumbai.
16. Ibid.

Afterword

Unlike a closed field of competition that obeys its own logic, Indian independent documentary, as I have shown, is marked by cultural and formal heterogeneity that undoes forms of categorisation associated with art and activism, critical and popular spectatorship, authorship and collaboration, expression and institution. Inside and yet struggling to maintain sovereignty from social authority systems, the complexity of the practice is an expression of artistic consciousness that reflects the reflexive social and artistic histories of the form. Independence notably articulates the multitude of documentary practices that patently examine heteronomous authority systems of art, culture, social and political institutions and reflexively, the histories, canons and traditions of the documentary form. It is through multiple levels and scales of intervention, social and textual, that independent documentary attempts to produce alternative sets of meanings that represent a challenge to the systems that govern subject positions, experiences, possibilities and desires. Heterogeneity, difference or particularity of functions, values and imaginaries is central to this conceptualisation of independence and its diverse meanings.

Admittedly, my focus on the practice and films of selected filmmakers does not claim to be representative of the plurality of the practice. However, it focuses upon a sustained and substantive trajectory of filmmaking by practitioners who have continued to make films in the independent mode over three decades, with nearly seventy-five films between them. Whilst making a significant contribution to public visual culture and narrative formation, documentary filmmakers, I have argued, hold the key to our understanding of independence, occupying the position of agent and subject, whose position can be understood primarily by examining responses to narrow definitions of 'function' that have plagued documentary film and filmmakers historically and in contemporary times. Where 'functions' carries meanings that harness images and image-makers to measurable phenomena of profit-making, institutional communication, consumption or mass persuasion, independent documentary works to challenge the teleological meaning of 'function' and its use as a yardstick to evaluate the value and legitimacy of cultural production and cultural producers. Examined from the point of view of artistic practice, a mobile and dynamic bricolage of non-standard, asystematic and reflexive practices emphasises a reconceptualisation of the function of culture. I have shown how these practices constitute a response and challenge to normative and regularised cultural narratives, social relations and political institutions in the nation but more broadly offer a way of thinking about what constitutes resistance to the cultures produced and shaped in contact with functionalist neoliberal socio-economic rationale. Providing knowledge about independence beyond its semiotic effects, the practices reveal a set of actions that appropriates and transforms from within seemingly closed systems to assign different meanings to positions of cultural producer, audience, participant and the media production process itself.

I have mapped a definition of independence, through three interlinked concepts, that shows the constitution of independence as a practice that cuts across the subjective, historical and social realms. As an artisanal practice, independent documentary filmmaking in India is anchored in individual subjectivities and knowledge positions emerging from personal experience, artistic skills and processes of reflection. In its effort to shift relations between viewers, culture and history, independent documentary filmmaking is constitutive of the social order rather than a discrete sphere of cultural activity. Challenging the separation of art from the social sphere and its commodification through industrial production, independent films and filmmakers counter the assignation of binary and exclusionary definitions and spaces of art and activism, factuality and imagination, and the public and private. The exhibition of excerpts from Anjali Monteiro and K. P. Jayasankar's *Saacha* (2001) at the Tate Modern's 'Word. Sound. Power' installation during 2013 is a case in point. Celebrated for its sensory visual and sonic qualities, the film's soundtrack is an imaginative auditory mix of poetry, archival popular music tracks and Marathi-language folk music in a political critique of the neoliberal takeover of the left-wing working-class culture of Mumbai. Independence, as I have argued, is identified through its dialectic nature that comprises resistance and adaptation, at once embedded in quotidian practices, norms and structures, which it also seeks to critique and reorganise.

Focusing on practice and its relation to the current political–historical moment allows us to locate Indian independent documentary not simply as an aesthetic practice with representation as its main function, but also within the broader field of the effects of modernity transmitted through the everyday. Modernity in the Indian context has implied a move towards Western political and social systems, technology-centred development and consumption, an activity that according to Appadaurai and Breckenridge (1995) draws our attention to 'new forms of expenditure and social identity' (5). Independent films demonstrate the ways in which documentary as a medium, whilst inaugurated and promoted by infrastructure, systems and practices and technologies of modernisation, reflexively re-examines received discourses of modernity for the vocalising of local political concerns. Representationally, this tension is captured in films such as *This or That Particular Person* (2012), in which filmmaker Subasri Krishnan conducts an evaluation of the seemingly transformative promise of technological modernity by raising contentious issues of surveillance and fixing of identity that are tied up with modern technologies such as that of biometric identification, being rolled out across India.[1]

Symbolically, independent films resist appropriation as objects of exchange, commodity value and cultural consumption, in the marketplace which is a central institution of neoliberal modernity. An underpinning foundation of this critique can be explained by examining the subject position of the filmmaker, wherein documentary practice is frequently embedded in social participation, the expression of citizenship and the mobilisation of publics around larger formations of democracy and rights. Clearly evident in the 'Not in My Name' coalition formed in July 2017 and spearheaded by filmmaker Saba Dewan and documentarist Rahul Roy, the multivalent campaign responds to a sharp turn towards strengthening systems of authoritarian governance beset by the rising 'majoritarianism' and 'anti-pluralism' of the Bharatiya Janta Party government (Ahmad 2017). Mobilising around the Right to Life and Equality enshrined in the Constitution, the non-party affiliated protest movement has rallied a cross-section of society through an appeal to the power of collective, democratic conscience and action. Sounded in a Facebook post on 24 June 2017, Dewan's call for a citizen gathering at the historic Jantar Mantar in New Delhi, against a campaign of Hindutva mob lynching of Muslim young men, reverberated throughout the nation. Citizens marched in Kolkata, Trivandrum and Bangalore, with eleven other Indian cities and London and Toronto joining in the days after. The emphasis of the filmmaker-led movement upon independence from institutional support and financial sponsorship has played a pivotal role in mobilising the support of ordinary citizens. Coming together as independent citizens rather than as group or political party-affiliated representatives, the individuals subsequently formed publics around a shared cause, the 'protection of democratic values enshrined in the constitution' ('The Principles We Followed' 2017).

Most significantly, the movement presents a counter-narrative to the hard identity-based state rhetoric to instead initiate the formation of a collective publics of individuals that step outside of conventional group formations of family, caste, religion, economics or language. Enlisting cultural forms such as a wide array of poster art, music, poetry, dance and film alongside public speech, the movement depicts the attempt to produce a structure of feelings, meanings and values that reinvest in collective formation and action against systemic individualist beliefs (Williams 1977: 132). Beyond the formulation of specific issues, the continued efforts to legitimise the social existence of independent Indian cultural forms including documentary film reinforces the significance of alternate lived experiences and discourses for a truly representative public domain and holds the key to our understanding of the polyvalent, non-paradigmatic nature of resistance that culture performs.

It is in the present context, marked by hardening ideological and identity-based boundaries and hierarchies wrought by populist governments, that we must consider the contribution and future directions of independent documentary filmmaking in India. Whilst on the one hand, technologies and transnational flows of knowledge, culture and resources become accessible to construct global shadow networks of production and circulation, the techniques and discourse of regulation continues to fragment and dissipate local publics. In 2017, for instance, the IDSFFK rejected three films from the festival on account of their interrogatory perspectives about the failure of governance and state-led violence against ordinary citizens. The banning of the films, in an ironic way, visualises the central contention of one of the banned films, *March, March, March* (2017), about the systematic stifling of student dissent on the New Delhi Jawaharlal Nehru University campus by state-sponsored media and police. While the filmmakers promptly uploaded the films online, testifying their commitment to public access, the act of banning and the subsequent actions demand cohesive responses to a thickening national discourse of core and periphery, legitimate and illegitimate, mainstream and marginal cultures.

In response, by forming informal alliances with interested individuals, organisations, social activists, civil society, academics, journalists, artists, cultural activists and citizens, independent documentary presents a model of collective organisation that presents different discourses of social interdependence. Independent filmmaking presents us with an instructive model to witness how individual artistic vision is constituted and realised through mutualistic alliances between filmmakers and the wider society not restricted to industry-based social groupings. The value of these negotiated, mobile and dispersed associations must also be understood in the context of modern democratic systems and a mediatised public domain and its role in neoliberal governmentality. As the Cinema of Resistance model demonstrates, countering the media marginalisation of populations from cultural representation and participation is a process that requires tactical association across the traditional binaries of institutions, geographic location, class and taste cultures.

This is why it is imperative to identify independence not simply through representation, but to consider equally the sites of interactions and encounters with the social order and ask what alternative epistemes these signify when market freedom is associated with notions of freedom and democracy? To answer this question, we must consider how independent documentary filmmakers re-evaluate the legitimisation of 'enterprise' that is reorganising the 'relationship of the individual to himself, time, those around him, the group, and the family' (Foucault 2008: 242). Drawing a different system of references in a recent interview following a screening of *The Factory* (2015), his film about the trade union movement in the Maruti Suzuki factory in New Delhi, Roy defines tactical practice in a decidedly non-entrepreneurial framework:

> What I keep arguing in India is that there is a merit to not becoming commercialized . . . By not being commercialized, we escape some of the pressure to conform to that.
>
> We do films which we want to do. We don't have that kind of pressure on us to generate profits. We can get away with saying and doing whatever we want, and we don't even get censored that often and we still show the films all over. The moment you go into that larger scale, the state has an interest – they will look at it and give you certification, all those issues. So I think that the documentary has to survive as a rich and varied genre. Then it's important that it doesn't follow the route of the commercial fiction cinema. (Quoted in Parsons 2015)

Against the '*homo economicus*' who views 'individual entrepreneurial freedom' as the best way to achieve human wellbeing, independent documentary filmmakers sketch discourses related to more fundamental notions of freedom, autonomy and personal expression (Gooptu 7).

It is in this context that I wish to draw attention to crowdfunding, an emerging form of patronage constituted through specific structures of authority and accountability that signals profound implications for independent documentary in India.[2] Recent Indian crowdfunding successes include *An Insignificant Man* (2016), crowdfunded by over 800 Indian and international contributors who raised nearly 600% over the nominated amount of 1.2 million Rupees.[3] With eleven crowdfunding platforms currently offering filmmakers a range of marketing and promotion services, crowdfunding is increasingly organising documentary production and circulation alongside the diminishing role of traditional public and corporate philanthropy arts funding (Dhar 2014: 113; A. Ghosh 2013). Emerging from the broader phenomenon of crowdsourcing or using the crowd to obtain ideas, feedback and solutions to develop corporate activities, crowdfunding relies on web 2.0 tools of social networking (Twitter, Facebook, LinkedIn and various specialised blogs) to seek funding from individuals rather than institutional investors (Belleflamme et al. 2014). The absence of institutional distribution and financing viewed as critical obstacles are reworked as the strength of crowdfunding in a discourse of democracy and creative control (Malik and Menon 2016). Studies in the UK (Sørenson 2015), which reveal that crowdfunding is driving the re-formulation of critical issues of artistic autonomy and documentary form, point towards a need for further examination of the discursive and material implications of the practice, particularly for the issues of artistic freedom and gatekeeping that plague independent Indian documentary.

In India, crowdfunding evidently presents opportunities for independent filmmakers to bypass NGO and institutional gatekeeping and raise funds from a dispersed body of local, national and international supporters to potentially increase the visibility of issues marginalised by mainstream media. However, increasingly institutionalised systems of crowdfunding structured through the principles of web-based economics demand further investigation into the practices of regulation and organisation particular to these environments. This may, for instance, include project selection processes, the role of promotion and marketing, taste and viewing preferences of web investors and publics, regimes of web-based competition and forms of valuation, each of which introduce new regulatory apparatus and modes of systemisation. Needless to say, this raises significant questions about the 'institutional' meaning and discourse of documentary constructed through crowdfunding practices and by casting public as patron, implicating the nature of accountability between documentary, publics and society. I pose these questions in the context of my study that identifies independence as tactical practice constituted through reflexivity, historical awareness, and continued adaptation of industrial and institutional norms within and against which filmmakers have sought to achieve autonomy and represent an alternate relation between culture, institutions and the individual.

My hope is that this book serves a dual purpose. It illuminates the ways in which particular practices of Indian documentary are connected to the questions of history, socio-political shifts and economic policy environments in the post-reform period. The examination of independent documentary from a practice standpoint reveals the ways in which the modern ensemble of social, industrial and political institutions and discourses produces subjects and subject positions, and the heterogeneous ways in which individuals resist through an array of aesthetic and social practices. On the other hand, it provides a position from where documentary studies can extend its knowledge of contemporary documentary practice and the evolving meaning of 'political' in relation to the socio-economic, cultural and technological transitions occurring in India and the Global South. In particular, I hope that these accounts of practice provide alternative geopolitical and cultural sites from which to consider new provocations about the mobility and mutation of terminologies, practices, theorisation and grammar of documentary film cultures in diverse contexts.

Notes

1. The Government of India has embarked upon an ambitious exercise to provide a 'unique identification' (UID) number to every resident of the country. Each number is to be connected with three types of biometric data: iris scans, fingerprints (all ten fingers) and a picture of the face. UID, it is claimed, will act as a useful identification facility and help the government to root out corruption from social distribution programmes (Chacko and Khanduri 2011).
2. Defined expansively, crowdfunding is 'an open call, essentially through the internet, for the provision of financial resources either in the form of donation or in exchange for some reward and/or voting rights in order to support initiatives for specific purposes' (Schwienbacher and Larralde 2012: 371).
3. According to data published on <http://insignificantman.com>, accessed 12 July 2017.

Filmography

Selected Filmmakers

Amudhan R. P.

Dollar City (2015), dir. Amudhan R. P. Amudhan R. P., DVD.
Leelavathi (1996), dir. Amudhan R. P. Amudhan R. P., videocassette.
Mercury in the Mist (2011), dir. Amudhan R. P. Amudhan R. P., DVD.
Notes from the Crematorium (2005), dir. Amudhan R. P. Amudhan R. P., DVD.
Radiation Stories, Part 1, 2, 3 (2010–12), dir. Amudhan R. P. Amudhan R. P., DVD.
Serruppu/Footwear (2006), dir. Amudhan R. P. Magic Lantern Movies, DVD.
Shit/Pee (2003), dir. Amudhan R. P. Amudhan R. P., DVD.

K. P. Jayasankar and Anjali Monteiro

Irani Restaurant Instructions (2008), dir. Anjali Monteiro and K. P. Jayasankar. TISS, DVD.
Kahankar: Ahankar (1995), dir. Anjali Monteiro and K. P. Jayasankar. Magic Lantern Movies, DVD.
Naata/The Bond (2003), dir. Anjali Monteiro and K. P. Jayasankar. Magic Lantern Movies, DVD.
Our Family (2007), dir. Anjali Monteiro and K. P. Jayasankar. Magic Lantern Movies, DVD.
Saacha (2001), dir. Anjali Monteiro and K. P. Jayasankar. Magic Lantern Movies, DVD.
Se Heddan So Hoddan/Like Here, Like There (2011), dir. Anjali Monteiro and K. P. Jayasankar. Public Sevice Broadcasting Trust, DVD.
SheWrite (2005), dir. Anjali Monteiro and K. P. Jayasankar. Magic Lantern Movies, DVD.
Tanda (1988), dir. Anjali Monteiro and K. P. Jayasankar. TISS, DVD.
YCP 1997 (1997), dir. Anjali Monteiro and K. P. Jayasankar. Magic Lantern Movies, DVD.
The Young Workers (1987), dir. Anjali Monteiro and K. P. Jayasankar. Anjali Monteiro and K. P. Jayasankar, DVD.

Rahul Roy

The City Beautiful (2003), dir. Rahul Roy. Magic Lantern Movies, DVD.
Dharmyuddha/Holy War (1989), dir. Saba Dewan and Rahul Roy. Saba Dewan and Rahul Roy, DVD.
The Factory (2015), dir. Rahul Roy. Aakar Trust, DVD.
Invisible Hands, Unheard Voices (1988), dir. Saba Dewan and Rahul Roy. U-Matic.
Majma (2001), dir. Rahul Roy. Magic Lantern Movies, DVD.
Nasoor/Festering Wound (1991), dir. Saba Dewan and Rahul Roy. Saba Dewan and Rahul Roy, U-matic.
Till We Meet Again (2013), dir. Rahul Roy. Aakar Trust, DVD.
When Four Friends Meet (2000), dir. Rahul Roy. Magic Lantern Movies, DVD.

Paromita Vohra

Annapurna: Goddess of Food (1995), dir. Paromita Vohra and T. Jayashree. Magic Lantern Movies, DVD.
Connected Hum Tum (2013), dir. Paromita Vohra. Zee Television.
Cosmopolis (2004), dir. Paromita Vohra. Magic Lantern Movies, DVD.
Morality TV Aur Loving Jehad/Morality TV and the Loving Jehad (2007), dir. Paromita Vohra. PSBT, DVD.
Partners in Crime (2011), dir. Paromita Vohra. Magic Lantern Movies, DVD.
Q2P (2006), dir. Paromita Vohra. Magic Lantern Movies, DVD.
Unlimited Girls (2002), dir. Paromita Vohra. Magic Lantern Movies, DVD.

General Filmography

7 Islands and a Metro (2006), dir. Madhusree Dutta. Magic Lantern Movies, DVD.
A Woman's Place (1999), dir. Maria Nicolo, Paromita Vohra, Catherine Stewart, and Patricia Van.
Adha Aasman/Half the Sky (1996), dir. Samina Mishra. Magic Lantern Movies, DVD.
An Indian Story (1981), dir. Tapan Bose and Suhasini Mulay. Cinemart, videocassette.
An Insignificant Man (2016), dir. Khushboo Ranka and Vinay Shukla. Memesys Culture Lab, DVD.
Barf/Snow (1997), dir. Saba Dewan. Saba Dewan, VCD.
The Battle of Chile (1975–8), dir. Patricio Guzmán. Icarus Films, film.
Bhoomika/The Role (1977), dir. Syam Benegal. Video Sound, DVD.
Bhopal: Beyond Genocide (1985), dir. Suhasini Mulay, Tapan Bose, and Salim Shaikh. Cinemart, videocassette.
Bombay, Our City (1985), dir. Anand Patwardhan. Anand Patwardhan, DVD.

Caste on the Menu Card (2015), dir. Ananya Gaur and Anurup Khillare. Tata Institute of Social Sciences, DVD.
Development at Gunpoint (2007), dir. Pramod Gupta. Pramod Gupta, DVD.
Dharavi (1992), dir. Sudhir Misra. NFDC-Doordarshan, DVD.
Dharavi: Slum for Sale (2010), dir. Lutz Konermann and Rob Appleby. CatandDocs, DVD.
**Dohra Bojh/A Double Burden* (1982), dir. CENDIT and Delhi Dehat Mazdoor Union/Delhi Rural Workers Union. The Other Picture Catalogue.
Eleven Miles (1992), dir. Ruchir Joshi. Ruchir Joshi, DVD.
En Dino Muzaffarnagar/These Days in Muzaffarnagar (2014), dir. Shubhradeep Chakravorty and Meera Chaudhary. Meera Chaudhary, DVD.
Explorer (1974), dir. Pramod Pati. Films Division, DVD.
Eyes of Stone (1990), dir. Nilita Vachani. FilmSixteen, DVD.
Father, Son And Holy War (1995), dir. Anand Patwardhan. Anand Patwardhan, DVD.
Final Solution (2004), dir. Rakesh Sharma. Rakesh Sharma, DVD.
Flashback (1974), dir. S.N.S. Sastry. Films Division, DVD.
The Girl Child: The Prisoner of Gender (1991), dir. Shikha Jhingan and Ranjani Mazumdar. PTI-TV, laser disc.
The Great Indian Yatra/The Great Indian Journey (2000), dir. Shweta Kishore and Yask Desai. Shweta Kishore and Yask Desai, DVD.
Half Life (1985), dir. Dennis O'Rourke. Alexander Street, DVD.
Harvest of Hunger (2004), dir. Rupashree Nanda. Actionaid International, DVD.
The Hidden Story (1995), dir. Shikha Jhingan and Ranjani Mazumdar. Women Make Movies, DVD.
The Hour of the Furnaces (1968), dir. Fernando E. Solanas, Octavio Getino. Grupo Cine Liberacion/Solanas Productions.
**Hum Bhi Insaan Hain/We Are Also Human* (1980), prod. CENDIT, dir. Delhi Dehat Mazdoor Union/Delhi Rural Wokers Union. The Other Picture Catalogue.
The Immoral Daughters in the Land of Honour/Izzatnagar Ki Asabhya Betiyaan (2012), dir. Nakul Singh Sawhney. Nakul Singh Sawhney, DVD.
In Secular India (1986), dir. Mediastorm Collective. Mediastorm Collective, DVD.
India '67/An Indian Day (1968), dir. Sukhdev Sandhu. Films Division, DVD.
India Cabaret (1986), dir. Mira Nair. Alexander Street, DVD.
Jai Bhim Comrade (2012), dir. Anand Patwardhan. Anand Patwardhan, DVD.
Kamlabai (1992), dir. Reena Mohan. Reena Mohan, DVD.
Khamosh Pani/Silent Waters (2003), dir. Sabiha Kumar. Les Films du Losange, DVD.
Kumar Talkies (1999), dir. Pankaj Rishi Kumar. Icarus Films, DVD.
Kya Hua Is Shehar Ko?/What Has Happened To This City? (1986), dir. Deepa Dhanraj. Deepa Dhanraj, DVD.

Mahila Mela Tilonia/Women's Fair Tilonia (1985), prod. CENDIT, dir. Social Work and Research Centre. The Other Picture Catalogue.

Many People, Many Desires (2004), dir. T. Jayashree. Magic Lantern Movies, DVD.

March, March, March (2017), dir. Kathu Lukose. Kathu Lukose, DVD.

Memories of Fear (1995), dir. Madhusree Dutta. Majlis Productions, DVD.

The Men in the Tree (2002), dir. Lalit Vachani. Magic Lantern Movies, DVD.

Mirch Masala/Spices (1987), dir. Ketan Mehta. National Film Development Corporation, DVD.

Muzaffarnagar Baaqi Hai /Muzzafarnagar Eventually (2015), dir. Nakul Singh Sawhney. Nakul Singh Sawhney, DVD.

Ram Ke Naam/In the Name of God (1992), dir. Anand Patwardhan. Anand Patwardhan, DVD.

Red Ant Dream (2013), dir. Sanjay Kak. Octave Communications, DVD.

The Rising Wave (2004), dir. Shweta Kishore and Yask Desai. Documentary Education Resources, DVD.

Saa (1991), dir. R. V. Ramani. Magic Lantern Movies, DVD.

Sita's Famly (2002), dir. Saba Dewan. Public Sevice Broadcasting Trust, DVD.

Sona Maati/A Very Ordinary Gold (1995), dir. Sehjo Singh. Magic Lantern Movies, DVD.

Tales from Planet Kolkata (1993), dir. Ruchir Joshi. South Productions, VCD.

Tales of the Night Fairies (2002), dir. Shohini Ghosh. Magic Lantern Movies, DVD.

The Textures of Loss (2013), dir. Pankaj Butalia. Magic Lantern Movies.

This or That Particular Person (2012), dir. Subasri Krishnan. Public Service Broadcasting Trust, DVD.

Three Women and a Camera (1998), dir. Sabeena Gadihoke. Doordarshan, DVD.

A Time to Rise (1981), dir. Anand Patwardhan. Anand Patwardhan, DVD.

Voices from Baliapal (1988), dir. Vasudha Joshi and Ranjan Palit. Vector Productions, DVD.

War and Peace/Jang Aur Aman (2002), dir. Anand Patwardhan. Anand Patwardhan, DVD.

Waves of Revolution (1975), dir. Anand Patwardhan. Anand Patwardhan, 1975. DVD.

The Women Betrayed/Atmaghat (1993), dir. Sehjo Singh. Magic Lantern Movies, DVD.

* These titles are listed in the catalogues mentioned in the citation; however, the original tapes on U-Matic analogue video format are either untraceable or damaged to an extent that they are not convertible to digital formats.

Works Cited

Aakar (2010), 'Contract: Let's Talk Men 2.0', Rahul Roy's personal documents, New Delhi.

Acland, Charles R., and Haidee Wasson (2011), 'Introduction', in Charles R. Acland and Haidee Wasson (eds), *Useful Cinema*, Durham, NC: Duke University Press, pp. 1–16.

Action Aid India, 'Who We Are', <https://www.actionaidindia.org/whoweare/>, accessed 11 December 2014.

Adaman, Fikret, and Yahya M. Madra (2014), 'Understanding Neoliberalism as Economization: The Case of the Environment', in Yıldız Atasoy (ed.), *Global Economic Crisis and the Politics of Diversity*, London: Palgrave Macmillan, pp. 29–51.

Agnihotri, Indu, and Vina Mazumdar (2005), 'Changing Terms of Political Discourse: Women's Movement in India 1970s–1990s', in Mala Khullar (ed.), *Writing the Women's Movement: A Reader*, New Delhi: Zubaan Books, pp. 48–79.

Agrawal, Ajay K., Christian Catalini, and Avi Goldfarb (2011), 'The Geography of Crowdfunding', National Bureau of Economic Research, <http://www.nber.org/papers/w16820>, accessed 21 August 2017.

Ahmad, Irfan (2017), 'Modi's Polarising Populism Makes a Fiction of a Secular, Democratic India', *The Conversation*, 12 July, <http://theconversation.com/modis-polarising-populism-makes-a-fiction-of-a-secular-democratic-india-80605>, accessed 18 August 2017.

Ahmed, Waquar, Amitabh Kundu, and Richard Peet (2010), *India's New Economic Policy: A Critical Analysis*, New York: Routledge.

Aitken, I. (2013), *Film and Reform: John Grierson and the Documentary Film Movement*, London and New York: Routledge.

Akerkar, Supriya (2005), 'Rights, Development and Democarcy: A Perspective from India', in Paul Gready and Jonathan Ensor (eds), *Reinventing Development?: Translating Rights-Based Approaches from Theory Into Practice*, Zed Books, pp. 144–55.

Akomfrah, John (1997), 'Storming the Reality Asylum', *Pix* 2, <http://patwardhan.com/?page_id=381>, accessed 22 January 2016.

Alexander, E. R. (2001), 'The Planner-Prince: Interdependence, Rationalities and Post-Communicative Practice', *Planning Theory & Practice* 2.3: 311–24.

Alter, Nora M. (2002), *Projecting History: German Nonfiction Cinema, 1967–2000*, Ann Arbor: University of Michigan.

Ambedkar, B. R. (1971), *Annihilation of Caste, with a Reply to Mahatma Gandhi*, Jullundur City: Bheem Patrika Publishers.

Anand, Dibyesh (2011), *Hindu Nationalism in India and the Politics of Fear*, New York: Palgrave Macmillan.

Anderson, Carolyn, and Thomas Benson (1991), 'Direct Cinema and the Myth of Informed Consent: The Case of Titicut Follies', in Larry Gross, John Stuart Katz, and Jay Ruby (eds), *Image Ethics: The Moral Rights of Subjects in Photographs, Film, and Television*, New York: Oxford University Press, pp. 58–90.

Annual Report 1982–1983: Ministry of Information and Broadcasting (1983), New Delhi: Ministry of Information and Broadcasting, Government of India.

Annual Report 2013–2014: Telecom Regulatory Authority of India (2014), New Delhi: Telecom Regulatory Authority of India, Government of India.

Appadurai, Arjun (1990), 'Disjuncture and Difference in the Global Cultural Economy', *Theory, Culture & Society* 7.2–3: 295–310.

Appadurai, Arjun (2011), 'Cosmopolitanism from Below: Some Ethical Lessons from the Slums of Mumbai', *The Johannesburg Salon* 4: 32–43.

Appadurai, Arjun, and Carol Breckenridge (1995), 'Public Modernity in India', in Arjun Appadurai and Carol Breckenridge (eds), *Consuming Modernity: Public Culture in a South Asian World*, Minneapolis: University of Minnesota Press, pp. 1–22.

Armatage, Kay, 'Feminist Film-Making: Theory and Practice', *Canadian Woman Studies* 1.3 (1979): 49–50.

Asian Development Bank (2009), *Overview of Civil Society Organisations: India*, Civil Society Briefs, <https://www.adb.org/sites/default/files/publication/28966/csb-ind.pdf>, accessed 19 April 2018.

Athique, Adrian (2012), *Indian Media*, Cambridge: Polity.

Atton, Chris (2002), *Alternative Media*, London: Sage Publications.

Babu, Abhilash (10 November 2014), personal interview, New Delhi.

Bala, Madhu (21 November 2014), personal interview, New Delhi.

Barbash, I., and L. Taylor (1997), *Cross-Cultural Filmmaking: A Handbook for Making Documentary and Ethnographic Films and Videos*, Berkeley: University of California Press.

Barthes, R. (1978), *Image-Music-Text*, trans. S. Heath, New York: Farrar, Straus and Giroux.

Battaglia, Giulia (2014), 'The Video Turn: Documentary Film Practices in 1980s India', *Visual Anthropology* 27.1–2: 72–90.

Baumgärtel, Tilman (2011), *Southeast Asian Independent Cinema*, Hong Kong: Hong Kong University Press.

Behar, Amitabh, and Aseem Prakash (2004), 'India: Exapanding and Contracting Democratic Space', in Muthiah Alagappa (ed.), *Civil Society and Political Change in Asia: Expanding and Contracting Democratic Space*, Stanford, CA: Stanford University Press, 191–222.

Belleflamme, Paul, Thomas Lambert and Armin Schwienbacher (2014), 'Crowdfunding: Tapping the Right Crowd', *Journal of Business Venturing* 29.5: 585–609.

Benjamin, Walter (1970), 'The Author as Producer', *New Left Review* 62: 83–96.

Benjamin, Walter (2008), *The Work of Art in the Age of Its Technological Reproducibility, and Other Writings on Media*, Cambridge, MA: Harvard University Press.

Bernier, Catherine (2013), '*Jai Bhim Comrade*: Tales of Oppression and Songs of Resistance', *Jump Cut* 55, <https://www.ejumpcut.org/archive/jc55.2013/BernierJaiBhim/index.html>, accessed 19 April 2018.

Berra, John (2010), 'Introduction', in John Berra (ed.), *American Independent*, Chicago: Intellect Books, pp. 6–8.

Berry, Chris (2003), 'The Documentary Production Process as a Counter-Public: Notes on an Inter-Asian Mode and the Example of Kim Dong-Won', *Inter-Asia Cultural Studies* 4.1: 139–44, <https://www.tandfonline.com/doi/abs/10.1080/1464937032000060276>, accessed 5 June 2015.

Berry, Chris (2006), 'Independently Chinese: Duan Jinchuan, Jiang Yue, and Chinese Documentary', in Paul Pickowicz and Yingjin Zhang (eds), *From Underground to Independent: Alternative Film Culture in Contemporary China*, Maryland: Rowman and Littlefield, pp. 109–22.

Berry, Chris, Lu Xinyu, and Lisa Rofel, eds (2010), *The New Chinese Documentary Film Movement: For the Public Record*, Hong Kong: Hong Kong University Press.

Bhowmick, Someswar (2002), 'From Coercion to Power Relations: Film Censorship in Post-Colonial India', *Economic and Political Weekly* 38.30: 3148–52.

Biswas, Soutik (2015), 'Why Indian Author Perumal Murugan Quit Writing', BBC, 15 January, <http://www.bbc.co.uk/news/world-asia-india-30808747>, accessed 19 February 2016.

Bordwell, David (1996), 'Contemporary Film Studies and the Vicissitudes of Grand Theory', in David Bordwell and Noel Carroll (eds), *Post-Theory: Reconstructing Film Studies*, Madison: University of Wisconsin Press, pp. 3–36.

Bose, Tapan, and Suhasini Mulay (1988), video interview by Thomas Waugh.

Bourdieu, Pierre (1977), *Outline of a Theory of Practice*, New York: Cambridge University Press.

Bourdieu, Pierre (1993), *The Field of Cultural Production: Essays on Art and Literature*, Cambridge: Polity Press.

Bourdieu, Pierre (1996), *The Rules of Art: Genesis and Structure of the Literary Field*, trans. Susan Emanuel, Stanford, CA: Stanford University Press.

Bourdieu, Pierre (1998), *Practical Reason*, trans. Randall Johnson, Stanford, CA: Stanford University Press.

Bourdieu, Pierre, and Hans Haacke (1995), *Free Exchange*, Cambridge: Polity Press.

Bourdieu, Pierre, and Loïc J. D. Wacquant (1992), *An Invitation to Reflexive Sociology*, Cambridge: Polity Press.

Boyle, Deirdre (1990), 'A Brief History of American Documentary Video', in Sally Jo Fifer and Doug Hall (eds), *Illuminating Video: An Essential Guide to Video Art*, New York: Aperture, pp. 51–69.

Brosius, C. (2012), *India's Middle Class: New Forms of Urban Leisure, Consumption and Prosperity*, London: Routledge.

Burchell, Graham, Colin Gordon, and Peter Miller (1991), *The Foucault Effect: Studies in Governmentality*, Chicago: University of Chicago Press.

Cecil, Dawn, and Jennifer Leitner (2009), 'Unlocking the Gates: An Examination of MSNBC Investigates – Lockup', *The Howard Journal of Criminal Justice* 48(2): 184–99.

Central Board of Film Certification (n.d.), 'The Principles for Guidance in Certifying Films', Ministry of Information and Broadcasting, Government of India, New Delhi.

Chacko, Simi, and Pratiksha Khanduri (2011), 'A Critical Primer on India's UID', Kafila, 12 September, <https://kafila.online/2011/09/12/uid-for-dummies-simi-chacko-and-pratiksha-khanduri/>, accessed 24 May 2016.

Chakrabarty, Dipesh (2000), *Provincializing Europe: Postcolonial Thought and Historical Difference*, Princeton, NJ: Princeton University Press.

Chamorro-Premuzic, Tomas, and Andrea Kallias (2014), 'What Type of Person Are You?' in James C. Kaufman and Dean Keith Simonton (eds), *The Social Science of Cinema*, New York: Oxford University Press.

Chandhoke, Neera (2003), *The Conceits of Civil Society*, Delhi: Oxford University Press.

Chandhoke, Neera (2009), 'Putting Civil Society in Its Place', *Radical Politics Today* 1.15 (n.p.).

Chant, Sylvia, and Cathy McIlwaine (2015), *Cities, Slums and Gender in the Global South: Towards a Feminised Urban Future*, Abingdon: Routledge.

Chapman, Jane (2009), *Issues in Contemporary Documentary*, Cambridge: Polity Press.

Chatterji, Shoma (2009), 'Fair Choice', *The Tribune*, 14 June, <http://www.tribuneindia.com/2009/20090614/spectrum/main5.htm>, accessed 16 May 2015.

Chowdhury, Kanishka (2011), *The New India: Citizenship, Subjectivity, and Economic Liberalization*, New York: Palgrave Macmillan.

Ciochetto, L. (2009), 'Advertising in a Globalised World', in K. M. Gokulsing and W. Dissanayake (eds), *Popular Culture in a Globalised India*, Abingdon: Routledge, pp. 192–204.

Corner, John (2009), 'Documenting the Political: Some Issues', *Studies in Documentary Film* 3.2, 113–29.

Corner, John, and Alan Rosenthal (2005), *New Challenges for Documentary: Second Edition*. Manchester: Manchester University Press.

Crusz, Robert, and Priyath Liyanage (1983), 'Anand Patwardhan: An Interview', *Framework* 38/39: 118–32.

Dash, Surya Shankar (10 August 2013), personal interview, New Delhi.

Davies, Rodrigo (2015), 'Three Provocations for Civic Crowdfunding', *Information, Communication & Society* 18.3: 342–55.

Davis, Aeron (2008), 'Investigating Cultural Producers', in Michael Pickering (ed.), *Research Methods for Cultural Studies*, Edinburgh: Edinburgh University Press, pp. 53–67.

de Certeau, Michel (1988), *The Practice of Everyday Life*, trans. Steven Rendall, Berkeley: University of California Press.

Deprez, Camille (2015), 'A Space in Between: The Legacy of the Activist Documentary Film in India', in Camille Deprez and Judith Pernin (eds), *Post-1990 Documentary*, Edinburgh: Edinburgh University Press.

Dewan, Saba (2010), interview by Sabeena Gadihoke, Magic Lantern Foundation, 26 February, <http://magiclanternfoundation.in/saba-dewan-and-sabeena-gadihoke/>, accessed 15 July 2015.

Dewan, Saba (23 August 2013), personal interview, New Delhi.

Dhanraj, Deepa (1986), interview by Julia Lesage, *Jump Cut* 31 (March 1986): 40–2.

Dhanraj, Deepa (2014), 'Transcending Testimony', interview by Shweta Kishore, *The Conversation*, 13 August, <https://theconversation.com/transcending-testimony-an-interview-with-filmmaker-deepa-dhanraj-29763>, accessed 12 January 2015.

Dhar, Jyoti (2014), 'India', *ArtAsiaPacific Almanac* 9: 111–14.

'Documentary on Muzaffarnagar Riots Screened at 60 Venues across 50 Towns in Protest', (2015), twocircles.net, 26 August, <http://twocircles.net/2015aug26/1440530926.html>, accessed 6 May 2016.

Doron, Assa, and Robin Jeffrey (2013), *The Great Indian Phone Book*, Cambridge, MA: Harvard University Press.

Duggal, Ashima (2013), 'Conversations of the Everyday Political in Paromita Vohra's Documentary Films', *Chapati Mystery*, 25 October, <http://www.chapatimystery.com/archives/potpurri/conversations_of_the_everyday_political_in_paromita_vohras_documentary_films.html>, accessed 8 October 2014.

Dutta, Madhusree (2004), 'Curating Political Art: Collating Political Aesthetics', <http://www.madhusreedutta.com/images/Curating%20Political%20Art_%20Collating%20Political%20Aesthetics.pdf>, accessed 12 June 2014.

Dutta, Madhusree (2007), 'Truth and the Indian Documentary', *Himal Mag*, October, accessed 14 May 2015.

Dutta, Madhusree (2013), 'Narrating Actuality', *Frontline*, 18 October, <http://www.frontline.in/arts-and-culture/cinema/narrating-actuality/article5186111.ece>, accessed 23 April 2015.

Ellis, John (2007), *TV FAQ: Uncommon Answers to Common Questions About TV*, London: I. B. Tauris.

Emigh, John, and Ulrike Emigh (2003), 'A Joker in the Deck', in Joel Schechter (ed.), *Popular Theatre: A Sourcebook*, London: Routledge, pp. 149–64.

Espinosa, Julio García (1979), 'For an Imperfect Cinema', trans. Julianne Burton, *Jump Cut* 20, <https://www.ejumpcut.org/archive/onlinessays/JC20folder/ImperfectCinema.html>, accessed 1 May 2016.

Faden, Ruth R., and Tom L. Beauchamp (1986), *A History and Theory of Informed Consent*, Oxford: Oxford University Press.

Feige, Daniel Martin (2010), 'Art as Reflexive Practice', *Proceedings of the European Society for Aesthetics* 2: 125–42.

Films Division (2017), 'Citizen's Charter', Ministry of Information and Broadcasting, Government of India, <http://filmsdivision.org/citizens-charter.html>, accessed 6 September 2017.

Fisher, William F. (1997), 'Doing Good? The Politics and Antipolitics of NGO Practices', *Annual Review of Anthropology* 26.1: 439–64, <https://www.annual reviews.org/doi/abs/10.1146/annurev.anthro.26.1.439>, accessed 19 April 2018.

Fisher, William (2001), 'Theories of Intellectual Property', in Stephen Munzer (ed.), *New Essays in the Legal and Political Theory of Property*, Cambridge: Cambridge University Press, pp. 168–99.

Forum for Independent Film and Video (1996), 'A Vision for Television', New Delhi: Forum for Independent Film and Video.

Foucault, Michel (1982), 'The Subject and Power', *Critical Inquiry* 8.4: 777–95.

Foucault, Michel (2008), *The Birth of Biopolitics: Lectures at the Collège de France, 1978–1979*, London: Palgrave Macmillan.

Gadihoke, Sabeena (2003), 'The Struggle to "Empower": A Woman behind the Camera', in Shirley White (ed.), *Participatory Video: Images That Transform and Empower*, New Delhi: Sage Publications, pp. 271–85.

Gadihoke, Sabeena (2012), 'Secrets and Inner Voices: The Self and Subjectivity in Contemporary Indian Documentary', in Alisa Lebow (ed.), *The Cinema of Me: The Self and Subjectivity in First Person Documentary*, New York: Columbia University Press, 144–57.

Gaines, Jane (1999), 'Political Mimesis', in Jane Gaines and Michael Renov (eds), *Collecting Visible Evidence*, vol. 6, Minneapolis: University of Minnesota Press, pp. 84–102.

Ganesh, Shiv (2005), 'The Myth of the Non-Governmental Organisation: Governmentality and Transnationalism in an Indian NGO', in George Cheney and George Barnett (eds), *International and Multicultural Organisational Communication*, New York: Hampton Press, pp. 193–219.

Ganguly-Scrase, Ruchira, and Timothy J. Scrase (2008), *Globalisation and the Middle Classes in India: The Social and Cultural Impact of Neoliberal Reforms*, London: Routledge.

Ganti, Tejaswini (2004), *Bollywood: A Guidebook to Popular Hindi Cinema*, London: Routledge.

Garcia, David, and Geert Lovink (1997), 'The ABC of Tactical Media', <http://amsterdam.nettime.org/Lists-Archives/nettime-l-9705/msg00096.html>, accessed 19 April 2018.

Geetha, J. (1992), 'Feminism and Cinema', *Deep Focus* 4.1: 43–55.

Geetha, V. (1998), 'Periyar, Women and an Ethic of Citizenship', *Economic and Political Weekly* 33.17, WS9–WS15, <https://www.jstor.org/stable/4406695>, accessed 12 August 2014.

Getino, Octavio, and Fernando Solanas (1976), 'Towards a Third Cinema', in Bill Nichols (ed.), *Movies and Methods: An Anthology*, vol. 1, Berkeley: University of California Press, pp. 44–64.

Ghosh, Akhila (1974), 'Films and Families', *Nigah* 2: 17–24.

Ghosh, Akhila (1984), 'Media and Rural Women', in Kamla Bhasin and Bina Agarwal (eds), *Women and Media: Analysis, Alternatives and Action*, New Delhi: Kali for Women.

Ghosh, Arundhati (2013), 'Arts funding in India: Hard times require furious dancing', 14 January, <http://blogs.lse.ac.uk/southasia/2013/01/14/arts-funding-in-india/>, accessed 29 July 2017.

Ghosh, Bishnupriya (2009), 'We Shall Drown, but We Shall Not Move: The Ecologics of Testimony in NBA Documentaries', in Janet Walker and Bhaskar Ghosh (eds), *Documentary Testimonies: Global Archives of Suffering*, New York: Routledge, pp. 59–82.

Ghosh, Shohini, Sabeena Gadihoke, and Sabina Kidwai (2012), in Latika Padgaonkar and Shubha Singh (eds), *Making News, Breaking News, Her Own Way*, Chennai: Westland.

Ghosh, Snehashish (2013), 'The State is snooping: Can you escape?', India Together, 26 June, <http://www.indiatogether.org/cms-human-rights>, accessed 21 July 2017.

Giri, A. (2003), 'Audited Accountability and the Imperative of Responsibility', in M. Strathern (ed.), *Audit Cultures: Anthropological Studies in Accountability, Ethics and the Academy*, London: Routledge, pp. 173–95.

Gooptu, Nandini (2013), *Enterprise Culture in Neoliberal India: Studies in Youth, Class, Work and Media*, London: Routledge.

Govil, Nitin (2015), *Orienting Hollywood: A Century of Film Culture Between Los Angeles and Bombay*, New York: New York University Press.

Grimshaw, Anna, and Nikos Papstergiadis (1995), 'David Macdougall', in *Conversations with Anthropological Film-Makers*, Cambridge: Prickly Pear, pp. 9–55.

Gross, Larry, John Stuart Katz and Jay Ruby (1991), 'Introduction: A Moral Pause', in Larry Gross, John Stuart Katz and Jay Ruby (eds), *Image Ethics: The Moral Rights of Subjects in Photographs, Film, and Television*, New York: Oxford University Press.

Grunenberg, Christoph (1999), 'The Modern Art Museum', in Emma Barker (ed.), *Contemporary Cultures of Display*, London: Yale University Press, pp. 26–49.

Gupta, Trisha (2013), 'Difficult Loves', *Caravan*, 1 November, <http://www.caravanmagazine.in/reviews-and-essays/difficult-loves>, accessed 13 November 2015.

Gurumurthy, Anita, C. Nandini and T. Sanjana (2016), 'Unpacking Digital India: A Feminist Commentary on Policy Agendas in the Digital Moment', *Journal of Information Policy* 6: 371–402.

Hanlon, Dennis (2014), 'Making Waves: Anand Patwardhan, Latin America, and the Invention of Indian Third Cinema', *Wide Screen* 5.1: 1–24.

Harvey, David (2005), *A Brief History of Neoliberalism*, Oxford: Oxford University Press.

Harvey, David (2008), 'The Right to the City', *New Left Review* 53: 23–40.

Holmlund, Chris, and Justin Wyatt, eds (2005), *Contemporary American Independent Film: From the Margins to the Mainstream*, New York: Routledge.

Imran, Rahat (2016), *Activist Documentary Film in Pakistan: The Emergence of a Cinema of Accountability*, London: Routledge.

Indian Association for Women's Studies (1991), *Special Issue on Report of the 5th National Conference on Religion, Culture and Politics*, Calcutta: Indian Association for Women's Studies.

Ingawanij, May Adadol, and Benjamin McKay, eds (2012), *Glimpses of Freedom: Independent Cinema in Southeast Asia*, Ithaca, NY: Southeast Asia Program Publications.

Insdorf, Annette (1981), 'Ordinary People, European-Style, or How to Spot an Independent Feature', *American Film* (1 September): 59–62.

Iosifidis, Petros, and Mark Wheeler (2016), 'Social Media, Public Sphere and Democracy', in Petros Iosifidis and Mark Wheeler (eds), *Public Spheres and Mediated Social Networks in the Western Context and Beyond*, London: Palgrave Macmillan, pp. 13–37.

Jaffee, Valerie (2006), '"Everyman a Star": The Ambivalent Cult of Amateur Art in New Chinese Documentaries', in Paul Pickowicz and Yingjin Zhang (eds), *From Underground to Independent: Alternative Film Culture in Contemporary China*, Lanham, MD: Rowman & Littlefield, pp. 77–108.

Jain, Rajive (1975), 'Video in Saharanpur', *Nigah* (July): 47–50.

Jain, Ranu (2014), *Mumbra: A Status Report*, Tata Institute of Social Sciences.

Jakimow, Tanya (2012), *Peddlers of Information: Indian Non-Government Organisations in the Information Age*, Sterling, VA: Kumarian Press.

Jameson, Frederick (1992), 'Postmodernism and Consumer Society', in Peter Brooker (ed.), *Modernism/Postmodernism*, London: Longman, pp. 163–79.

Jayal, Niraja (2007), 'The Role of Civil Society', in Sumit Ganguly, Larry Diamond, and Marc F. Plattner (eds), *The State of India's Democracy*, Baltimore: Johns Hopkins University, pp. 143–60.

Jeffrey, Robin (2008), 'The Mahatma Didn't Like the Movies and Why It Matters: Indian Broadcasting Policy, 1920s–1990s', in Nalin Mehta (ed.), *Television in India: Satellites, Politics and Cultural Change*, Abingdon: Routledge, pp. 13–31.

Johari, Aarefa (2014), 'Attack on Film Festival in Kerala's Cultural Capital Shows Rising Hindutva Presence in Liberal State', Scroll.in., 1 March, <https://scroll.in/article/657425/attack-on-film-festival-in-keralas-cult

ural-capital-shows-rising-hindutva-presence-in-liberal-state>, accessed 25 February 2016.

Johnson, David W. (2003), 'Social Interdependence: Interrelationships Among Theory, Research, and Practice', *American Psychologist*: 934–45.

Johnson, D., and R. Johnson (2006), 'New Developments in Social Interdependence Theory', in *Genetic, Social and General Psychology Monographs*, Washington, DC: Heldref Publications, pp. 285–358.

Johnston, Claire [1973] (1985), 'Women's Cinema as Counter-Cinema', in Bill Nichols (ed.), *Movies and Methods*, Berkeley: University of California Press, pp. 208–17.

Juhasz, Alexandra (1999), 'They Said We Were Trying to Show Reality – All I Want to Show Is My Video: The Politics of the Realist Feminist Documentary', *Collecting Visible Evidence*, vol. 6, Minneapolis: University of Minnesota Press, pp. 190–215.

Kamat, Sangeeta (2004), 'The Privatization of Public Interest: Theorizing NGO Discourse in a Neoliberal Era', *Review of International Political Economy*, vol. 11, no. 1: 155–76.

Kaplan, Cora (1986), *Sea Changes: Essays on Culture and Feminism*, London: Verso.

Kaplan, E. Ann (1983), 'Theories and Strategies of the Feminist Documentary', *Millennium Film Journal* 12: 44–67.

Kapur, Geeta (2008), 'A Cultural Conjuncture in India: Art into Documentary', in Terry Smith, Okwui Enwezor, and Nancy Condee (eds), *Antinomies of Art and Culture: Modernity, Postmodernity, Contemporaneity*, Durham, NC: Duke University Press, pp. 30–59.

Kapur, Jyotsna (2003), 'Why the Personal Is Still Political: Some Lessons from Contemporary Indian Documentary', *Jump Cut* 46, <https://www.ejumpcut.org/archive/jc46.2003/indiandocs.kapur/>, accessed 2 June 2015.

Kapur, Jyotsna (2006), 'Love in the Midst of Fascism: Gender and Sexuality in the Contemporary Indian Documentary', *Visual Anthropology* 19.3–4: 335–46.

Kapur, Jyotsna, and Keith B. Wagner (2011), *Neoliberalism and Global Cinema: Capital, Culture, and Marxist Critique*, London: Routledge.

Kaur, Raminder, and William Mazzarella (2009), *Censorship in South Asia: Cultural Regulation from Sedition to Seduction*, Bloomington: Indiana University Press.

Kaviraj, Sudipta (2010), *The Trajectories of the Indian State: Politics and Ideas*, Ranikhet, India: Permanent Black.

Khagram, S., James Riker and Kathryn Sikkink (2002), 'From Santiago to Seattle: Transnational Advocacy Groups Restructuring World Politics', in S. Khagram, J. V. Riker, and K. Sikkink (eds), *Restructuring World Politics: Transnational Social Movements, Networks, and Norms*, Minneapolis: University of Minnesota, pp. 3–22.

Khan, Sameera (2004), 'Who Is a Feminist?', India Together, 1 May, <http://www.indiatogether.org/feminist-women>, accessed 18 June 2017.

Khopkar, Arun (2011), 'Moments of Creation', in Kevin Macdonald and Mark Cousins (eds), *Imagining Reality*, London: Faber & Faber.

Kilborn, Richard (1992), *Television Soaps*, London: B. T. Batsford.

Kilborn, Richard, and John Izod (1997), *Confronting Reality: An Introduction to Television Documentary*, Manchester: Manchester University Press.

King, Geoff (2012), *American Independent Cinema: Indie, Indiewood and Beyond*, London: Routledge.

King, Homay (2007), 'Matter, Time, and the Digital: Varda's The Gleaners and I', *Quarterly Review of Film and Video* 24.5: 421–9.

Kiran, S. (2016), 'An Analysis of Lifting the Veil (A Collection of Short Stories) by Ismat Chughtai', *Journal of South Asian Studies*, 4.2: 51–60.

Kishore, Shweta (2014), interview with filmmaker Deepa Dhanraj (13 August), *The Conversation*, accessed 12 July 2017.

Kishore, Shweta (2016), 'Participation, Poetry and Song: Anand Patwardhan and New Latin American Cinema', *Jump Cut* 57, <https://www.ejumpcut.org/currentissue/-KishoreIndiaDoc/index.html>, accessed 19 April 2018.

Kishore, Shweta (2017), 'Reframing the Margin: Regional Film Festivals in India, a Case Study of the Cinema of Resistance', in Tyson Wils and Sonia Tascón (eds), *Activist Film Festivals: Towards a Political Subject*, Bristol: Intellect, pp. 159–79.

Kleinhans, Chuck (1984), 'Forms, Politics, Makers and Contexts: Basic Issues for a Theory of Radical Political Documentary', in Thomas Waugh (ed.), *Show Us Life: Toward a History and Aesthetic of the Committed Documentary*, Metuchen, NJ and London: Scarecrow Press, pp. 318–43.

Korde, Bhau (17 December 2014), personal interview, Mumbai.

Korossi, Georgia (2015), interview with Anand Patwardhan (5 May), British Film Institute, <http://www.bfi.org.uk/news-opinion/bfi-news/earth-vision-interview-anand-patwardhan>, accessed 3 May 2016.

Kothari, Rajni (1986), 'NGOs, the State and World Capitalism', *Economic and Political Weekly*, 2177–82.

Koves, M. (1997), 'Telling Stories of Partition and War: Saadat Hasan Manto and Istvan Orkeny', *Economic and Political Weekly* 33/34: 2147–53.

Lal, Vinay (2005), 'Travails of the Nation', *Third Text* 19.2: 177–87.

Larkin, Brian (2013), 'The Politics and Poetics of Infrastructure', in D. Brenneis and K. B. Strier (eds), *Annual Review of Anthropology*, vol. 42: 327–43.

Latour, Bruno (2005), *Reassembling the Social – An Introduction to Actor-Network-Theory*, Oxford and New York: Oxford University Press.

Lees, Loretta (2014), 'Gentrification in the Global South', in Susan Parnell and Sophie Oldfield (eds), *The Routledge Handbook on Cities of the Global South*, London: Routledge, pp. 506–21.

Lefebvre, Henri (1991), *Critique of Everyday Life*, London: Verso.

Lesage, Julia (1984), 'The Feminist Documentary – Politics and Aesthetics', in Thomas Waugh (ed.), *Show Us Life: Toward a History and Aesthetic of the Committed Documentary*, Metuchen, NJ and London: Scarecrow Press.

Litton, Addison (2015), 'The State of Surveillance in India: The Central

Monitoring System's Chilling Effect on Self-Expression', *Washington University Global Studies Law Review* 14.4: 799–822.

Lobato, Ramon (2012), *Shadow Economies of Cinema*, London: Palgrave Macmillan.

Loynd, Maxine (2008), 'Politics without Television: The Bahujan Samaj Party and the Dalit Counter-Public Sphere', in Nalin Mehta (ed.), *Television in India: Satellites, Politics and Cultural Change*, Abingdon: Routledge, pp. 62–86.

Ludden, David (2015), 'Explaining Historical Patterns of Inequity in South Asia: Empire Meets Globalisation', *Economic and Political Weekly* 47.30.

Lunch, Nick, and Chris Lunch (2006), *Insights Into Participatory Video: A Handbook for the Field*, InsightShare.

Lyotard, Jean-François (1984), *The Postmodern Condition: A Report on Knowledge*, Minneapolis: University of Minnesota Press.

MacCabe, Colin (1974), 'Realism', *Screen* 15.2: 7–27.

Macdougall, David (1970), 'Prospects of the Ethnographic Film', *Film Quarterly* 23.2: 16–28.

Maclay, Kathleen (2004), 'Anand Patwardhan, the "Michael Moore of India," Brings His Hard-hitting Documentary Films to Campus', *UC Berkeley News*, 13 October, <https://www.berkeley.edu/news/media/releases/2004/10/13_patwardhan.shtml>, accessed 7 May 2016.

Majumdar, Rochona (2012), 'Debating Radical Cinema: A History of the Film Society Movement in India', *Modern Asian Studies* 46.3: 731–67.

Mandel, Ernest (1975), *Late Capitalism*, London: New Left Books.

Mankekar, Purnima (1999), *Screening Culture, Viewing Politics: An Ethnography of Television, Womanhood, and Nation in Postcolonial India*, Durham, NC: Duke University Press.

Martin, Randy (1990), *Performance as Political Act: The Embodied Self*, Greenwood Publishing Group.

Mazumdar, Ranjani (1991), 'Dialectic of Public and Private: Representation of Women in Bhoomika and Mirch Masala', *Economic and Political Weekly* 26.43, WS81–WS84.

Mazumdar, Vina (1985), 'Emergence of the Women's Question in India and the Role of Women's Studies', occasional paper, Centre for Women's Development Studies.

Mazzarella, William (2013), *Censorium: Cinema and the Open Edge of Mass Publicity*, Durham, NC and London: Duke University Press.

McGuigan, J. (2010), *Cultural Analysis*, London: Sage Publications.

McGuigan, J. (2016), *Neoliberal Culture*, Springer.

Mefalopulos, Paolo (2008), *Development Communication Sourcebook: Broadening the Boundaries of Communication*, World Bank Publications.

Meghnath (1997), 'Akhra Redefined', 2 April, *Media Mail* 1.2, Magic Lantern Foundation, <http://magiclanternfoundation.in/media-mail-volume-1-issue-2/>, accessed 19 September 2014.

Mehta, Nalin (2008), 'Introduction: Satellite Television, Identity and

Globalisation in Contemporary India', in Nalin Mehta (ed.), *Television in India: Satellites, Politics and Cultural Change*, Abingdon: Routledge, pp. 1–12.

Menon, K. S. V., and Garima Malik (2016), *Funding Options for Startups: A Conceptual Framework and Practical Guide*, Chennai: Notion Press.

Minh-ha, Trinh T. (1992), *Framer Framed*, New York: Routledge.

Moemeka, Andrew A. (1994), *Communicating for Development: A New Pan-Disciplinary Perspective*, Albany: State University of New York Press.

Mohan, Reena, and Dibya Choudhuri (1996), 'Of Wayward Girls and Wicked Women', *Deep Focus* 6: 4–14.

Mohanty, Amlan (2011), 'A Love Story about Piracy – Movie Review: Partners in Crime', Spicy IP, 31 May, <https://spicyip.com/2011/05/love-story-about-piracy-movie-review.html>, accessed 11 February 2016.

Monteiro, Anjali, and K. P. Jayasankar (1998), interview, *Media Mail* 2.4, Magic Lantern Foundation, <http://magiclanternfoundation.in/media-mail-volume-2-issue-4/>, accessed 4 July 2015.

Monteiro, Anjali, and K. P. Jayasankar (14 March 2013), personal interview, Mumbai.

Monteiro, Anjali, and K. P. Jayasankar (10 June 2013), telephone interview.

Monteiro, Anjali, and K. P. Jayasankar (19 December 2014), personal interview, Mumbai.

Monteiro, Anjali, and K. P. Jayasankar (2015), *A Fly in the Curry: Independent Documentary Film in India*, New Delhi: Sage Publications India.

Mulay, Suhasini (1988), interview by David Stratton, 6 October, *The Movie Show*, SBS Australia.

Naficy, Hamid (2001), *An Accented Cinema: Exilic and Diasporic Filmmaking*, Princeton, NJ: Princeton University Press.

Nagpaul, Dipti (2015), 'Voices Silenced', *The Indian Express*, 11 March, <http://indianexpress.com/article/india/india-others/voices-silenced/>, accessed 12 May 2015.

'National Policy on the Voluntary Sector' (2007), New Delhi: Planning Commission.

Nichols, Bill (1991), *Representing Reality: Issues and Concepts in Documentary*, Bloomington: Indiana University Press.

Nichols, Bill (2010), *Introduction to Documentary*, 2nd ed., Bloomington: Indiana University Press.

Ortner, Sherry B. (2011), 'On Neoliberalism', *Anthropology of this Century* 1, <http://aotcpress.com/articles/neoliberalism/>, accessed 7 March 2016.

Ortner, Sherry B. (2012), 'Against Hollywood: American Independent Film as a Critical Cultural Movement', *Journal of Ethnographic Theory* 2.2, 1–21, <https://www.haujournal.org/index.php/hau/article/view/hau2.2.002>, accessed 22 March 2016.

O'Shea, Tom (2011), *Consent in History, Theory and Practice*, The Essex Autonomy Project, <https://autonomy.essex.ac.uk/resources/consent-in-history-theory-and-practice/>, accessed 30 July 2017.

Pandey, K. (2017), 'Breaking the Prolonged Silence of Agonies: A Glimpse into Ismat Chughtai's Short Stories', *The Achievers Journal* 3.2, <https://

www.theachieversjournal.com/index.php/taj/article/view/165>, accessed 24 August 2017.

Pandit, Sushmita (2011), 'Ideological Network Apparatus: Media and the Indian Public Sphere', *Global Media Journal: Indian edition*, <http://connection.ebscohost.com/c/articles/71947163/ideological-network-apparatus-media-indian-public-sphere>, accessed 19 April 2018.

Park, Young-a (2011), 'New Activist Cultural Production: Independent Filmmaker, the Post Authoritarian State, and New Capital Flows in South Korea', in Gi-Wook Shin and Paul Y. Chang (eds), *South Korean Social Movements: From Democracy to Civil Society*, Abingdon: Routledge, pp. 190–205.

Parsons, Lee (2015), interview with Indian filmmaker Rahul Roy, director of The Factory, 7 December, <https://www.wsws.org/en/articles/2015/12/07/fact-d07.html>, accessed 19 April 2018.

Patel, G. (2001), 'Marking the Quilt: Veil, Harem/Home, and the Subversion of Colonial Civility', *Colby Quarterly* 37.2: 174–88.

Patnaik, U. (2007), 'Neoliberalism and Rural Poverty in India', *Economic and Political Weekly* 42 (30).

Patwardhan, Anand (1984), 'The Guerilla Film – Underground and in Exile: A Critique and a Case Study of Waves of Revolution', in Thomas Waugh (ed.), *Show Us Life: Toward a History and Aesthetic of the Committed Documentary*, Metuchen, NJ and London: Scarecrow Press, pp. 444–64.

Patwardhan, Anand (1986), interview by Sean Cubitt, *Framework* 30/31 (1 January): 60–7.

Patwardhan, Anand (1988), interview by Thomas Waugh (videorecording).

Patwardhan, Anand (2013), 'Dissent!', <http://www.augusteorts.be/discourse/10/DISSENT-Anand-Patwardhan>, accessed 8 June 2016.

'Pedpics' (2007), Pedestrian Pictures web log post, 19 December, <https://pedestrianpictures.wordpress.com/>, accessed 9 November 2013.

Pendakur, Manjunath (1995), 'Cinema of Resistance: Recent Trends in Indian Documentary Film', Yamagata International Documentary Film Festival, <https://www.yidff.jp/docbox/7/box7-4-e.html>, accessed 10 June 2015.

Philips, D., and G. Whannel (2013), *The Trojan Horse: The Growth of Commercial Sponsorship*, New York: Bloomsbury.

Polan, Dana B. (1974), 'Brecht and the Politics of Self-Reflexive Cinema', *Jump Cut* 1, <https://www.ejumpcut.org/archive/onlinessays/JC17folder/BrechtPolan.html>, accessed 19 April 2018.

Polanyi, Michael (1998), *Personal Knowledge: Towards a Post-Critical Philosophy*, London: Routledge.

Prakash, Gyan (2013), 'Tragic Fable of Mumbai Mills', *The New York Times*, 28 October, <https://india.blogs.nytimes.com/2013/08/28/tragic-fable-of-mumbai-mills/>, accessed 28 April 2016.

Prashad, Vijay (2007), 'Janam's Commitments', *Critical Asian Studies* 39.4: 635–48, <https://www.tandfonline.com/doi/abs/10.1080/14672710701686083?journalCode=rcra20>, accessed 12 July 2015.

'The Principles We Followed to Organise the 28 June #Notinmyname Protest in Delhi' (3 July 2017), Not in My Name Facebook page, <https://www.facebook.com/notes/not-in-my-name/the-principles-we-followed-to-organise-the-28-june-notinmyname-protest-in-delhi/238228443352390/>, accessed 19 April 2018.

Pryluck, Calvin (1976), 'Ultimately We Are All Outsiders: The Ethics of Documentary Filming', *Journal of the University Film Association* 28.1: 21–9.

Rabiger, Michael (2004), *Directing the Documentary*, fourth ed., Burlington, VT: Elsevier.

Rahbaran, S. (2016), *Iranian Cinema Uncensored: Contemporary Film-makers since the Islamic Revolution*, London: I. B. Tauris.

Rajagopal, Arvind (2001), *Politics After Television: Hindu Nationalism and the Reshaping of the Public in India*, Cambridge: Cambridge University Press.

Rajagopal, Arvind, and Paromita Vohra (2012), 'On the Aesthetics and Ideology of the Indian Documentary Film: A Conversation', *BioScope: South Asian Screen Studies* 3.1: 7–20.

Rao, Shakuntala, and Herman Wasserman (2015), 'A Media Not for All', *Journalism Studies* 16.5: 651–62.

Renninger, Bryce (2013), 'Cara Mertes, Head of Ford Foundation's JustFilms, Explains Why Thinking about Impact Will Make Your Doc Better', *Indiewire*, 13 December, <http://www.indiewire.com/2013/12/cara-mertes-head-of-ford-foundations-justfilms-explains-why-thinking-about-impact-will-make-your-doc-better-yes-really-241342/>, accessed 10 February 2016.

Revathi (6 May 2013), personal interview, Chennai.

Robinson, Luke (2013), *Independent Chinese Documentary*, London: Palgrave Macmillan.

Robinson, Mark (1997), 'Privatizing the Voluntary Sector: NGOs as Public Service Contractors', in David Hulme and Michael Edwards (eds), *NGOs, States and Donors: Too Close for Comfort?*, London: St Martin's Press.

Rosenthal, Alan (2007), *Writing, Directing, and Producing Documentary Films and Videos,* fourth ed., Carbondale: Southern Illinois University Press.

Rothwell, Jerry (2012), 'Producing', in Wilma de Jong, Erik Knudsen, and Jerry Rothwell (eds), *Creative Documentary: Theory and Practice*, Abingdon: Routledge, pp. 185–200.

Rouse, Joseph (2000), 'Practice Theory', in Dov Gabbay and Paul Thagard (eds), *Handbook of the Philosophy of Science* 15: 499–540.

Roy, Indrajit (2003), 'Development and Its Discontents: Civil Society as the New Lexicon', *Development* 46.1: 80.

Roy, Rahul (6 April 2013), personal interview, New Delhi.

Roy, Rahul (20 September 2013), personal interview, New Delhi.

Roy, Rahul (7 October 2013), personal interview, New Delhi.

Roy, Rahul (14 January 2015), personal interview, New Delhi.

Roy, Rahul, Deepak Mehta, and Sudha Vasan (2008), *Delhi International Ethnographic Film Festival*, University of Delhi Department of Sociology.

Roy, Srirupa (2007), *Beyond Belief: India and the Politics of Postcolonial Nationalism*, Durham, NC: Duke University Press.

R. P., Amudhan (3 May 2013), personal interview, Chennai.

R. P., Amudhan (5 May 2013), personal interview, Chennai.

Ruby, J. (1980), 'Exposing yourself: Reflexivity, anthropology, and film', *Semiotica* 30 (1–2).

Ruby, J. (2005), 'The Ethics of Image Making; or They're Going to Put Me in the Movies. They're Going to Make a Big Star Out of Me', in Alan Rosenthal and John Corner (eds), *New Challenges for Documentary: Second Edition*, Manchester, UK: Manchester University Press, pp. 209–19.

Russell, Catherine (1999), *Experimental Ethnography*, Durham, NC: Duke University Press.

Rutherford, Anne (2006), '"Buddhas Made of Ice and Butter": Mimetic Visuality, Transience and the Documentary Image', *Third Text* 20.1: 27–39.

Saravanan, T. (2006), 'Different Strokes for Different Folks', *The Hindu*, 18 February.

Sarkar, Bhaskar, and Nicole Wolf (2012a), 'Documentary Acts: An Interview with Madhusree Dutta', *BioScope: South Asian Screen Studies* 3.1: 21–34.

Sarkar, Bhaskar, and Nicole Wolf (2012b), 'Editorial', *BioScope: South Asian Screen Studies* 3.1: 1–6.

Schatzki, Theodore R. (2001), 'Introduction: A Practice Theory', in Theodore R. Schatzki, Karin Knorr-Cetina, and Eike von Savigny (eds), *The Practice Turn in Contemporary Theory*, London: Routledge, pp. 1–14.

Schramm, Wilbur (1973), *Big Media, Little Media*, Stanford, CA: Stanford University Institute for Communication Research.

Schwienbacher, Armin, and Benjamin Larralde (2012), 'Alternative Types Of Entrepreneurial Finance', in Douglas Cumming (ed.), *The Oxford Handbook of Entrepreneurial Finance*, Oxford: Oxford University Press, pp. 369–91.

Scroll.in (2015), 'Video: After Screening Is Halted, Anand Patwardhan Releases 'Ram Ke Naam' on YouTube', 5 January, <https://scroll.in/article/698707/video-after-screening-is-halted-anand-patwardhan-releases-ram-ke-naam-on-youtube>, accessed 14 May 2015.

Sen, Gargi, and Supriyo Sen (2012), 'Indian Documentaries Today: Changing Field, Scope and the Practice of Documentary', in Jane H. C. Yu (ed.), *Asian Documentary Today*, Busan: Busan International Film Festival, pp. 76–107.

Sen, Ronojoy (2016), 'Narendra Modi's Makeover and the Politics of Symbolism', *Journal of Asian Public Policy* 9.2: 98–111.

Sen, Siddhartha (1993), 'Defining the Nonprofit Sector: India', in L. M. Salamon and H. K. Anheier (eds), *Working Papers of the Johns Hopkins Comparative Nonprofit Sector Project*, no. 12, Baltimore: The Johns Hopkins Institute for Policy Studies.

Seshu, Geeta (2016), 'Women and the Internet in India: Denial of Access and the Censorship of Abuse', in Sunetra Sen Narayan and Shalini Narayanan (eds), *India Connected: Mapping the Impact of New Media*, New Delhi: Sage, pp. 237–260.

Shafik, Viola (2007), *Arab Cinema: History and Cultural Identity*, Cairo: American University in Cairo Press.

Sharma, Kalpana (2004), 'Censor Board Bans Film on Gujarat Violence', *The Hindu*, 6 August, <http://www.thehindu.com/2004/08/06/stories/2004080604471200.htm>, accessed 19 September 2015.

Sharma, Rakesh (2014), 'Film-maker Releases a Dozen Clips of Controversial Modi Speeches Made Just after Gujarat Riots', Scroll.in interview by Sumana Ramanan, 10 March, <https://scroll.in/article/658119/film-maker-releases-a-dozen-clips-of-controversial-modi-speeches-made-just-after-gujarat-riots>, accessed 19 September 2015.

Shore, Cris, and Susan Wright (2015), 'Governing by Numbers: Audit Culture, Rankings and the New World Order: Governing By Numbers', *Social Anthropology* 23.1: 22–8.

Sinclair, John, and Mark Harrison (2004), 'Globalization, Nation, and Television in Asia: The Cases of India and China', *Television and New Media* 5.1: 41–54.

Singh, Bhrigupati, and Ashok Bhargava (2002), 'Documentaries and Change: Review of and Commentary on Three of Anand Patwardhan's Films', *Critical Asian Studies* 34.4: 623–36.

Skaria, Ajay (2003), 'Development, Nationalism and the Time of the Primitive: The Dangs Darbar', in K. Sivaramakrishnan and Arun Agrawal (eds), *Regional Modernities: The Cultural Politics of Development in India*, Stanford, CA: Stanford University Press, pp. 215–36.

Sørenson, Inge E. (2015), 'Go Crowdfund Yourself: Some Unintended Consequences of Crowdfunding for Documentary Film and Industry in the UK', in Geert Lovink, N. Tkacz, and P. de Vries (eds), *MoneyLab Reader: An Intervention in Digital Economy*, Amsterdam: Institute for Networked Cultures, pp. 268–80.

Spivak, Gayatri (1988), 'Can the Subaltern Speak?', in Cary Nelson and Lawrence Grossberg (eds), *Marxism and the Interpretation of Culture*, Urbana: University of Illinois Press, pp. 271–313.

Stanley, L., and S. Wise (1983), *Breaking Out: Feminist Consciousness and Feminist Research*, London: Routledge.

Sundaram, Ravi (2009), *Pirate Modernity: Delhi's Media Urbanism*, Abingdon: Routledge.

Sutoris, Peter (2016), *Visions of Development: Films Division of India and the Imagination of Progress, 1948–75*, New York: Oxford University Press.

Swami, Sridala (2008), 'Indian Documentary: Introduction', *Pratilipi: A Bilingual Quarterly Magazine* 1:4, <http://pratilipi.*in*/2008/10/indian-documentary/>, accessed 10 May 2015.

de Tocqueville, Alexis [1835–40] (2002), *Democracy in America*, trans. Henry Reeve, vol. 1, University Park, PA: Pennsylvania State University Press.

Taylor, Charles (1985), *Philosophical Papers: Volume 2, Philosophy and the Human Sciences*, Cambridge: Cambridge University Press.
Telecom Regulatory Authority of India (2016), *Annual Report 2015–16*, New Delhi: Telecom Regulatory Authority of India.
'Textile Workers Withdraw Fast' (1991), *Times of India*, 11 October, accessed 8 May 2015 via ProQuest Historical Newspapers.
Turner, Stephen (1994), *The Social Theory of Practices: Tradition, Tacit Knowledge, and Presuppositions*, Chicago: University of Chicago Press.
UNESCO (2008), *Participatory Content Creation for Development: Principles and Practices*, ed. Jerry Watkins and Jo Tacchi, New Delhi: UNESCO.
Upadhyay, Vineet (2015). 'Nainital Film Fest to Screen 'Caste on the Menu Card' – Times of India', *The Times of India*, 3 November, <https://timesofindia.indiatimes.com/city/dehradun/Nainital-film-fest-to-screen-Caste-on-the-Menu-Card/articleshow/49649147.cms>, accessed 25 March 2016.
Uroskie, Andrew (2014), *Between the Black Box and the White Cube: Expanded Cinema and Postwar* Art, Chicago: University of Chicago Press.
Vanita, Ruth (1986), 'For the Right to Exist: Pavement Dwellers in Bombay', *Manushi* 35, <http://www.manushi-india.org/pdfs_issues/PDF%20files%2035/16.%20For%20the%20right%20to%20exist-%20Interview%20with%20Anand%20Patwardhan.pdf>, accessed 12 June 2014.
Vasudevan, Ravi (2011), *The Melodramatic Public: Film Form and Spectatorship in Indian Cinema*, New York: Palgrave Macmillan.
Velayanikal, Malavika (2012), 'Amudhan R. P.: A Rebel, an Activist and a Filmmaker', Daily News and Analysis, 16 December, <http://www.dnaindia.com/lifestyle/report-amudhan-rp-a-rebel-an-activist-a-filmmaker-1777982>, accessed 30 July 2017.
Vilanilam, J. V. (2005), *Mass Communication in India: A Sociological Perspective*, New Delhi: Sage Publications.
Vohra, Paromita (2011), 'Dotting the I: The Politics of Self-less-ness in Indian Documentary Practice', *South Asian Popular Culture* 9.1: 43–53, <https://www.tandfonline.com/doi/abs/10.1080/14746689.2011.553887>, accessed 10 May 2013.
Vohra, Paromita (12 March 2013), personal interview, Mumbai.
Vohra, Paromita (5 September 2013), personal interview, Mumbai.
Vohra, Paromita (4 January 2015), personal interview, Mumbai.
Waldman, Diane, and Janet Walker (1999), 'Introduction', in Diane Waldman and Janet Walker (eds), *Feminism and Documentary*, Minneapolis: University of Minnesota Press, pp. 1–36.
Waugh, Thomas (1991), 'Lesbian and Gay Documentary: Minority Self-Imaging in Oppositional Film Practice and the Question of Image Ethics', in Larry Gross, John Stuart Katz and Jay Ruby (eds), *Image Ethics: The Moral Rights of Subjects in Photographs, Film, and Television*, New York: Oxford University Press, pp. 248–72.
Waugh, Thomas (2011), 'Words of Command: Cultural and Political Inflections of Direct Cinema in Indian Independent Documentary', in Thomas Waugh (ed.),

The Right to Play Oneself: Looking Back on Documentary Film, Minneapolis: University of Minnesota Press, pp. 239–65.

White, Shirley A. (2003), 'Participatory Video: A Process That Transforms the Self and the Other', in Shirley A. White (ed.), *Participatory Video: Images That Transform and Empower*, New Delhi: Sage Publications, pp. 63–101.

Whiteman, David (2004), 'Out of the Theaters and Into the Streets: A Coalition Model of the Political Impact of Documentary Film and Video', *Political Communication* 21.1: 51–69.

Willemen, Paul (1989), 'The Third Cinema Question: Notes and Reflections', in Jim Pines and Paul Willemen (eds), *Questions of Third Cinema*, London: British Film Institute, pp. 1–29.

Williams, Raymond (1977), *Marxism and Literature*, Oxford: Oxford University Press.

Williams, Raymond (1981), *The Sociology of Culture*, London: Fontana Paperbacks.

Williams, Raymond (1983), *Culture and Society, 1780–1950*, New York: Columbia University Press.

Winston, Brian (1991), 'The Tradition of the Victim in Griersonian Documentary', in Larry P. Gross, John Stuart Katz and Jay Ruby (eds), *Image Ethics*, New York: Oxford University Press, pp. 34–57.

Winston, Brian (1995), *Claiming the Real: The Griersonian Documentary and Its Legitimations*, London: British Film Institute.

Winston, Brian (2000), *Lies, Damn Lies and Documentaries*, London: British Film Institute.

Winston, Brian (2008), *Claiming the Real II: The Griersonian Documentary and Its Legitimations*, 2nd ed., London: British Film Institute.

Wolf, Nicole (2013), 'Foundations, Movements and Dissonant Images: Documentary Film and Its Ambivalent Relations to the Nation State', in K. Moti Gokulsing and Wimal Dissanayake (eds), *Routledge Handbook of Indian Cinemas*, London: Routledge, pp. 910–48.

World Bank (1995), *World Bank Participation Sourcebook* (1995), Washington, DC: World Bank.

World Bank (2016), 'Internet Users (per 100 People)', <http://data.un.org/Data.aspx?d=WDI&f=Indicator_Code%3AIT.NET.USER.P2>, accessed 11 May 2016.

Wragg, D. (1994), *The Effective Use of Sponsorship*, London: Kogan Page.

Zachariah, Mini (2007), 'Making Business Sense of Documentary Filmmaking', *Hindustan Times*, 9 February, <https://www.hindustantimes.com/india/making-business-sense-of-documentary-filmmaking/story-GgsQZ0iXfVJAyEae24PhdJ.html>, accessed 23 June 2015.

Index

Note: *italic* page numbers refer to illustrations